VIETNAM STUL

SHARPENING THE COMBAT EDGE:

THE USE OF ANALYSIS TO REINFORCE MILITARY JUDGMENT

by

Lieutenant General Julian J. Ewell

and

Major General Ira A. Hunt, Jr.

DEPARTMENT OF THE ARMY
WASHINGTON, D.C. 1974

Library of Congress Catalog Card Number: 74–14649

First Printing

For sale by the Superintendent of Documents, U.S. Government Printing Office
Washington, D.C. 20402 – Price $3.05 (paper cover)
Stock Number 008–020–00554–1

Foreword

The United States Army has met an unusually complex challenge in Southeast Asia. In conjunction with the other services, the Army has fought in support of a national policy of assisting an emerging nation to develop governmental processes of its own choosing, free of outside coercion. In addition to the usual problems of waging armed conflict, the assignment in Southeast Asia has required superimposing the immensely sophisticated tasks of a modern army upon an underdeveloped environment and adapting them to demands covering a wide spectrum. These involved helping to fulfill the basic needs of an agrarian population, dealing with the frustrations of antiguerrilla operations, and conducting conventional campaigns against well-trained and determined regular units.

Although this assignment has officially ended, the U.S. Army must prepare for other challenges that may lie ahead. While cognizant that history never repeats itself exactly and that no army ever profited from trying to meet a new challenge in terms of the old one, the Army nevertheless stands to benefit immensely from a study of its experience, its shortcomings no less than its achievements.

Aware that some years must elapse before the official histories will provide a detailed and objective analysis of the experience in Southeast Asia, we have sought a forum whereby some of the more salient aspects of that experience can be made available now. At the request of the Chief of Staff, a representative group of senior officers who served in important posts in Vietnam and who still carry a heavy burden of day-to-day responsibilities has prepared a series of monographs. These studies should be of great value in helping the Army develop future operational concepts while at the same time contributing to the historical record and providing the American public with an interim report on the performance of men and officers who have responded, as others have through our history, to exacting and trying demands.

All monographs in the series are based primarily on official records, with additional material from published and unpublished secondary works, from debriefing reports and interviews with key participants, and from the personal experience of the authors. To facilitate security clearance, annotation and detailed bibliography have been omitted from the published version; a fully documented account with bibliography is filed with the Office of the Chief of Military History.

The reader should be reminded that most of the writing was accomplished while the war in Vietnam was at its peak, and the monographs frequently refer to events of the past as if they were taking place in the present.

Lieutenant General Julian J. Ewell, one of the coauthors of this monograph, has been a combat infantryman during his entire Army career. He served as a battalion and regimental commander in the 101st Airborne Division in World War II. He ended the Korean War as a regimental commander in the 2d Infantry Division. After a tour in Combat Developments Command, where he gained insights into the use of operations research, he commanded the 9th Infantry Division in the delta area of Vietnam in 1968 and 1969. He then commanded II Field Force Vietnam in the area around Saigon until April 1970.

Major General Ira A. Hunt, Jr., was assigned to the Corps of Engineers upon graduation from the United States Military Academy in 1945. He has served as an engineer battalion commander in the 8th Infantry Division in Europe and as a Military Assistant in the Office of Organization and Management Planning, Office of the Secretary of Defense. In Vietnam, he served with General Ewell as Chief of Staff of the 9th Infantry Division and as the 1st Brigade Commander. He is currently assigned as Deputy Chief of Staff for Training and Schools, Headquarters, United States Army Training and Doctrine Command, Fort Monroe, Virginia.

Washington, D.C.   VERNE L. BOWERS
15 October 1973   Major General, USA
                                          The Adjutant General

Preface

This monograph focuses on the use of analysis in combat operations and concentrates on the utilization of techniques in situations with which the authors were personally familiar. It covers primarily the systematic blending of military judgment, data collection, and simple problem solving techniques as utilized in the 9th Infantry Division and II Field Force, Vietnam in 1968, 1969 and 1970. The approach is rather tentative because it was not possible in many cases to determine exactly what factors made the operations go so well. Rather we have laid out the most important and interesting factors in the hopes that the readers will be stimulated and perhaps decide for themselves what the critical points were. Fortunately, a large amount of basic data was available to support the manuscript. On the other hand, some basic data has been lost. In these cases we drew on memory and tried to double check the accuracy of our recollections. We think any general statements are reasonably accurate.

In order to hold the length of the manuscript down to reasonable limits, the authors found it necessary to assume that the reader was generally familiar with the Vietnamese war and had a good grasp of the operations, tactics and techniques of the combined arms. A knowledgeable professional military reader should find the material fairly easy to grasp. A reader with more limited military background may find it rather hard going.

The analytic approach when tried on the battlefield seemed to help produce sizable increases in both overall performance and efficiency. Whether these improvements were due more to good basic concepts or to good execution or both is difficult to determine.

We can say that first class officers and first class soldiers are capable of outstanding battlefield performance. To list the thousands of people who contributed to this tremendous team effort would be impossible. However, the monograph is dedicated to all those members of the 9th Infantry Division and of II Field Force Vietnam who acquitted themselves so well in Vietnam.

To assist the reader in placing the events discussed in this monograph in proper time perspective, a chronological list of milestones is included as an Appendix.

We wish to thank Colonel Charles Hayward, who did much of the original work on the II Field Force Vietnam portion of this monograph, and Colonel Archibald W. McFadden, Colonel Leonard Spirito, Lieutenant Colonel James Lindsay, Lieutenant Colonel Fred Mahaffey, Dr. David Wigdor, and Mr. Alfred Beck for their assistance in the preparation and review of the manuscript.

Washington, D.C.   JULIAN J. EWELL
15 October 1973   Lieutenant General, U.S. Army

                                    IRA A. HUNT, JR.
                                    Major General, U.S. Army

Contents

Charts

Maps

Tables

Illustrations

Page

Illustrations are from Department of the Army files except for the five pieces of artwork by members of the Combat Art Team of the 19th Military History Detachment: the photograph on page 49 of an ink drawing by Sergeant Thomas Sherwood, the photograph on page 59 of a painting by Specialist Edward Rohrbach, the photograph on page 187 of a pencil drawing by Specialist Rohrbach, the photograph on page 215 of an oil painting by Specialist Donald Orosz, and the photograph on page 226 of another oil painting by Specialist Orosz.

SHARPENING THE COMBAT EDGE: THE USE OF ANALYSIS TO REINFORCE MILITARY JUDGMENT

CHAPTER I

Introduction

At its inception this monograph was visualized as a brief treatment of "Operations Research Techniques as Applied to the Battlefield in Vietnam." Initially, it was assumed that there was little documented use of these techniques in Vietnam. However, initial research disclosed that there was a fairly common use of the simpler types of such techniques and consequently more material than could be managed usefully. The primary difficulty lay in evaluating second hand the extent to which military judgment on the one hand and analytical techniques on the other contributed to the final result of various studies and operations.

It was therefore decided that this monograph should be narrowed to focus on the use of analysis in combat operations and to concentrate on the use of such techniques in situations with which the authors were personally familiar. The monograph therefore covers primarily the systematic blending of military judgment, data collection, and simple problem-solving techniques as performed in the 9th Infantry Division and II Field Force Vietnam in the period 1968–1970. Considerable success was achieved in improving combat effectiveness fairly rapidly by these means. However, this use of analysis was neither systematic nor sophisticated. A more organized effort might have had a greater payoff.

There is a tendency in the Army to distrust operations research due to some rather unpleasant experiences with its use (or misuse) during the Robert S. McNamara-Dr. Alain C. Enthoven regime. However, one can take little exception to the definition of operations research contained in AR 320–5, Dictionary of United States Army Terms: "The analytical study of military problems, undertaken to provide responsible commanders and staff agencies with a scientific basis for decision on action to improve military operations. Also known as operational research, operations analysis."

Quite simply, operations analysis is an approach to problem solving that makes it possible to use systematic logic and often mathematical techniques to arrive at a decision which will optimize an operation or objective. The key factor in a decision problem is to determine the objective. The task of the decision maker then is

THE LEADER IN ACTION

to choose a course of action which optimizes this objective function.

Every decision problem involves one or more inputs which are subject to the control of the decision maker. Any combination of controllable variables is called a course of action. Therefore, the essence of decision making is the selection of the appropriate controllable inputs. As we will discuss later our most important inputs were infantry units and aviation assets. There may often be uncontrollable variables also. This can lead to real problems.

Quite often a problem has conflicting objectives. In Vietnam, almost all decisions had at least these three objectives: (1) to protect our own personnel and material resources, (2) to damage the enemy, and (3) to assist in the pacification of an area. These objectives were almost always in conflict in greater or smaller proportion. Therefore, one had to rely to a great extent on the judgment and skill of commanders.[1]

Although the element of judgment is crucial, perhaps the most critical of all attributes for decision making is the intellectual toughness to make a decision in a timely fashion. In the Vietnamese environment with its great amount of risk, uncertainty, and conflict, where an improper decision cost human lives, decisions were difficult.

We, like the other combat units, determined our objectives, gathered as best we could the data required, analyzed the data, considered alternatives, and made decisions. These analyses were as detailed as one might expect in a combat environment, but they were not sophisticated. We barely scratched the surface of combat analysis techniques. In this monograph *we do not elaborate on the normal military decision making methods which are well understood and were utilized extensively.* We stress the extension of these more normal decision making devices by analytical methods. It is our contention that when these analytical methods were properly used in Vietnam they were very helpful.

Dr. Enthoven has stated in his latest book, *How Much Is Enough?*, that operations research was used very little in Vietnam. He is probably correct if he was referring to systems analysis and cost effectiveness which are normally used to analyze high-level problems. The Vietnamese war was so complex, so varied, and so changeable that these high-level approaches tended to be very difficult to use with any confidence. However, simple, straightforward operations analysis, while not easy to use, posed less of a problem and was used extensively. The Army Combat Operations Vietnam study was a good example. By combining military judgment, data collection, and use of operations research methods, it was able to rationalize a standard infantry battalion organization which saw good service during the latter stages of the Vietnamese

---

[1] This point has been emphasized by most analyses of operations, reference the Army Combat Operations Vietnam and Mechanized and Armored Combat Operations Vietnam studies cited subsequently.

war (see the Four-Rifle Company Conversion, page 18). The Mechanized and Armored Combat Operations Vietnam study conducted in late 1966, studied armored and mechanized organization, equipment, tactics and techniques and served as a vehicle to update knowledge in these areas. Both of these used operations research (or operations analysis) techniques to a certain extent. Major General George L. Mabry, Jr., the Army Combat Operations Vietnam study chief, stated:

I found that:
  a. Analytical methods used during the ARCOV study were very useful up to a point.
  b. Results of an analysis could assist one in reaching conclusions and developing alternative courses of action.
  c. Results of an analysis could not replace military judgment.

Major General Arthur L. West, Jr., the Mechanized and Armored Combat Operations Vietnam study leader, concluded:

My major point is that military judgment was, at all stages of MACOV, the controlling factor ... MACOV was structured from the outset to *combine* military judgment with the techniques of operations research and systems analysis. . . . In summary, I submit that military judgment, though being the controlling factor, must often times be validated by analytical methods. In the case of MACOV the analytical methodologies utilized were essential for the support of one military judgment against an opposing military judgment.

Perhaps one of the earliest published accounts of Operations Research in Vietnam was the war gaming directed by General William C. Westmoreland and conducted by II Field Force Vietnam under command of Lieutenant General Jonathan D. Seaman. The study was initiated when senior personnel became concerned about the adequacy of the defense of Tan Son Nhut Air Base and other key areas in the spring of 1966. The purpose of the war games was to determine the capability inherent in a maximum effort by the Viet Cong and North Vietnamese Army against U.S. Forces in the late spring and summer of 1966. Actual tactical changes, made as a result of these war games, later paid off in an impressive fashion.

The 25th Infantry Division under Major General Ellis W. Williamson carried on a great amount of operations analysis during the period August 1968 to September 1969, which almost parallels the period of this monograph. The 25th Division also utilized computers to a great extent to study such problems as countermine warfare, target acquisition, and operational planning.

In addition to the analyses conducted by in-country military units and by Department of the Army support agencies excellent research was also sponsored by the Office of the Assistant Secretary of Defense for International Affairs and the Advanced Research Projects Agency. Some of these studies, such as "A Look at the VC Cadres: Dinh Tuong Province, 1965–1966," were conducted by the Rand Corporation and had a direct and specific application to the 9th Division area of operations in the delta.

The Army Concept Team in Vietnam consistently used the soldier-scientist team approach to solve military problems.

From this small sample of the more prominent studies it can be seen that the use of low level operations analysis was fairly widespread throughout Vietnam. This monograph gives examples of organized critical analysis of operations in a small sector of the Vietnam War—the 9th Infantry Division area of operations in the Mekong Delta and also in the larger II Field Force and III Corps area around Saigon. As this approach was not, strictly speaking, a classical use of operations research or analysis, we have described it as combat analysis. This is a reasonably accurate description of the actual process.

Strategic Background

The strategy and grand tactics of the Vietnamese war will probably not be well understood for years. In general, the war and its total environment were so foreign to classical western experience, military and civilian, that one could not grasp it well at the time much less understand it. In addition much of the writing concerning the war has concentrated on specific aspects to the extent that general lessons have not been clearly deduced. The press, in particular, was greatly handicapped by the dispersed and obscure nature of the war and, with some praiseworthy exceptions, found it difficult to report accurately what was actually taking place. Objective works on the Vietnam war are few and far between.

However, recognizing these pitfalls, one might conclude tentatively that the Communist strategy in Vietnam followed the traditional Maoist three stage theory. When it became apparent, after the Geneva agreements, that South Vietnam would not submit to the Lao Dong (North Vietnamese Communist) party of its own accord, the first or organizational phase was put in high gear by the North Vietnamese and the Viet Cong. In the chaos following the overthrow of the Ngo Dinh Diem regime, the second or guerrilla phase came on strong, and by 1964 the third or open warfare phase was well underway. The North Vietnamese intervention with regular units in 1964 and thereafter was probably designed to top the third phase off with a rapid victory.

On the South Vietnamese and Allied side the strategy was very uncertain and experimental. The succession of coups necessarily led to a rather spasmodic approach. After many false starts, the effective organization of the government and the people began in 1967 and 1968. The defensive operations against the North Vietnamese Army and the Viet Cong main force units began to take effect with the introduction of U.S. units in 1965 and was going well by 1967. The general mobilization of South Vietnam to flesh out the seriously understrength army and to form hundreds of new Regional and Popular force units did not start until the summer of 1968 and was not fully effective until 1970.

However, the Allied strategy became fairly clear at this stage. The Communist main force units were progressively fragmented and driven away from the populated areas in the period 1965–1969. Starting with the accelerated pacification campaigns of 1968 and 1969, the control of the rural population was largely taken away from the Communists. By late 1969 the Communist seaborne supply routes had been cut and their in-country supply routes heavily interdicted. The Cambodian operation in early 1970 cut the Sihanoukville seaborne supply route, leaving the Ho Chi Minh trail as the only route for support of in-country Communist forces. The Vietnamization program to turn the primary responsibility for their own defense over to the South Vietnamese people was progressing well in 1970.

With this overview as a backdrop let us look at the ground tactics of the war in recent years. In the big unit period of the Vietnamese war (1965–1967), the North Vietnamese evidently felt that they could defeat United States and South Vietnamese units in face-to-face combat in engagements of their own choosing. During this period, while it was not easy to bring the enemy to combat, it was a manageable problem. During this phase the Communists sustained a continuous series of major defeats and, as a result, in mid or late 1967, went to ground and changed their approach to a degree. The Communists devoted the bulk of their energies to rebuilding while avoiding contact, and accepted combat only when cornered or when the odds looked particularly favorable. During this period the tactics which had worked well for U.S. units for several years became less effective. The enemy, then, shifted gears, changing their tactics by adopting a "high point" policy which resulted in weeks or months of "evasion" followed by a "high point" of attacks. The best known "high point" was, of course, the *Tet* 1968 attacks. It gradually became clearer that the situation called for a change in tactics by the friendly troops.

Thus, in 1968 the problem became one of bringing evading enemy units to battle during the quiet periods, and limiting their damage during the high points so that they could not interfere with the pacification program, which was just going into high gear. This was particularly true at division level.

The Mouth of the Dragon

Prior to the move of the 9th Division Headquarters to the Delta at Dong Tam, the Division had a tactical area of interest about the size of New Jersey both south and east of Saigon. This large area was very difficult to handle because of its size and complexity and the rather light friendly troop density. The move to the delta greatly reduced our Tactical Area of Interest giving us primary responsibility for only four provinces: Long An in southwestern III Corps Tactical Zone south of Saigon and Dinh Tuong, Kien Hoa and Go Cong in northeastern IV Corps Tactical Zone, the northern delta region. Dinh Tuong is one of the most heavily populated of the Vietnamese provinces with almost 700,000 inhabitants. (Map 1) It is closely followed by Kien Hoa with well over a half million. Both of these provinces had only approximately one-third of their people under the control of the Vietnamese government in 1968. Long An with over 400,000 people has long been a key province because of its rich rice crops, its closeness to the capital, Saigon, and its control of the highway routes to the delta. The total population of the four provinces is 1,815,000, about 18 percent of the country's population, of which almost 80 percent or 1,470,000 are rural and mostly farmers.

The land surface is extremely low and flat, averaging about two meters above sea level. The main crop is rice, but palm, coconut, and assorted fruit trees are grown around the canals and streams. The surface drainage is poor due to the lack of gradients necessary to create a good run off condition. Six major rivers constitute the major drainage network. A great number of canals and streams connect these rivers. There are four major highways: QL–4 running the length of Dinh Tuong and Long An Provinces is one of the major highways of the delta, carrying produce from the delta to Saigon; TL–24 connects My Tho city with Go Cong city; TL–26 connects with Ben Tre city and Ba Tri city in Kien Hoa Province; and LTL–5A connects Go Cong with Saigon, although it was not usable for much of its length at that time because of ferry and bridge destruction by the VC.

The most common relief features in the area are the rice paddy dikes which are 0.3 to 1.0 meters high and 0.3 to 0.6 meters wide.

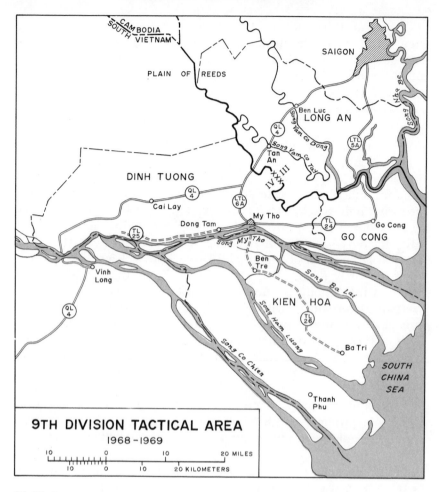

MAP 1

Scattered throughout the area are many small higher areas that have localized elevations from 1 to 3 meters above the terrain. The hamlets and villages are generally located on these higher areas.

Cover and concealment are determined by the interplay of land forms and vegetation and for the most part concealment is best in the palm groves generally found spotted across the country-side in the vicinity of canals and rivers. Most of the palm canopy provides fair concealment from aerial observation. Ground observation is limited by light undergrowth although the rice fields offer little concealment. The Plain of Reeds, stretching from northern Dinh Tuong to Cambodia, offers excellent ground concealment everywhere due to tall reeds and grasses. By Vietnamese standards,

THE PLAIN OF REEDS

the country is relatively open, but the Viet Cong were most skillful at utilizing what cover and concealment were available.

The suitability of this area for military operations varies seasonally. Contrary to popular belief, light infantry can operate year round within the area although their capabilities are limited in the marshes and mangroves near the coast. During the wet season small boats (sampans) can be used widely. The canals and streams are usable for sampan movement year around. Airmobile operations are facilitated during the dry season by numerous helicopter landing zones. During the wet season the excess surface water and mud hamper heliborne operations somewhat. Tactical air operations are hampered by early morning low cloudiness and fog during both seasons. Armored operations are not possible. Mechanized vehicles (armored personnel carriers) can be utilized with care in the dry season and with extreme difficulty in the wet season.

The climate is characterized by two major seasons: the southwest (wet season) monsoon from mid-May through October and the northeast (dry season) monsoon from early November to mid-March. The average rainfall from May to October is about five

Typical Delta Terrain

inches a month, but the number of days with precipitation in the six-month period from November through April is normally less than a dozen. Thunderstorm activities are prevalent May through October and can be accompanied by gusty winds strong enough to hamper helicopter operations. The temperature varies but slightly throughout the year, the average monthly mean high temperature is about 90° Fahrenheit and the mean low temperature is about 75° Fahrenheit.

The major waterways, canals, and streams offer excellent routes for sampans and thus facilitate rapid movement of communist troops and supplies. The tidal range is as much as six to seven feet and its effect on military operations must be taken into consideration.

In summary, the Upper Delta is a densely populated, flat, almost swampy area with a dense waterway network and limited concealment. Because of its rural nature, closeness to Cambodia and good water transportation it facilitates enemy combat operations and resupply. On the other hand, the level, open terrain enhances Allied airmobile operations. The climate is divided into a wet and a dry season. During the wet season overland movement is extremely difficult, whereas in dry season the ground is capable of supporting armored personnel carriers of the M–113 type (but not medium tanks).

This then was the area of operations of the 9th Infantry Division, unusual perhaps in the annals of warfare for U.S. forces in sustained combat and unusual even in Vietnam.[2] This Delta region of the Mekong (The Nine Dragon) River is sometimes referred to as "The Mouth of the Dragon."

A Twofold Quest

From the beginning we initiated a double barrelled effort to enhance the operational capabilities of the 9th Infantry Division. One effort was directed towards providing the maximum number of fit, motivated, well-equipped and properly supported infantry soldiers to the field on a daily basis, night and day. In other words, we wanted to optimize our working assets. In fundamental or basic terms, our success in resources management could be measured by the number of fighting men in the paddy on a daily basis. This depended upon good personnel, logistical, and unit management and included such items as strength accounting, aircraft availability,

---

[2] Such terrain was encountered in the Seminole Indian War and at times during World War II in the Southwest Pacific.

and the use of facilities. Aircraft availability was a most important factor. Concurrently, another effort was directed towards making these fighting infantrymen in the field as efficient as possible in the performance of their missions. The enhancement of combat capabilities depended upon the improved performance of units and derived from our intelligence, tactics, combat activities and pacification efforts.

In our twofold quest to optimize our assets and improve combat efficiency, we used operations analysis to reinforce our military judgment and thus "Sharpen the Combat Edge"

CHAPTER II

Unit Management and Personnel Actions

In a counterinsurgency environment commanders rarely have all the resources required. One can always use more men to secure and pacify an area, or air assets to carry on operations, or more supplies, and on and on. Nevertheless, assets are of necessity limited and therefore commanders must often choose between conflicting goals and most of the time must settle for suboptimization in their courses of action. We realized early that it was impossible to optimize the thousands of factors that enter into running an infantry division. To stay on top of the game, decisions had to be satisfactory and timely rather than optimal. We settled for satisfying a large number of subsystems: awards and decorations, leaves, repair parts, sensor devices, POL (petroleum, oils, and lubricants) storage, vehicular transportation, guard, post exchange support, artillery, and hundreds of others. However, two areas were identified that had such an impact on the combat effectiveness of the division that we sought to optimize rather than satisfy these areas to insure that the total system was maximized. These areas were: (1) the number of infantrymen in the field on a daily basis; and (2) the number of aviation assets available to support the infantrymen in the field. The first part of our double barrelled effort was to provide the largest number of healthy, motivated, well-equipped, properly supported infantry soldiers to the field commanders on a daily basis. In this chapter are described unit management and personnel actions; in the next chapter maximizing army aviation assets and support facilities will be discussed. These will tell the story of how we optimized our assets.

The 9th Division in the late spring of 1968 found itself with its fighting edge somewhat dulled as the consequences of an extensive area of operations, static missions, its table of organization, the tempo of operations, a split Division Headquarters and the losses sustained in *Tet* and the Mini-*Tet* of May 1968. The factors which reduced the number of infantrymen in the field were the result of an organizational situation and the severe combat of *Tet* and were not controllable at the time by the able commanders who had preceded us in the 9th Infantry Division. However, as mentioned earlier in our strategic analysis, the post-*Tet* situation was different. We were in a position to take advantage of restructuring of the division along the lines recommended in the Army Combat Operations Vietnam study as well as completing the final phase of relocation to the delta envisioned by General Westmoreland several years earlier. This move enabled us to reduce our static missions and to operate much more efficiently on interior lines with a smaller area of responsibility. In all, there were six major actions involving unit management and personnel that materially increased the number of infantrymen in the rice paddies on a daily basis: changing the mix between straight-leg and mechanized infantry battalions; converting from three to four company rifle battalions; obtaining a tenth rifle battalion; getting a handle on strength accountability; attacking our foot disease problems; and unloading static missions. All of these efforts jelled in the winter and spring of 1968–1969, greatly increasing the combat power and flexibility of the division. With a greater number of well-equipped and supported infantrymen in the paddy, we were able to forge a much longer and keener cutting edge to our combat sword.

Refining the Organization

The 9th Division was initially organized with seven rifle (foot) battalions and two mechanized infantry battalions. This was probably the correct mix for its original mission and area around Saigon. As the division moved south into the delta and as the enemy was broken up and began to evade, the need for two mechanized battalions became less pressing. In fact, it became more and more difficult to employ two such units usefully. The muddy terrain affected their mechanized vehicles too much. This was particularly true after the enemy gave up trying to ambush on the highways and mechanized highway patrols were consequently no longer needed. The last time that the mechanized battalions fully earned their keep was during the Mini-*Tet* attack on Saigon when both battalions made forced marches into the southern Saigon suburbs and really hurt the enemy due to their firepower and shock action. After that, the mechanized units were almost more of a hindrance than a help. These battalions were also handicapped by only having three rifle companies, which reduced their ability to control large areas and their staying power. In fact, we finally had to keep them partially unhorsed in order to force them into learning to conduct effective offensive small-unit foot operations. As it became obvious that we needed more foot infantry, we were able to swap one of our

THE COMBAT EDGE

mechanized battalions for a foot battalion of another division and settled down with nine foot battalions and one mechanized. (We had in the meantime gained a tenth battalion from the Continental U.S. base.) In late 1968 and 1969, ten foot battalions would have been preferable in the delta, but it was too late in the Vietnamese operation for force structure changes, however desirable.

The Four-Rifle Company Conversion

The 9th Infantry Division was brought to Vietnam under a personnel ceiling that made it necessary to hold all the rifle battalions to three-rifle companies. This triangular organization, while quite workable in Europe and Korea, with their essentially linear wars, was very awkward in Vietnam. The need to cover terrain and the desirability for constant pressure on the enemy were hard to accomplish with a triangular organization. Many of the difficulties were rather hard to quantify but the Army Combat Operations Vietnam evaluation conducted in 1966–67 pinned the problem down and clearly demonstrated the need for a square (four-rifle company) battalion.

Having been exposed to the full effect of triangular battalions for some months in Vietnam, we will limit ourselves to saying that it is a miserable organization for semi-guerrilla operations. (As a matter of interest, one difficulty that most South Vietnamese Army divisions must overcome is that their battalions are triangular. Only the "elite" units—airborne, ranger, Marines, and parts of the 1st South Vietnamese Army Divisions—are square.) Fortunately, the desirability (or necessity) of "squaring" the 9th had been recognized and the program had been set into motion for the fall of 1968 and spring of 1969. Thus, the 9th Division during this period gained about 33 percent in rifle strength and somewhat more than that in flexibility and staying power.

The Windfall

In early 1968 the Cavalry Squadron of the 9th Division (3d Squadron, 5th Cavalry) was moved to northern I Corps (Quang Tri area) to give more armored weight to that area. While the cavalry was quite useful in the division's orginal area east of Saigon, its usefulness south of Saigon was limited due to the rice paddy terrain. However, its transfer to I Corps resulted in a net loss of three company size (troop) maneuver units. In the spring of 1968, a new infantry battalion (originally earmarked for the Americal Division, we believe) was arriving in-theater. Due to the tremendous geographical spread of the 9th Division and possibly the loss of its Cavalry Squadron, this battalion (6th Battalion, 31st Infantry) was assigned to the 9th Division. At the time, the increase of one square battalion meant an 11 percent increase in rifle battalions and a 14 percent increase in rifle companies for the division. More importantly, when the division settled down in the delta, it allowed each brigade to have three battalions (3 × 3 = 9) with one left over to secure the rather exposed division base at Dong Tam.

Brigade organization is an interesting subject in itself. In our opinion, a two-battalion brigade in Vietnam was of marginal usefulness. A three-battalion brigade handled reasonably well (from the brigade commander's point of view). From occasional experience, a four-battalion brigade seemed the most effective arrangement.

As an important afterthought, when the 3d Squadron, 5th Cavalry was detached, its Air Cavalry troop remained with the division. This was fortunate, as a division in Vietnam without an air cavalry troop was blind. In addition, the absence of the Cavalry Squadron, perforce, placed the air cavalry troop under division control, which was a very responsive arrangement.

Paddy Strength

In March of 1968, it was not readily apparent that the rifle company strength of the 9th Division was critically low, although it in fact was. The overall strength of the division and even the battalions was quite high, but on critical examination, it could be seen that the shortages were concentrated in the rifle companies. The division had seen hard fighting during the *Tet* battles as well as in the post-*Tet* counteroffensive in Dinh Tuong Province. The average loss per company may have been higher than in other

PADDY STRENGTH

divisions as the 9th was one of the few units in the theater with three-rifle company battalions. In hard fighting, the exposure rate of each company to losses tended to be higher than in a four-rifle company battalion. Also, the number of replacements available per division dropped due to the overall losses throughout Vietnam so that losses outweighed gains by an appreciable amount. As a result of all of these factors, many companies ended up with a "paddy strength" of 65 or 70. ("Paddy strength" is the term we used in the wet delta for the number of riflemen present for duty on the battlefield.) A company this size did not handle well in combat and could not stand up well to constant pressure.

Although the men and their commanders did their best without grumbling, it was readily apparent that the strength situation of the division at the combat level would have to be improved markedly if the combat effectiveness of the units was to be increased.

Once we found that our offensive strike capability had been severely blunted by lack of combat infantrymen in the field, we had to establish procedures to increase the paddy strengths of the tactical units. We did not have to look far for improvement because it became obvious that the division headquarters was too fat. First, we eliminated all augmented strengths and temporary duty personnel, except for the Division Headquarters and Headquarters Company and the Division Administration Company. Then we hacked away at these two headquarters units. We pruned the temporary duty personnel by more than half until they totaled about 300 personnel, or less than two percent of the total division strength. Since U.S. Army Vietnam tried to keep all divisions at approximately 102 percent strength, this enabled all of our divisional units to remain at their full Table of Organization and Equipment authorizations—an important factor.

In attacking the problem, we started using the normal personnel reports based on the Morning Report. Unfortunately, this system has a built-in time lag of several days which is aggravated during combat conditions and, while going into gains and losses in detail, does not show exactly how many men are *actually* in combat. We therefore devised a rather simple daily report suitable for radio reporting, called the Paddy Strength Report, which reflected in real time, on a daily basis, exactly how many men were in the paddy. Initially, this information was a rather bitter brew to take, as it showed that our fighting units were much lower strength-wise than our more normal reports suggested.

There were four major problem areas. First, unit losses due to rotation and battle casualties were not being replaced in a responsive fashion. Second, there were diversions of infantry soldiers from line units to brigade and battalion headquarters. Third, there were diversions to run fire support bases where the necessary security and morale activities such as guard, clubs, and post exchange, soaked up enlisted men in alarming amounts. Fourth, there were unexpectedly large numbers of enlisted men attending sick call or with permanent physical profiles which precluded their use in field combat.

To get a handle on these problem areas, the Paddy Strength Report, requiring all maneuver units including brigade headquarters to report their combat strengths on a daily basis, was revised. A very simple format was evolved utilizing morning report data to the maximum extent possible and a set of guidelines was established. The following table and discussion succinctly summarizes the paddy strength reporting procedures and goals:

TABLE 1—PADDY STRENGTH REPORT

Problem	Monitorship Responsibility	Guideline Maximum Leeway	Resulting Rifle Company Strength	Items Reported (Nomenclature)
			164	Authorized Strength
Replacements not properly assigned.	G–1, Division Headquarters	4% or 7 enlisted men	157	Assigned Strength
Diversions to Brigade and Battalion Headquarters, leave, and Temporary Duty.	Brigade Headquarters	10% or 16 enlisted men	141	Present for Duty Strength
Diversions to cover unit overheads, sick call, physical profiles, guard, etc.	Battalion Headquarters	15% or 21 enlisted men	120	Paddy Strength

The Division G–1 was responsible for insuring that all maneuver battalions had assigned at least 96 percent of their authorized strength. The Brigade Commander was then responsible for insuring that brigade and battalion headquarters did not siphon off too many assigned personnel. His guideline was that only 10 percent of assigned personnel could be absent from duty. Thus, the present-for-duty strength per rifle company should have been approximately 141 enlisted men.

The Battalion Commander was responsible for insuring that 85 percent of the present-for-duty personnel were available for combat

THE DELTA ENVIRONMENT—FINDING A CACHE

operations. This meant that a maximum of 21 enlisted men could be diverted to unit overhead. The battalion and company commanders had to keep a tight rein on sick call and physical profiles. Thus the paddy strength of the rifle companies should be at or above 120 enlisted men. This was our key strength figure—one which every company commander knew well.

Actually, the first Paddy Strength Reports were real shockers. They showed, as stated earlier, not only the expected diversions to headquarters units but, more importantly, that there were a large number of combat infantrymen hitting sick call almost daily or walking around with permanent profiles which barred them from field duty. Some units had as many as 50 percent of their unit strength non-available for combat duty because of foot problems alone. Although it was recognized that foot disease had been a severe medical problem in the wet delta, it had not dawned on anyone that the problem was as widespread or as important as the Paddy Strength Reports indicated. Two actions were immediately initiated. The first was to reassign those combat infantrymen with long-term or permanent profiles. In this respect, U.S. Army Vietnam was extremely helpful because they accepted the transfer of 11 Bravos (riflemen) to other units in Vietnam such as depots, where the soldiers would not be required to work constantly in water and where they could perform their jobs adequately in sandals if necessary. The second effort was the initiation of "Operation Safe Step" for the purpose of controlling and minimizing foot problems. This medical research effort proved to be the most important single factor in increasing the paddy strength of the 9th Division.

By holding our feet to the fire, literally and figuratively, our strength situation began to correct itself. After some months the rifle companies were putting 120 men in the paddy routinely and the problem became self-solving and needed only occasional re-emphasis.

Operation Safe Step

The Paddy Strength Report indicated that there was a significant loss of manpower due to sickness that was not being reported through medical channels. Upon investigation, it was found that this loss was due to skin disease, largely of the feet and lower leg, and that not only was the medical reporting system inadequate to measure the losses, but medical personnel lacked the specialized training to make accurate diagnosis or to develop effective preventive measures.

As noted previously, the 9th Division Area of Operations in the delta of Vietnam consisted primarily of inundated terrain including rice paddies and swamp land cut by an intricate complex of canals and streams. As a consequence, skin disease was consistently the major single medical cause of combat noneffectiveness in the 9th Infantry Division. During Fiscal Year 1969, skin diseases of the foot and the boot area accounted for an average of 47 percent of the total combat man-days lost, or an average of 2,238 man-days lost per month. (*Table 2 and Chart 1*) These statistics, although alarming, follow the norm to be expected, because in wars disease usually incapacitates far more soldiers than wounds. Historically, in the tropics, skin disease has been a leading cause of morbidity and lost man-days. During World War II, about 16 percent of the soldiers evacuated from the South Pacific were sent back to the United States for diseases of the skin. In the tropical Southeast Asia area in the British Malayan campaign, skin diseases were the largest single cause of hospital admissions. During their nine years in Indochina (1945–1954), the total French force of 1,609,987 soldiers suffered 689,017 hospital admissions for skin diseases. In Vietnam overall, the four leading causes of noneffectiveness from disease in

TABLE 2—COMBAT MAN-DAYS LOST, 9TH INFANTRY DIVISION MANEUVER
BATTALIONS, 1968–1969

Date	Total Medical/Surgical	Dermatological Foot/Body	Dermatological: Percent of Total
1968			
JULY	3147	1843	59%
AUGUST	3585	1953	54%
SEPTEMBER	4904	2641	54%
OCTOBER	5472	3846	70%
NOVEMBER	3952	2119	54%
DECEMBER	4185	1584	38%
1969			
JANUARY	6237	3063	49%
FEBRUARY	6784	3125	46%
MARCH	5510	2227	40%
APRIL	4812	1811	38%
MAY	4845	1482	31%
JUNE	3605	1167	32%

the U.S. Army were acute respiratory infections, diarrhea, skin diseases, and malaria.

Once the crippling loss of combat strength due to skin diseases was fully appreciated, this factor received strong command interest. We initiated multiple approaches to save time—studying this complex problem on several fronts concurrently. We needed a quick fix. Medical personnel under Colonel Archibald W. McFadden investigated three areas: the nature and causes of these diseases, the actual manpower lost, and simple yet effective control measures. From the outset two facts were obvious. First, only infantry soldiers developed severe incapacitating diseases of the foot and lower leg area and second, it was almost impossible to avoid when operating in the wet terrain of the Mekong Delta.

Our three pronged attack on skin disease was called "Operation Safe Step." It included a controlled series of experimental testing of different models of foot gear, skin protective ointments, and timed exposure to paddy water by a group of enlisted volunteers within the perimeter of the Dong Tam Base. The latter was a most interesting aspect of the investigations, and probably unique in an infantry division in an active combat zone. During the period August 1968 through June 1969, approximately 100 infantrymen were detailed for varying periods to the Division Surgeon for this project in three separate increments. These volunteers included men fresh in the country, experienced paddy soldiers with up to 10 months in the field, combat veterans without skin problems, and

CHART 1—Combat Man-Days Lost, Maneuver Battalions,
9th Infantry Division, 1968–1969

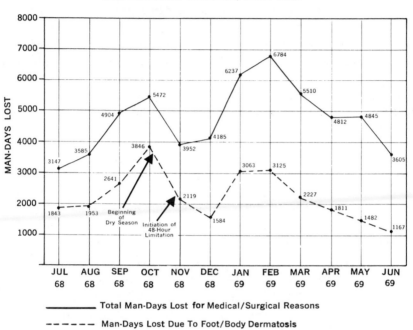

Total Man-Days Lost for Medical/Surgical Reasons

— — — — — — Man-Days Lost Due To Foot/Body Dermatosis

men newly recovered from severe skin disease. This experiment in practical research was suggested by Colonel William A. Akers, Chief of Dermatology Research Division, Letterman Army Institute of Research, and Professor David Taplin, Dermatology Department, University of Miami, and was conducted by the Division Surgeon, assisted by personnel from the 9th Medical Battalion. This was extremely interesting research, and personnel who are knowledgeable in medical research techniques could well afford to inquire into this approach in more detail. Overall, it was a multi-disciplined analysis and, and because of Professor Taplin's pragmatic approach, we rapidly delved into what the diseases actually were and determined more effective treatments.

Through "Operation Safe Step" we initially tried to discover the single "magic" solution to this serious skin disease problem, which would solve it without interfering with the standard infantry tactics of five or more days of unrelenting, aggressive pressure on the Viet Cong. Imaginative and ingenious variations of the standard tropical boot, which were suggested by the Division Surgeon and developed by the U.S. Army Laboratory, Natick, were extensively tested. Unfortunately, these experimental boots were not too helpful. The testing proved that no easy answer existed and that we must experiment with modifications of standard infantry tactics and troop management.

The experiments were conducted in rice paddies, banana groves, and swamp areas within Dong Tam Base, which exactly duplicated the inundated terrain of the delta without the hazards of combat. These tests continued throughout this period and yielded valuable results and confirmation of suggestions from the field. Utilizing volunteer soldiers, six experimental boot models, four experimental boot socks and three protective ointments and lotions were evaluated. The average skin tolerance to water was tested and several anti-leech and mosquito repellants were tested. Experiments were conducted by volunteers barefooted, wearing standard boots and socks, and wearing different boots and socks under controlled timed conditions. Details of the testing of footwear are indicated in the report below:

HEADQUARTERS 9th INFANTRY DIVISION
OFFICE OF THE DIVISION SURGEON
APO SAN FRANCISCO 96370

TESTING OF FOOTWEAR FOR THE MEKONG DELTA
OPERATION SAFE STEP: PHASE II, 1969

In an effort to decrease the skin and foot problems which result from extensive tactical operations in the wet terrain of the Mekong Delta, several new items of footwear were assigned to the Office of the Division Surgeon for testing under simulated combat conditions. Experimental testing of a new Zipper Boot, a 100% Nylon sock (stretch) and a Nylon mesh sock, and a Comfort Slipper has been carried out since early February. The testing and evaluation of these items has recently been concluded and the results are discussed below.

In the first of four separate experiments, the new Zipper Boot was compared to the standard issue Tropical Boot when worn with regular issue O.D. wool socks. No clinical difference in the progression or severity of foot disease was detected between the two boots. However, the volunteers felt that the Zipper Boot drained and dried faster than the Tropical Boot. The thin synthetic material of the Zipper Boot tended to "give" in tension areas, especially around the seams.

The second test compared the 100% Nylon stretch sock with the regular issue wool sock, worn with the standard issue Tropical Boot. The 100% Nylon sock was found to be definitely superior in retarding foot disease due to its fast drying qualities. The men also felt the Nylon sock to be much more comfortable because it didn't hold water or "bunch up" under the foot. They suggested that if the Nylon sock were thicker, it might offer protection from abrasion inside the boot, although this problem was not significant.

The third test compared the Zipper Boot to the Tropical Boot when worn with 100% Nylon stretch socks. The Zipper Boot was found to be on balance superior to the Tropical Boot in this test. Presumably, the increased ventilation of the Zipper Boot became effective in combination with the fast-drying qualities of the Nylon sock. It was again noted that the material of the Zipper Boot frayed easily in stress areas of the Boot. A few men complained that the Nylon sock permitted fine sand to enter between the sock and foot, causing an abrasive effect.

The fourth experiment compared the 100% Nylon stretch sock to the Nylon mesh sock, both worn with the Tropical Boot. The mesh sock was found to be inferior to the stretch sock in preventing foot problems. The mesh sock permitted sand and grit to enter easily, and the abrasive effect of the sand and grit was probably responsible for the early breakdown of the skin. The mesh sock also tore in several cases.

Comfort Slippers Types I and II (lace type and velcro fastener type) have been given initial field tests. The lace type Comfort Slipper proved to stay on the foot better when actually running through paddy type terrain. The fastener type was easier to take on and off, and thus more suitable for base camp conditions. When the fastener type Slipper was laced through the auxiliary eyelets, it too remained on the foot during the paddy run.

Long range field studies of the Zipper Boot, the 100% Nylon stretch sock, the Nylon mesh sock, and the Comfort Slipper are now in progress among the maneuver battalions of the Division. These studies should be concluded within one month.

> A. W. MC FADDEN, MD
> COL, MC
> C, DC&CHCS

A summary of findings of "Operation Safe Step" follows:

(1) Normal healthy skin can tolerate about 48 hours of continuous exposure to paddy water and mud before developing Immersion Foot Syndrome.

(2) Fungal infection of the severe inflammatory type due to Trichophyton Mentagrophytes did not develop until after about three months of paddy duty.

(3) Nylon boot socks were markedly better than the issue wool boot socks in reducing skin disease, quick drying, comfort and troop acceptance.

(4) Soft, tennis shoe-like NOMEX comfort shoes were valuable in replacing combat boots in base camp for the same reasons as noted above.

(5) No experimental boot tested was completely suitable for use in the Mekong Delta terrain. Suggestions for improvement in the standard boot included the adoption of the "Panama Sole"

design, reduction of the amount of leather, replacement of canvas with strong NOMEX fabric and zippers instead of laces.

(6) Miscellaneous experiments resulted in the following conclusions or recommendations:

(a) Silicone protective ointments were useless due to discomfort and troop rejection.

(b) A protective lotion supplied by Colonel William A.

TAKING TEN

IMMERSION FOOT?

CHART 2—Fungal Disease (Foot and Boot Area)

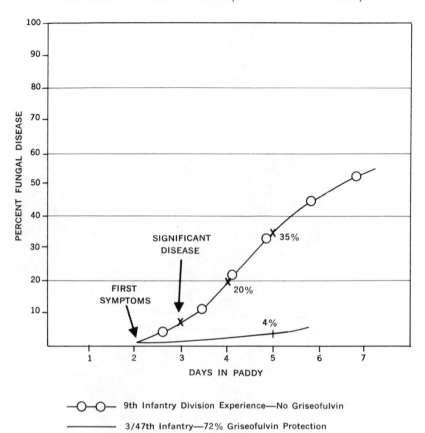

Akers, MC, showed promise in delaying the onset of Immersion Foot Syndrome.

(c) The anti-leech lotion was not acceptable to the troops and therefore not effective.

Three important diseases were identified through investigations in the field and practical research in "Operation Safe Step." These diseases all affected the foot and boot area; yet, each required a specific treatment:

(1) Fungal Infection. In the tropics fungal infections on the body usually begin as small reddish scales around the ankles, on the top of the foot, on the buttock and on the groin. Itching is mild at first but can become unusually severe. Tiny vesicles appear and when the patient scratches off the top of the vesicles bacteria invade, causing secondary infections. Although the patient with extensive or very inflamed fungal infection may be quite miserable

and incapacitated for several weeks, his general health is unharmed and he will fully recover. Fungal infection can be both treated and prevented, to a substantial degree, by Griseofulvin, an anti-fungal antibiotic. The graph in chart 2 indicates the disabling effects of fungal infections.

(2) Immersion Foot. Immersion foot in its classic form is unique to the 9th Division in the delta. It almost inevitably develops in approximately 95 percent of all personnel exposed. Its late results are similar to cold weather trench foot of World War II with damaged circulation and intolerance to cold weather. It is caused by prolonged exposure to rice paddy, water, and mud in the tropical environments of the delta while wearing the standard issue tropical boots plus the issue wool cushioned socks. To clarify this point—the native rice farmer rarely develops the condition because he wears sandals or goes barefooted and dries out his feet periodically during the day and at night. Its early symptoms are swelling of the entire boot area. The soles of the feet are dead white and soggy with deep wrinkles associated with moderate pain on walking. The rather severe symptoms resemble the foot of a drowning victim—the foot has swelling and is dead white in appearance. There is a painful burning surface when the feet hang down and they are exquisitely tender to touch. Frequently the top layer of skin comes off in silver dollar size patches where it is rubbed off at boot friction points. The entire sole is hardened, swollen and painful to walk on. The best treatment of this disease is prevention. Soldiers need bed rest and then gradual ambulation without boots. No medicine used internally or on the skin will influence immersion foot. The effects appear to be cumulative and several moderate episodes will result in the inability to wear boots and the men then require a permanent profile and are lost to infantry duty. Chart 3 shows the disabling effects of tropical immersion foot syndrome. This chart indicates that shortly after two days in the rice paddies a unit could generally become as much as 50 percent disabled. Thus the syndrome can be almost completely avoided by limiting exposure to 48 hours.

(3) Pyoderma Bacterial Skin Infections. There are always bacteria on the skin and the heat and humidity of the tropics is an excellent incubator. Minor skin injuries under these conditions are prone to secondary infections. No really effective solution was found to treat or to prevent bacterial skin infections, although a Walter Reed Army Institute of Research team had developed some very promising information just before the 9th Division departed

CHART 3—TROPICAL IMMERSION FOOT SYNDROME

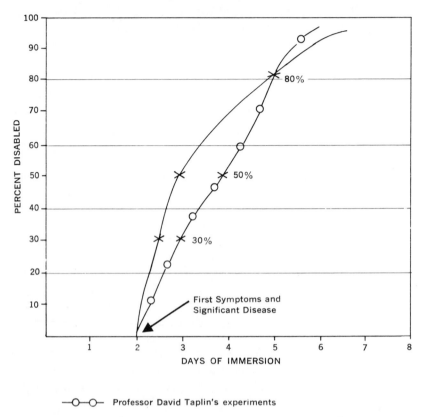

─○─○─　Professor David Taplin's experiments

─────　9th Infantry Division experience and operation Safe Step

Vietnam. Chart 4 is an indication of the disabling effects of pyoderma bacterial infection.

The results of the tests for the 3rd Battalion, 47th Infantry are indicated in chart 5 for the period July through December 1968. It can be seen that once the 48 hour rule was initiated the incidence of immersion foot dropped to almost zero and that at no time did fungal infections become a major problem. However, the incidence of pyoderma continued to rise and became the major cause of lost time due to dermatological diseases. (The onset of the dry season also tended to depress the end figures).

The medical reporting system within the 9th Division was initially found to be defective in three major aspects. First, statistics reflecting time lost from duty because of disease were grossly inaccurate since they normally included only soldiers sick in quarters in medical battalion facilities and hospital admissions. Secondly,

CHART 4—Pyoderma—Bacterial Infection (Foot and Boot Area)

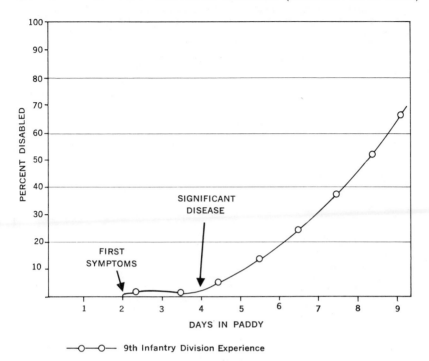

—O—O— 9th Infantry Division Experience

these reports were tabulated monthly and were not suited for the close day by day monitoring of a serious disease problem. Finally, the information often was based on inaccurate diagnoses because of the lack of dermatological experience in the physicians. To overcome these shortcomings a daily Dermatological Sick Call Report was required from each divisional medical treatment facility. This material was tabulated (*Table 3*) and forwarded to Division Headquarters with comments in a Weekly Dermatology Sick Call Summary. The same information in a shorter form was presented in the Weekly Administrative Briefing. These reports accomplished several important functions: they provided an accurate measure of the loss of combat strength due to skin disease, they provided a timely monitoring system for the commander, and served to increase the interest of medical officers and unit commanders in this serious problem.

The complete preventive dermatology program was interrelated, including medical diagnosis and treatment, administrative reporting and monitoring, and the most important component of command support. The single most important contribution to the solution of the problem was a directive on 28 October 1968 which limited

CHART 5—COMBAT MAN-DAYS LOST DUE TO DERMATOSIS,
3D BATTALION, 47TH INFANTRY, JULY–DECEMBER 1968.

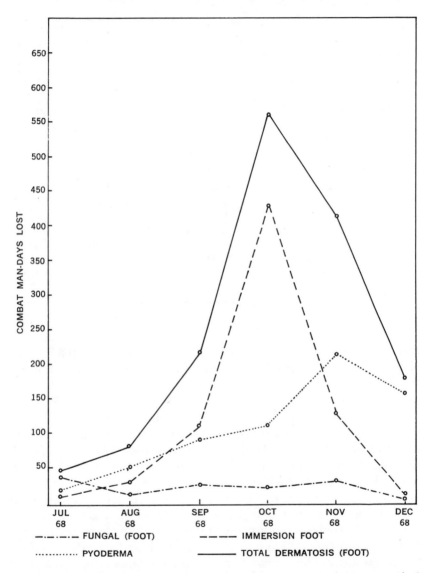

combat operations to 48 hours (except in real tactical emergencies) followed by a 24-hour drying out period. This was a radical departure from normal Vietnamese practice which favored longer periods in the field for various cogent reasons.

"Operation Safe Step" proved that command supported practical medical research of significant medical problems was feasible in a

TABLE 3—NINTH INFANTRY DIVISION WEEKLY DERMATOLOGY SICK CALL REPORT SUMMARY
PATIENTS/MAN DAYS LOST [a]
PERIOD 19–25 JUNE 1969

| Ninth Division Units | MDL All Med/Surg Causes | Dermatology Body | | Foot Disease—Patients/Man Days Lost | | | | | | | | Total Ft. Dis | |
| | | | | A. Pyoderma | | B. Fungal | | C. Immersion Foot | | D. Other (Misc) | | | |
		Pts	MDL	Pts	MDL	Pts	MDL	Pts	MDL	Pts	MDL	Pts	MDL
6/31 Inf	9	43	—	3	—	1	—	4	—	4	—	12	—
2/39 Inf	175	10	15	14	20	1	1	12	14	—	—	27	35
3/39 Inf	52	8	—	—	—	10	10	1	1	12	9	23	20
4/39 Inf	99	19	30	10	1	1	—	9	2	5	2	25	5
2/47 Inf	139	53	16	7	7	7	1	—	—	13	4	27	12
3/47 Inf	139	11	24	12	17	4	4	7	15	5	7	28	43
4/47 Inf	137	7	2	25	22	16	19	39	19	1	—	81	60
2/60 Inf	32	12	—	4	—	8	—	3	—	1	—	16	—
3/60 Inf	62	10	8	—	—	2	—	8	3	1	—	11	3
5/60 Inf	92	15	11	1	—	1	—	—	—	16	20	18	20
Man Bn Tot	936	188	106	76	67	51	35	83	54	58	42	268	198
Average	93.6	18.8	10.6	7.6	6.7	5.1	3.5	8.3	5.4	5.8	4.2	26.8	19.8
Oth	390	203	64	4	—	4	5	—	—	13	2	21	7
Div Totals	1326	391	170	80	67	55	40	83	54	71	44	289	205

[a] Man Days Lost (MDL) reports each day a soldier is medically unfit to perform in his MOS, includes Quarters, Limited Duty and No Paddy Duty

combat division in the field. The 9th Infantry Division rapidly developed a highly successful integrated program to manage the serious skin disease problems in the Mekong Delta that had eluded control in previous conflicts in tropical Southeast Asia.

Management of Unit Missions

As we began to get our unit strengths under control through use of the Paddy Strength Report, it became apparent that we had defensive missions assigned which were adversely affecting our ability to conduct offensive operations. For example, at one time, we had the following diversions: protecting U.S. Army, Vietnam, ammunition unloading point, 1 company; defending signal relay site, (1 platoon), ⅓ company; defending POL tank farm (1 battalion), 3 companies; defending a remote artillery position, 1 company; defending two major bridges, 1 company; and convoy protection, 1 company—a total of 7⅓ companies.

These missions had accumulated over a period of time and were necessary. Initially, they were not too burdensome, as units which were tired or cut up could be diverted to these tasks and while

DEFENSIVE VIGIL

performing the defensive missions could rebuild and retrain. However, we began to see that regardless of the way it was handled that slightly over one-quarter of our divisional infantry units (7.3/27 = 27+ percent) were defending critical installations and not carrying the fight to the enemy directly. Fortunately, the division, in the spring and summer of 1968, was shifting into the delta, and some of these tasks were passed off to other units. As the overall security situation improved, some were simply terminated as no longer necessary. When the Government of Vietnam mobilized in 1968, regular South Vietnamese Army units or Regional Force and Popular Force units became available and took over some of the remaining tasks. Suffice it to say that after about six months, they had all been closed out, and the division was able to concentrate practically all of its units on offensive operations.

The effect of these efforts was most dramatically brought out in Long An Province. In early 1968 there were six rifle and three mechanized companies in Long An Province (three battalions). Three of these companies were on these defensive operations. As a result, each battalion had only two companies available for mobile offensive operations and all other missions. In effect, they were just barely keeping the enemy off balance and worried. During the Mini-*Tet* offensive against Saigon, the enemy was able to move three or four of the five Main Force battalions in Long An against Saigon and to put on a fairly creditable attack. In addition, Long An while the most populous and richest (rice-wise) province in all of III Corps was the least pacified. We decided we had to do better in Long An, and as a result in late June 1968, we moved our best brigade into the province with two very good "strike" battalions (2d Battalion, 39th Infantry and 2d Battalion, 60th Infantry) plus a mechanized battalion. Due to the previous culling out of defensive missions, these two battalions were able to devote almost 100 percent of their effort to mobile offensive operations and were able to break up the enemy battalions in Long An over a period of months.

The Mathematics of Troop Management

Each of the efforts mentioned previously achieved measurable results in isolation. However, taken all together, the increase in unit or troop availability was most impressive.

	March 1968 Unit Base	3 to 4 Company Reorganization	6th Battalion, 31st Infantry Addition	Mechanized Battalion Swap
Infantry Companies	$7 \times 3 = 21$	$7 \times 4 = 28$	$8 \times 4 = 32$	$9 \times 4 = 36$
Mechanized Companies	$2 \times 3 = 6$	$2 \times 3 = 6$	$2 \times 3 = 6$	$1 \times 3 = 3$
	27 Cos. 100%	34 Cos. 125.9%	38 Cos. 140.7%	39 Cos. 144.4%

In looking at it from this point of view, the Division gained 44 percent in rifle companies, the majority of which (26 percent) resulted from the "squaring" reorganization based on the Army Combat Operations Vietnam evaluation, with the remaining 18 percent due to the other changes.

By a combination of refining unit missions and concentrating on the offensive we were able to reduce defensive effort and increase offensive effort. The mathematical improvement on a division basis was impressive.

	Spring 1968	June 1968	Spring 1969
Available Cos.	27	31	39
Offensive Effort	50 percent	66 percent	66 percent
Companies on Offense	13.5	20+	26

It can be seen that from a purely mathematical point of view the increase in offensive effort from both organizational and management improvements was in the neighborhood of 100 percent.

Before the *Tet* battles, the 9th Division was scattered over a large area. Its Tactical Area of Interest, the area which it overwatched, included all or part of at least eight provinces, and its Tactical Area of Responsibility included all or part of four large provinces. By late 1968, as the division moved south to the Upper Delta, both of these areas had been reduced to more manageable proportions. The following gives an indication of this concentrating effect:

Pre-*Tet* TAOI (provinces)	Pre-*Tet* TAOR (provinces)	Late '68 TAOI (provinces)	Late '68 TAOR (provinces)
Long An	Long An	Long An	Long An
Dinh Tuong	Dinh Tuong	Dinh Tuong	Dinh Tuong
Go Cong		Go Cong	
Bien Hoa	Bien Hoa (eastern)		

Pre-*Tet* TAOI (provinces)	Pre-*Tet* TAOR (provinces)	Late '68 TAOI (provinces)	Late '68 TAOR (provinces)
Long Khanh	Long Khanh (western)		
Phuoc Tuy			
Binh Thuy			
Gia Dinh			
(parts from time to time)			
		Kien Hoa	Kien Hoa
Strategic Reserve IV Corps	Strategic Reserve IV Corps	Strategic Reserve IV Corps	Strategic Reserve IV Corps

It should be noted that the geographical assignment of missions was not as simple or tidy as suggested. However, the chart does bring out that the division's geographical responsibilities became much more limited, thus permitting it to essentially focus ten battalions on three provinces. (Go Cong required little effort.) The psychological and intellectual focus was probably of equal importance. With more manageable areas and missions all commanders felt more confident and became more able to influence their situations. As a result, the impact of the brigades was improved markedly. For example:

Long An Brigade

In early 1968 because of static details only six companies out of the three battalions in Long An were offensively oriented. After squaring the battalions and shaking out the defensive missions about 8 of the 11 companies were committed offensively. The actual improvement was more than the figures would suggest, as the brigade commander was able to put on more and constant pressure and to react more quickly with his own resources.

The Riverine Brigade.

The historical Riverine method of operating can be described as three days of full effort and five of rest, rehabilitation, and training, or 37.5 percent offensive effort for six companies. After we understood paddy foot better and changed to the 48-hour exposure rule and added one battalion, the brigade effort was increased and fluctuated between a 66 and 75 percent operating rate for twelve companies with a quadrupling of offensive effort. Quite a jump!

The Dinh Tuong Brigade.

In the spring of 1968 this brigade could muster 2 battalions totalling 6 companies with 4 on offensive effort. By late 1968 it had

RIVERINE FORCE

3 battalions totalling 12 companies with 9 on offensive operations. This more than doubled their offensive effort.

In summary, by a combination of reorganizations, tight personnel control, emphasis on offensive operations, "Operation Safe Step," and a more manageable mission, the division was able to increase its offensive effort at least one hundred percent across the board. These increased resources were then devoted to a more concentrated effort due to the smaller area of responsibility.

If one were to draw up a set of rules for the 9th Division area, it might be that the optimum solution would be:

A reasonable configuration for effective operations in a manageable area would be ten 4-company rifle battalions at full strength.

Three-company rifle battalions resulted in a marked loss of efficiency.

Seriously understrength rifle companies resulted in a loss of efficiency.

A thirteen-battalion division would probably be the best arrangement for operations giving a good balance between foxhole strength, flexibility, and effective control with a low overhead ratio.

This is partially an intuitive judgment although based on good results obtained with four-battalion brigades from time to time.

It might be added that our experience in this area was that tight management, plus a continuing analysis of missions, areas of operation and organization brought about a maximizing of effort and very good control of operations.

Tiger (Kit Carson) Scouts

An important element of our program for strengthening our units and improving their effectiveness was the Kit Carson Scout or Tiger Scout program. This program impinges on many aspects of our overall strengthening process and it is covered here only as a matter of convenience.

The Kit Carson Scout Program (which for unknown reasons was called the Tiger Scout Program in the 9th Division) was well known in Vietnam. It consisted of hiring Viet Cong or North Vietnamese Army soldiers who had defected (and were known as Hoi Chanhs), and integrating them in U.S. units. These defectors, who invariably were strongly anti-Communist once they had deserted, were used in rifle squads as riflemen or scouts. Their guerrilla skills, their local knowledge, familiarity with the local language, and their ability to communicate with the Vietnamese people made them invaluable. Unfortunately, their command of English was usually very limited, but after some contact with the unit in which they lived and fought, they were able to communicate rea-

TIGER SCOUT

sonably well. After having the advantage of good food, good medical care and the superior training of the U.S. units, they made first class soldiers.

In the spring of 1968, the 9th Division was authorized in the neighborhood of 250 Tiger Scouts. In theory, that put about two Tiger Scouts in each rifle platoon, but in practice we did not have as many as authorized. It had been our experience, heretofore, that it was difficult to recruit as many scouts as we were authorized. After assessing the advantages of the program and making a few trial runs, it was determined that the recruiting possibilities were actually quite good, but the program suffered from a combination of lack of attention by lower commanders and a certain subconscious uneasiness at having Communist defectors in frontline units. In any case, we started an organized recruiting campaign and were very rapidly able to have our authorization raised to somewhat over 400 scouts in the division. The direct cost to the U.S. Government was quite low as their pay scale, although attractive in Vietnamese terms, was quite modest.

The increased authorization and recruitment allowed us to put one Tiger Scout in each rifle squad, as well as specialists in intelligence and reconnaissance units and prisoner of war interrogation teams. One very direct bonus from this arrangement was that it automatically increased our rifle strength by ten percent, and counteracted the effect of U.S. soldiers being absent due to rest and recreation, sick call, and wounds. Not only did this device increase our rifle strength, but it had many indirect bonuses alluded to above. It obviously broke down the language barrier to a certain extent as the scouts could talk to prisoners, the local population, or to members of the Vietnamese armed forces. Not only could they converse with these people, but due to their knowledge of the country, they were able to solicit information from them that an American could never obtain in any case. They were also very good scouts—they had an intimate knowledge of Communist tactics and could, as a result, feel out situations by instinct which the inexperienced among the U.S. soldiers had to figure out the hard way. Interestingly enough, the Tiger Scouts proved to be extremely able and loyal members of the team. Although some of them were discharged due to illness or lack of ability, the number of scouts who deserted or were suspected of rejoining the Communist forces was extremely low, perhaps a handful at most. All in all, this was a most successful program as it not only strengthened our own units, but helped to soften some of the major difficulties inherent in a U.S. unit working in a strange country.

The Pay Off

A recapitulation of the aforementioned six actions indicates the terrific impact that close management of units and personnel can have upon the operational effectiveness of a Division. After the May offensive against Saigon we reoriented our thinking towards the Delta. Our movement from the Bearcat area to Dong Tam commenced in early June 1968 and was completed in July. When we started our reorientation we had 21 straight-leg and 6 mechanized infantry companies available for combat operations; of these, seven and one-third were tied up on static missions and each company could field not more than 80 riflemen. Our infantry companies operated in the delta environment and in the jungle areas around Bearcat fifty percent of the time. This amounted, then, to about 780 infantrymen aggressively seeking the enemy on a daily basis.

After our reorganization to four-rifle company battalions, the windfall of another infantry battalion and the exchange of one of our mechanized battalions for another infantry battalion we ended up with 39 infantry companies. Additionally, as the result of intensive personnel management by the use of the Paddy Strength Report these companies had a minimum combat strength of 120 men. The flexibility afforded by the reorganization plus improved techniques in night operations allowed us to increase the tempo of operations to three companies per battalion in the field on a daily basis. This amounted to about 3,500 infantrymen breathing down Charlie's neck every day and night of the year–an increase of about 350 percent in the resources available for combat operations.

This rather slow and difficult process took from six to nine months to bring to completion. Obviously, the division was more effective. However, the real gain was to get the division up to its design Table of Organization and Equipment strength where it became a responsive and effective fighting machine.

CHAPTER III

Optimizing Army Aviation Assets and Support Facilities

In the Mekong Delta combat capability was directly correlated with Army Aviation assets. We soon found that we had little tactical success without helicopters. They provided mobility and fire power as well as surprise. The Air Cavalry troop was the eyes of the division and the "slicks" gave us our maneuverability. Since the tactical success of the division hinged so much on aircraft support, great command emphasis was placed on this vital area. We successively analyzed five major aspects of aviation: maintenance, combat effectiveness, aircraft allocations, tactics, and aircraft utilization. Operations Analysis was utilized to maximize each of these aspects of air operations.

Maintenance

We knew we needed more aircraft on a daily basis if we were going to improve our operational success. But before going to higher headquarters for assistance we decided to get our own house in order. This meant maximum utilization of organic aircraft, and you can't fly them unless they are flyable. Applying the maintenance lessons learned in mechanized units in Europe we attacked our aircraft maintenance problems. Little by little, these efforts proved successful and by July 1968 an integrated maintenance program had evolved. However, we had to wait until about November 1968 for the completion of some of the maintenance hangars at Dong Tam to put our total program into effect. We formalized what we were doing as an "Eight Point Maintenance Program," consisting of:

(1) Direct Supervision by the Division Aviation Officer.
(2) Decentralized Maintenance.
(3) Reorganized Aircraft Distribution.
(4) Expanded Prescribed Load Lists.
(5) Aggressive Management of Authorized Stockage Levels.
(6) Weekly Maintenance Stand-down.

(7) Night Maintenance.
(8) Aggressive Management of Assets.

In actuality this proved to be the basic formula for the successful utilization of our aviation assets, both organic and attached. Since the program was so successful for our own aircraft, we later utilized it for attached and most supporting aircraft.

Direct Supervision by the Division Aviation Officer.

The operations of an infantry division are so diverse and there are so many decision-making centers that the organization almost violates the basic rule of sound management—manageable span of control. Under the normal division organization the commander must deal with many officers on aviation matters: the Aviation Officer, the Armored Cavalry Battalion Commander, the three brigade commanders, the Division Artillery Commander, and the Maintenance Battalion Commander. We decided early to place all our aviation assets under the supervision of the Division Aviation Officer for maintenance matters and to hold him responsible overall for the maintenance of aircraft. This did not include operational control which was retained by those units to which the aircraft were assigned. Every evening around 2200 hours the Division Aviation Officer was required to give a complete rundown of the status of all aircraft assigned to the division as well as his maintenance plans for the night. Since tactical planning depended to a great extent upon the availability of aircraft, this procedure allowed the G–3 to revise plans for the next day if necessary. Then again at 0700 hours at the morning briefing the Division Aviation Officer again provided a complete rundown of aircraft availability, incorporating all changes resulting from the night's maintenance. The summary chart utilized at the morning briefing is shown in table 4. Operational plans were again adjusted, if necessary, based on this information and on the intelligence picture.

Decentralized Maintenance.

Direct supervision by the aviation officer was greatly facilitated by attaching Company B, 709th Maintenance Battalion, the aviation maintenance company, to the 9th Aviation Battalion. We did this as part of a Department of the Army test that was supervised by the Army Concept Team in Vietnam. However, had there been no tests this step would have been taken because of the necessity to combine as much operations and maintenance as possible. We also expanded the maintenance operations of Delta Troop,

TABLE 4—9TH INFANTRY DIVISION DAILY AIRCRAFT AVAILABILITY

Unit	Type	Assigned	Opera-tionally Ready	Org Maint	Support Maint	% Available
A, 9th Aviation	UH–1D/H	28	24	1	3	86
B, 9th Aviation	UH–1C	4	4	0	0	
	AH–1G	6	5	1	0	
	LOH	4	3	1	0	
	U6–A	2	2	0	0	
		16	14	2	0	87
D Troop, 3d Battalion, 5th Cavalry	UH–1D/H	7	6	0	1	
	AH–1G	9	7	1	1	
	LOH	9	7	2	0	
		25	20	3	2	80
1st Brigade	LOH	4	3	1	0	75
2d Brigade	LOH	4	3	1	0	75
3d Brigade	LOH	4	3	1	0	75
Division Artillery ...	LOH	7	6	1	0	86
9th Division	TOTAL	88	73	10	5	83

3rd Battalion, 5th Cavalry and A Company, 9th Aviation Battalion so that they could perform third echelon maintenance. This decentralization of third echelon maintenance to three units was a real shot in the arm—the two major users maintained their own aircraft and B Company, 709th Maintenance Battalion provided maintenance for all the other units.

Reorganized Aircraft Distribution.

We soon learned that maintenance of a proper prescribed load list or authorized stockage level in a combat situation with the high turbulence in personnel and aircraft was a herculean task. To facilitate this task the aircraft within the division were redistributed to have, as far as posible, only a single type aircraft assigned to each unit. Table 5 indicates the final aircraft distribution. Of the nine units involved, six ended up with only one type of aircraft, one unit had no aircraft, and two units had multiple type aircraft assigned. This redistribution facilitated maintenance, since most mechanics needed to familiarize themselves with only one type of aircraft and most prescribed load lists reflected only the parts of one aircraft type. Only Bravo Company, 9th Aviation Battalion and Delta

Type Aircraft

TABLE 5—AIRCRAFT DISTRIBUTION

Unit	UH-1D/H		UH-1C		AH-1G		LOH		U6-A		TOTAL	
	TOE AUTH	ASGD	TOE AUTH	ASGD	TOE AUTH	ASGD	TOE AUTH	ASGD	TOE AUTH	ASGD	TOE AUTH	ASGD
Co A, 9th Aviation Battalion	25	28	0	0	0	0	0	0	0	0	25	28
Co B, 9th Aviation Battalion	2	0	0	4	6	6	4	4	0	2	12	16
B/709th Maintenance Battalion	2	0	0	0	0	0	0	0	0	0	2	0
D Trp, 3d Battalion 5th Cavalry	6	7	2	0	9	9	9	9	0	0	26	25
1st Brigade	0	0	0	0	0	0	4	4	0	0	4	4
2d Brigade	0	0	0	0	0	0	4	4	0	0	4	4
3d Brigade	0	0	0	0	0	0	4	4	0	0	4	4
Division Artillery	0	0	2	0	0	0	9	7	0	0	11	7
3d Battalion, 5th Cavalry	0	0	0	0	0	0	0	2	0	0	0	2
TOTAL	35	35	4	4	15	15	34	34	0	2	88	90

Troop, 3d Battalion, 5th Cavalry ended up with more than one type of aircraft.

Expanded Prescribed Load Lists.

Our two highest density units were Co A, 9th Aviation Battalion and Delta Troop, 3d Battalion, 5th Cavalry. We received permission to expand their prescribed load lists to double the normal stockage. These expanded prescribed load lists went hand and hand with third echelon maintenance capabilities and insured the division the capability of performing most of its sophisticated maintenance right in these units. The expanded prescribed load lists cut our maintenance down-time in half in these units.

Authorized Stockage Lists.

The Authorized Stockage List for aircraft parts was broken out from the card deck of the 709th Maintenance Battalion. The concept was to have two separate decks, both supported by the single repair parts dedicated NCR 500 computer. Ideally both decks (aviation and general parts) should have been run through a daily cycle but because the NCR 500 was overloaded and because we were running so many research programs on the machine it was possible to cycle only the aviation repair parts deck on a daily basis. Every day of the week parts runs were made by helicopter and by wheeled vehicle. We maintained a liaison sergeant at the Aviation Maintenance Management Center run by the 34th General Support Group. The liaison thus established was invaluable and the support provided by the 34th Group was of the highest order.

Weekly Maintenance Stand-down.

From the aforementioned one might presume that repair parts were the guts of maintenance. That is the truth! Yet even with enough repair parts we found out that operational necessity generally overrode maintenance procedures and aircraft were not getting their periodic inspections as scheduled. Therefore, we initiated an inviolate weekly maintenance stand-down—thus one-seventh of the choppers in the division stood down every day. This paid off handsomely because it enabled maintenance to be performed on minor faults before they became major problems. The weekly stand-down kept our choppers flying out of all proportion to the down-time lost.

Night Maintenance.

The majority of aircraft were utilized in daytime operations. The Light Observation Helicopter (LOH), for example, was generally not useful at night and unless there was a night raid

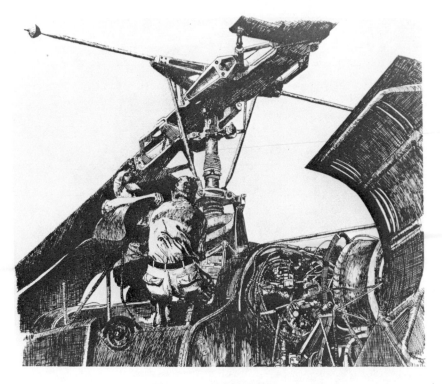

HELICOPTER MECHANICS

scheduled, very few Huey UH–1D or UH–1H models were utilized at night. Since the LOH's and Huey's were about 80 percent of our aircraft it was apparent we had to perform maintenance at night in order to fly more during the day. However, without adequate facilities nighttime maintenance was impossible. Therefore, the first order of priority in the construction of Dong Tam was the provision of adequate hangars. The lights in these hangars burned all night every night—mortar attack or not. Naturally this twenty-four-hour-a-day maintenance took careful personnel scheduling but the morale of the mechanics was high and the pride they took in their work was extraordinary. We rewarded the fine work of the aviation mechanics by various forms of recognition, but few people in the division realized how much they owed to this dedicated group of soldiers.

The aforementioned Eight Point Maintenance Program boils down to just common sense; centralized control, reorganization as required, efforts placed at critical points, and firm and aggressive management. Not apparent in this discussion are all the extremely complex operations required to milk repair parts out of a sluggish

PICKUP ZONE

system, to insure that reports were proper, to schedule periodics so that maintenance was performed, to keep Prescribed Load Lists up to date, to anticipate problem areas, and to inspire the men who performed this around-the-clock repetitive day-to-day maintenance. The net result of the Eight Point Maintenance Program was to raise the availability of aircraft in the 9th Division from around 50 percent to a level consistently above 80 percent. This increase in

PICKUP ZONE

aircraft availability provided commanders with a degree of flexibility that enabled several new tactical techniques requiring aviation support to be tested.

Aggressive Management of Assets.

The 9th Division did a lot of pre-planning but it also maintained maximum flexibility. We reacted quickly to good enemy intelligence; these reactions had to be swift to be effective. Most reactions were dependent upon aviation assets. Therefore we established within the Division Tactical Operations Center an organization with the responsibility for controlling every aircraft, both organic and attached, at all times. We called this our Air Control Team, whose acronym ACT was the essence of their responsibilities. They were provided with the best communications equipment available as well as sharp and aggressive officers. Through the ACT, aircraft could be diverted on a moment's notice from any portion of the division's area of operations to a new mission and we could expect that the subsequent mission would be accomplished rapidly because of the tight management of assets. Although Hueys were *assigned and utilized on a decentralized basis* it was understood that any aircraft could be recalled on the order of the Air Control Team. No aircraft was held in reserve or on standby.

Allocations

It was natural that our first analytic efforts concerning aircraft availability should be directed toward maintenance, because initially it affected our organic assets the most. However, the preponderance of our tactical aviation support was allocated to us by higher headquarters and our combat efficiency was in great part tied to these allocations. During the summer and fall of 1968, II Field Force Vietnam normally allocated us two assault helicopter companies and an air cavalry troop daily. Considering stand-downs and diversions to other units this averaged approximately 53 assault helicopter company days per month and 22 air cavalry troop days per month. When the II Field Force Vietnam air cavalry assets were combined with the organic Delta Troop 3d Battalion, 5th Cavalry it gave us about 48 air cavalry days per month. Thus with three brigades in the field at all times this meant that every day at least one of the brigades was without helicopter support. We had found that the best combination was to provide a brigade with both an air cavalry troop and an assault helicopter company under its operational control. During the summer of 1968 the main thrust of all our tactical planning was to determine the greatest enemy threat or the most lucrative intelligence target so that we could allocate our scarce air assets to obtain the maximum results. The brigade in Long An Province because of its strategic location south of Saigon and its nearness to the Cambodian Border received the lion's share of the helicopter assets—25 days a month. The brigade in Dinh Tuong Province had helicopter assets an average of 17 days a month and the Riverine Brigade operating in Kien Hoa Province received helicopter assets an average of only 8 days per month. Although the Viet Cong capabilities in Dinh Tuong and Kien Hoa were about the same, the riverine force had some "built-in" mobility due to their naval assault craft while the brigade in Dinh Tuong was on foot—thus the difference in the allocation of assets.

In mid-August 1968 we found that the use of the "People Sniffer" (Airborne Personnel Detector) was giving us good results in finding Viet Cong. At the time we were probably one of the few units in Vietnam that thought highly of the People Sniffer. In retrospect the reason was undoubtedly that the terrain in the delta was ideal for the device as compared to jungles and hilly country throughout most of the rest of Vietnam. Consequently, in the fall of 1968 we began to distribute People Sniffer equipment to each brigade on a daily basis to assist them in locating the enemy. In our normal tactical configuration the People Sniffers were carried in a slick belonging to the supporting Air Cavalry Troop and the People Sniffer runs were an integral part of the search techniques of the troop. To give each brigade a daily People Sniffer capability meant simply that we had to make up a reconnaissance team from organic aviation assets. This additional team paid off handsomely in operational results—it gave us an additional nose and pair of eyes but we were still limited in troop carrying assets and gunships. Thus, we followed up lucrative targets by diverting our scarce aviation assets to the hottest target.

It became obvious to any casual observer that when a brigade had aircraft assets, particularly both the air cavalry and the slicks, that its tactical success was greatly enhanced; consequently, we made a systematic study of the effectiveness of the helicopter in combat operations. This study, which is discussed in the next section, proved conclusively that a brigade with chopper assets was much more successful than one without chopper assets. So, we started beating the drums with higher headquarters to get more air assets. Fortunately, we received a welcome break from IV Corps Tactical Zone. Major General George S. Eckhardt, the IV Corps Senior Advisor, had conceived a "Dry Weather Campaign" whose purpose was to make an all out push during the dry weather season in the delta to deal a decisive blow to the Viet Cong in this heavily populated and rice rich area of Vietnam. Military Assistance Command, Vietnam, agreed to the major aspects of this program, including the provision of additional air assets. Commencing in January 1969 the 9th Division thus received a third Assault Helicopter Company and a second Air Cavalry Troop (for a total of three) on a daily basis. Thus, for approximately 26 days a month every brigade had the optimum helicopter support—an Air Cavalry Troop plus an Assault Helicopter Company. This roughly amounted to a 40 percent increase in gross supporting assets. In our opinion, receipt of these additional aircraft was perhaps the most important factor in increasing the combat efficiency of the division.

In addition to our attached helicopter support, by the fall of 1968 we had improved our aircraft maintenance to the point that our organic assets could provide slicks as well as additional improvised air cavalry to our brigades on the days that we did not receive our full ration of attached or supporting aviation. This gave us an additional 15 percent push in the use of aviation assets. On top of that it enabled us to increase our stand-by aircraft for counter-mortar alerts at night and it gave us the capability within division resources to implement some very sophisticated night tactics which evolved in the early part of 1969.

Commencing in January 1969, then, we had maximum coverage of our area of operations in every brigade area utilizing our daytime intensive reconnaisance and air assault techniques. Additionally, in at least two brigade areas we had night coverage which enabled us to interdict Viet Cong movement of supplies and personnel. As a result of this continuous day and night pressure Charlie became unglued in March 1969 and we took him apart completely in April 1969. The increased availability of aircraft as well as our finely honed tactical concepts were keys to these tactical successes.

Improvements in Combat Efficiency
Resulting from Additional Aviation Assets

As we began to get a good feel of those areas affecting combat operations that needed systematic analysis we decided to bring a sharp officer into the Command Section to perform operational analysis on a full time basis. During a period of little over a year we successively utilized three outstanding officers, Major Edwin A. Deagle, Jr., Major John O. B. Sewall, and Major Jack O. Bradshaw. Because of the importance of aviation assets we set Major Deagle on the problem of measuring the improvements in combat efficiency which could be directly related to the input of airmobile resources. Major Sewell performed several studies, one of which, "Jitterbugging Operations," he has presented at Fort Benning. Major Bradshaw produced an outstanding compendium of combat statistics and also documented historical data to support a Presidential Unit Citation submission.

The study concerning improvements in combat efficiency resulting from airmobile assets was particularly informative. We defined our combat environment as one in which the enemy sought to avoid contact. This was our normal situation after the high point of *Tet* 1968 and with few exceptions after that time did the enemy ever mass for major sustained attacks. We concluded then, and continued to believe, that the most direct statistical index of combat efficiency which could be isolated was the damage measured in the number of enemy losses (prisoners of war, Hoi Chanhs and killed-in-action) inflicted on the enemy by a unit in the field.

We recognized that combat efficiency, as defined here, provided no indication of the number of our own battle casualties sustained while inflicting losses on the enemy; therefore, we also included an analysis of our own casualty rates.

The term "airmobile assets" required precise definition. In literal terms, it would have to include assault lift elements, airborne and air transported fire support, command and control aircraft, reconnaissance aircraft, and airmobile logistic support elements. To simplify the analysis, it was assumed that the provision of all types of airmobile resources except assault helicopter units and air cavalry units was reasonably uniform and thus did not materially influence combat performance from day to day. "Airmobile assets" was therefore defined to include Assault Helicopter Companies and Air Cavalry Troops only.

It was the policy in the division to give commanders maximum control of their combat assets. As a result the Assault Helicopter Companies and Air Cavalry Troops were allocated to the brigades on a daily basis and placed under their operational control. Therefore, it was only natural to use the brigade as a basic maneuver unit in a measurement of combat effectiveness of air assets. The study included a total of 313 brigade-days of combat during the period 7 March through 15 August 1968. We hasten to point out that this was an early period of operations before our paddy strength was up and long before we had perfected our tactical innovations. The period was good for statistical purposes but in subsequent months we refined our operations to the point that we expected and received much better results than were obtained during this period.

With no airmobile or air cavalry support, the three brigades averaged 0.21 significant enemy contacts per day spent on field operations. When supported by either an Air Cavalry Troop or an Assault Helicopter Company, brigade performance did not change appreciably, or in any case was not statistically consistent. However, when supported by both an Air Cavalry Troop and an Assault Helicopter Company, average brigade performance more than doubled, to a figure of 0.49 contacts per day. In other words, with no air assets, a brigade averaged a significant contact with the enemy only once every five days; with an Air Cavalry Troop and an Assault Helicopter Company, it developed contact every other day on the average.

Analysis of Viet Cong losses per field day produced more definitive inferences. With no air assets, brigade performance averaged 1.6 Viet Cong losses per field day—hardly a creditable return. With an Air Cavalry Troop, this figure rose to 5.1 Viet Cong per day: an increase in performance of 218%. With an Assault Helicopter Company, performance averaged 6.0 Viet Cong losses per day. It is doubtful that the difference in performance between operations supported by an Air Cavalry Troop and those supported by an Assault Helicopter Company are statistically significant. However, when a brigade was supported by both an Air Cavalry Troop and an Assault Helicopter Company, brigade performance rose to 13.6 Viet Cong losses per day—an increase of 750%. The striking rise in efficiency when both assets were present supports the idea that performance with both assets tends to be somewhat more independent of the leadership styles of the brigade commanders than with either asset alone.

Enemy losses are most meaningful as an indicator of performance when they are compared with friendly losses. It was our desire in the 9th Infantry Division to maximize our capabilities to damage the enemy, with heavy emphasis on prisoners and Hoi Chanhs, and to minimize our own personnel losses. The ratio of enemy losses to friendly losses, then, was considered to be an excellent measure of combat output.

The following table compares the total Viet Cong eliminated with U.S. Killed by Hostile Action as well as U.S. Killed by Hostile Action and Wounded by Hostile Action during the period of the study in the spring and summer of 1968.

TABLE 6—COMBAT STATISTICS MARCH–AUGUST 1968

Forces	Ratio of Enemy Losses to U.S. KHA	Ratio of Enemy Losses to U.S. KHA plus U.S. WHA
With no air assets	8.2	0.54
With an Air-Cavalry Troop only	10.5	1.60
With an Assault Helicopter Company only ...	10.3	1.70
With both Air Cavalry Troop and Assault Helicopter Company	12.9	2.50

It is obvious that air assets not only enhanced the results of brigade operations, but they also enabled us to reduce our own casualties relatively thereby increasing our combat efficiency. We could not be insensitive to total U.S. casualties and Table 6 shows that the overall cost in wounded and killed U.S. personnel was radically reduced when air assets were available as compared to slugging it out on the ground. This is not particularly startling because the increase in maneuverability, fire power and observation was bound to make operations more effective and enable us to protect our troops to the utmost. Thus in terms of inflicting damage to the enemy as well as protecting our own personnel, the capability of an infantry brigade in Vietnam was greatly enhanced by the use of airmobile assets. (Later on it was possible to reduce friendly KHA absolutely as well as relatively.)

The brigade's statistics can be extended into a measurement of divisional effectiveness simply through an additive process. Using the situation in which no air assets are available as an index, the division's combat results would be:

1.6 + 1.6 + 1.6 = 4.8 Viet Cong losses per day

With one Air Cavalry Troop it would become:

1.6 + 1.6 + 5.1 = 8.3 Viet Cong losses per day

Similarly, with two Air Cavalry Troops the Viet Cong losses would increase to 11.8 per day, and with three Air Cavalry Troops the division could be expected to average 15.3 Viet Cong losses per day—an improvement of 218 percent over results with no aviation assets.

Similar calculations can be made for any combination of Assault Helicopter Companies and Air Cavalry Troops—up to three of each. It is pertinent, given the apparent complementary nature of the two assets, to look at the rate of increase in performances for increments of both assets:

> One Air Cavalry Troop and one Assault Helicopter Company
> 16.8 Viet Cong losses per day
>
> Two Air Cavalry Troops and two Assault Helicopter Companies
> 28.8 Viet Cong losses per day
>
> Three of each: 40.8 Viet Cong losses per day

From the 9th Division's point of view, the last figure is the most significant. During the periods examined, the division was allocated on the average slightly less than two Air Cavalry Troops and two Assault Helicopter Companies per day (including the organic Air Cavalry Troop). Had the allocation been three of each (one for each brigade), it is estimated that the division's combat effectiveness for that period would have increased by approximately 40 percent. Moreover, brigades could have been expected to improve further over time since planning would not have been disrupted by last-minute changes in support priorities among the three brigades. Daily operations with the same supporting air units greatly enhanced co-ordination and professionalism—the brigades in effect moved rapidly up the learning curve (a phenomenon which reportedly is inherent to airmobile division units). It is difficult to imagine how similar inputs of any other type of resources (artillery, infantry, etc.) would have generated an equivalent improvement in combat performance.

It is probable that not all divisions in Vietnam would have achieved statistical improvements similar to those of the 9th Division. The inundated flatlands of the Mekong Delta have a double edged impact on the mutual effectiveness between foot and airmobile operations. Marshy swamps and flooded rice paddies severely penalize ground troops. Units frequently are able to move no more than 500 meters per hour or less. On the other hand, the broad stretches of virtually flat delta country provide an ideal environment for the unrestricted employment of Army aviation. Presumably such would not be the case in other areas of Vietnam, but unquestionably the allocation of additional airmobile assets to provide each combat brigade on a daily basis with an Assault Helicopter Company and an Air Cavalry Troop would have increased combat results by a meaningful amount. The actual increases in combat efficiency resulting from the assignment of an Assault Helicopter Company and an Air Cavalry Troop to each brigade have been measured for 9th Division operations and will be discussed in a subsequent section on the payoff of increased Army aviation assets.

Innovative Aviation Tactics

The 9th Division, largely due to a large number of very skillful combat leaders, was particularly innovative in adapting standard tactical techniques to the delta terrain. With respect to the use of aviation assets we fostered several tactical techniques, but they all stemmed from two fundamental changes that materially enhanced our operational capabilities.

As was stated previously, by the fall of 1968 the Viet Cong in our area had broken down into small groups and were avoiding combat at all costs. Consequently, our airmobile assault techniques utilizing an entire Assault Helicopter Company with supporting air cavalry elements were proving ponderous. We wanted to break down into smaller more flexible units in order to be able to cover a larger area and to apply more constant pressure on the enemy. However, airmobile doctrine dictated that each assault be accomplished by 9 or 10 slicks covered by two light fire teams (4 Cobras or other gunships). Consequently, we mustered our thoughts in this matter and briefed Major General Robert R. Williams, the 1st Aviation Brigade Commander, on the desirability of switching to five slick insertions instead of the usual ten. This had drawbacks for the aviation personnel since it required twice as many trained lead ship personnel. However, General Williams gave us the go ahead on a trial basis and we commenced Jitterbugging with five slick insertions. The immediate effect was dramatic. We were able to check out twice as many intelligence targets. We were able to cover broader areas thereby almost doubling the amount of pressure brought to bear on the Viet Cong. Later on, in 1969, when we had chopped up the Viet Cong even worse and scattered them to a greater degree it was commonplace to make 2, 3 and 4 slick insertions without fear of undue casualties in either aircraft or infantry personnel. The single technique of breaking down into smaller assault groups in late October 1968 had extremely far reaching implications for our tactical success. Like many new ideas it had been done before but on a rather selective basis. The new idea was to do it all the time.

The second fundamental change in techniques involved our Air Cavalry Troops, perhaps the most important ingredient in strike operations. As our maintenance improved and the availability of aircraft became greater we split our organic 3d Battalion, 5th Cavalry Troop into two teams. Initially the purpose was to provide daylight reconnaissance for all three brigades when one of our normal supporting Air Cavalry Troops was standing down for maintenance. Subsequently, we evolved night tactics tailored to the

MINIGUNS

use of air cavalry which proved tremendously effective. Our Night Search, Night Hunter and Night Raid techniques, combined with infantry night ambushes, "Bushmaster" and "Checkerboard" tactics, enabled us to keep an around the clock pressure on the enemy. These tactical techniques will be discussed in detail later. Because of our day and night operations we needed two air cavalry teams— a day team and a night team. The nucleus of the day team were the scouts (LOH 6's). There was much argument over whether the scouts should work in pairs under the protection of one Cobra or should work as a Scout-Cobra team. It was our experience in the delta that scouts working in pairs gave optimum coverage and due to the nature of the terrain and sparseness of vegetation that one Cobra could more than adequately provide cover for two scouts. There were others, however, who were in favor of the usual Scout-Cobra Team. Our day teams, then, normally consisted of 1 Command and Control ship, 2 Cobras and 4 Scouts.

On the other hand the Night Search and Night Hunter technique required 1 Command and Control copter and a light fire team (2 Cobras and a Huey flare ship if the ambient light was insufficient to activate our night vision devices). The Night Raid required a Command and Control copter and a light fire team plus 2 or 3 Hueys to insert a small element of combat troops. The total requirements for the Air Cavalry Troop, night team plus day team, amounted to approximately 50 percent of their assets and was met easily on a daily basis.

When our organic as well as supporting units (we cannot speak too highly of the 7th Battalion, 1st Air Cavalry Squadron for their ability to support night operations and the 214th Aviation Battalion for their all-around support) had broken down into the two team concept it literally took the night away from the Viet Cong. This, coupled with the expanded daytime air assault capability, optimized our tactical use of Army aviation air assets.

The two aforementioned simple but highly effective techniques revolutionized airmobile operations in the delta and allowed us to apply relentless pressure, heavily interdicting Viet Cong troop and supply activities as well as weakening his forces to the maximum degree.

Utilization of Army Aviation Assets

As we improved our maintenance and got locked in on our new tactical techniques it appeared as if our major unresolved problem with army aviation was "How much average flying time does it take to adequately support tactical missions?." To get a handle on this question we did a rather exhaustive analysis taking into consideration the tactical techniques and actual aircraft support provided the division by organic and assigned aviation assets. The premise underlying our analysis was that we would have one Air Cavalry Troop and one Assault Helicopter Company per brigade daily plus our organic divisional aviation assets. We considered that maintenance was such that at least 70 percent of the aircraft would be "mission ready" daily. We went about the study on a mission oriented basis, analyzing optimum daily requirements.

Air Cavalry Troop.

We considered a day team and a night team as previously discussed. We felt that the day team should be augmented at least 15 days per month by either the Air Cavalry Troop aero rifle platoon or by 4 Air Cavalry Troop slicks to carry our own infantrymen since some of the air cavalry squadrons were not organized with an aero rifle platoon while others were. On Jitterbugging Operations the use of 4 slicks with aero scouts or organic troops would give us a 50 percent additional troop carrying capability, thus increasing area coverage.

With respect to night team operations we felt that we could conduct eight Night Raids a month when slicks would be required to transport the raiding troops. On the other hand the Night Search and Night Hunter would require only one Command and Control copter and a light fire team (two Cobras). The results of our analyses are shown in Table 7.

SLICKS

SLICKS

TABLE 7—UTILIZATION STATISTICS AIR CAVALRY TROOP

Daily Aircraft Requirements

	UH–1B/D/H C&C	Slicks	AH–1G	OH–6A	Total
Day Team	1	4 [a]	2	4	
Night Team	1	2 [b]	2	—	
Total Requirement	1	4	4	4	13 [c]
Assigned	8		8	9	25
% Aircraft utilized	62%		50%	44%	52%

a—15 days/month
b—8 nights/month
c—Only 1 C&C and 4 slicks need to be mission ready

Hours Per Aircraft Per Day

	UH–1B/D/H C&C	Slicks	AH–1G	OH–6A
Day Team	8	6	8	8
Night Team	4	3	4	—

Total Hours Per Month

	UH–1B/D/H C&C	Slicks	AH–1G	OH–6A	Total
Day Team	240	360	480	960	2040
Night Team	120	48	240	—	408
Total Hours	360	408	720	960	2448
Aircraft Assigned	8		8	9	25
Hours Per Aircraft	96		90	107	98

Pilot Hours Per Month

	UH–1B/D/H [d]	AH–1G [d]	OH–6A	Total
Total Aircraft Hours	768	720	960	2448
No. of Pilots	18	15	9	42
Avg Hrs per pilot	85	96	106	96

d—Two pilots per aircraft

It can be seen that on the average only 52 percent of the Air Cavalry Troop aircraft are committed on a daily basis and that the maximum flying time for any aircraft is 8 hours. The total hours per aircraft per month averaged out to approximately 98 hours. Pilot time averaged 96 hours per month, well below the 140 maximum stipulated by regulations.

Assault Helicopter Company.

The mission of the Assault Helicopter Company is rather cut and dried at first glance; they transport the troops and supplies to

TEAM OF AIR WORKHORSES

the target area. When utilized as a single entity, the Assault Helicopter Company normally provides one Command and Control copter, ten slicks, and two light fire teams comprised generally of four Charlie models (in 1968). However, the Jitterbugging tactics of the 9th Infantry Division normally involved five slick insertions. Under these circumstances it became routine to break the Assault Helicopter Company into two teams of five slicks each. However, the Command and Control copter and the light fire teams normally accompanied each insertion of the five slicks, so that in reality there was a shuffling effect with the troop-carrying choppers. When insertions were made in two dispersed geographical areas, it proved advantageous to have the Air Cavalry Troop cover one insertion and to have one Light Fire Team from the Assault Helicopter Company cover the other. The Bounty Hunters of the 191st Assault Helicopter Company did this with extraordinary results. In such a situation, the ten slicks and two Charlie models would set down awaiting a new insertion while the Command and Control copter circled overhead with the Assault Helicopter Company and infantry battalion commanders and the other Light Fire Team provided troop cover. The aircraft and hour requirements for an Assault Helicopter Company are indicated in table 8. It can be seen that daily aircraft requirements for the Assault Helicopter company are slightly above those for an Air Cavalry Troop, both in percent of

TABLE 8—UTILIZATION STATISTICS ASSAULT HELICOPTER COMPANY

Daily Aircraft Requirements

	UH–1B/D/H		UH–1C	Total
	C&C	Slicks		
Requirement	1	10	4	15
Assigned	19		7	26
% Aircraft utilized	58%		57%	58%

Hours Per Aircraft Per Day

	UH–1B/D/H		UH–1C
	C&C	Slicks	
Hours	10	5¾	6 a

a—Two at 6¼ hours and two at 5¾ hours.

Total Hours Per Month

	UH–1B/D/H		UH–1C	Total
	C&C	Slicks	•	
Hours	300	1725	720	2745
Aircraft Assigned	19		7	26
Hours per Aircraft	107		103	105

Pilot Hours Per Month

	UH–1B/D/H b	UH–1C b	Total
Total Aircraft Hours	2025	720	2745
No. of Pilots	44	23	67
Avg Hrs per Pilot	92	63	82

b—Two pilots per aircraft.

aircraft utilized and in total hours per month, although the average pilot hours per month are less. It is interesting to note that about October 1968 higher headquarters authorized the Division to use its supporting Assault Helicopter Companies 2700 hours per 30 day period. This gave the Division much greater flexibility in that our commanders could use the assault aircraft for long periods when there was a good contact and could cut the flying short when the enemy was not to be found. In order to do this we used a 30-day-moving-average of 2700 aircraft hours which smoothed out humps and valleys. Our own analysis showed that under optimum conditions the average monthly requirement per Assault Helicopter Company was 2745 hours. Quite often intuitive judgment hit requirements right on the head even at higher headquarters.

Organic Divisional Aviation Assets.

The missions of our organic divisional aviation assets varied greatly. By and large, slicks were used as Command and Control

TABLE 9—UTILIZATION STATISTICS ORGANIC DIVISION AVIATION ASSETS

Daily Aircraft Requirements

	UH–1B/D/H	UH–1C	AH–1G	OH–6A	Total
Requirement	18	2	4	15	39
Assigned	28	4	6	23	61
% Aircraft utilized	64%	50%	66%	65%	64%

Hours Per Aircraft Per Day

	UH–1B/D/H	UH–1C	AH–1G	OH–6A
Hours	6	4 [a]	5 [b]	5

a—Night stand-by
b—Night search, night hunts, Ranger insertions and extractions

Total Hours Per Month

	UH–1B/D/H	UH–1C	AH–1G	OH–6A	Total
Hours	3240	240	600	2250	6330
Aircraft Assigned	28	4	6	23	61
Hours per Aircraft	115	60	100	98	104

Pilot Hours Per Month

	UH–1B/D/H [a]	UH–1C [c]	AH–1G [c]	OH–6A	Total
Total Aircraft Hours	3240	240	600	2250	6330
No. of Pilots	63	8	18	24	113
Avg Hrs per Pilot	103	60	67	94	92

c—Two pilots per aircraft

aircraft and performed essential maintenance and administrative functions including courier runs, day and night utility runs, and night radar repair ship. The gunships and Cobras generally were utilized on night standby to react immediately to enemy initiated incidents and as a night air cavalry team in support of the brigades on either Night Search or Night Raid operations. Because of the diversity of tasks, our assessment of utilization was based on a reasonable slice of assigned aircraft. We thought that about two-thirds of all assigned aircraft should be operationally committed on a daily basis. The aircraft and our requirements are indicated in table 9. It can be seen that 64 percent of the aircraft were utilized and the total hours per aircraft per month were 104.

Summary.

Table 10 summarizes operational requirements and hours per month for aircraft for all type units:

TABLE 10—OPERATIONAL REQUIREMENTS, HOURS PER MONTH PER
AIRCRAFT

	UH–1B/D/H	UH–1C	AH–1G	OH–6A	Avg Total
Air Cavalry Troop	96	—	90	107	98
Assault Helicopter Companies.	107	103	—	—	105
Organic	115	60	100	98	104
USARV Avg (Feb 69)	74	64	59	68	67

The total average requirements varied between 98 and 105 hours.
We took a standard of 100 hours/aircraft/month, then, as a utilization rule of thumb. The U.S. Army Vietnam average was much
below this—approximately 67 hours per month. The utilization
standard we established would require a 50 percent increase in
general aircraft utilization over the U.S. Army Vietnam figure. As
a matter of interest, a detailed test was conducted in II Field Force
later on, which demonstrated that efficient aircraft usage peaked
at about 103 or 104 hours per plane per month, as contrasted to
the 70 hours per month previously considered as optimum.

Actually, the utilization of aircraft for the months of February
and March 1969 in support of the 9th Division amounted to 93.1
percent of this established standard. The only major shortfalls were
in the use of Scout aircraft by the Air Cavalry Troops and in the
use of organic Huey assets. The theoretical standard was based
upon proven tactical usage and reasonable aircraft availability
factors (about 60 percent daily). Since actual performance compared favorably with the standard, we felt that the aircraft utilization in the 9th Infantry Division was about optimized with respect
to flying hours.

A review indicated that by December 1968 the flying hours were
also about optimized. We got a big shot in the arm when our
organic and support aviation moved to Dong Tam, enabling us to
operate from a central base location. We also improved our techniques in pre-positioning fuel and ammunition at outlying base
camps in order to cut down on aircraft refueling and rearming time.
Therefore, our aircraft assets were operating as efficiently as we
knew how by making every flying hour count towards tactical
operations.

The Payoff

To improve our tactical effectiveness we knew that we had to
increase our aviation assets. We started out in our own backyard
by implementing the "Eight Point Maintenance Program." The

result was an increase of our aircraft availability, both organic and attached, from 50 to 55 percent to about 80 to 85 percent on a daily basis, enabling us to split our air cavalry assets, forming a day team and a night team. Initially, however, until we obtained a third Air Cavalry Troop we used both organic teams for daylight operations.

Fortunately, the IV Corps Dry Weather Campaign which commenced in January 1969 gave us an additional Assault Helicopter Company and an Air Cavalry Troop. This optimized our tactical aircraft support, allowing an Air Cavalry Troop and an Assault Helicopter Company to support each brigade on a daily basis. Again, improved maintenance of our Hueys allowed us to parcel out 4 or 5 slicks to one of the brigades on those days when a supporting Assault Helicopter Company was standing down, thus keeping up the operational momentum.

In the late fall of 1968 we obtained permission from the 1st Aviation Brigade to split our supporting Assault Helicopter Companies so that we could have twice as many insertions and thus cover a broader area bringing more pressure to bear on the enemy. Throughout this period we were refining our tactics, increasing our aircraft availability and upping our flying hour utilization so that by February and March 1969 we were averaging over 93 hours per aircraft per month. As a result of the move to Dong Tam and the pre-positioning of fuel and ammunition we were able to insure that our flying hours were most productive in supporting combat assaults.

All of this increased our combat performance. Recalling our study which measured the combat efficiency directly related to the inputs of airmobile resources, let us compare actual results with predictions. We found an appreciable increase in the efficiency of a brigade depending on the amount of aircraft under their operational control. In terms of actual results achieved by a brigade: with no air assets 1.6 Viet Cong would be eliminated per day; with an Air Cavalry Troop only 5.1 should be eliminated (we have projected that this figure is valid for both daytime and nighttime operations) ; with one Assault Helicopter Company only, 6.0 Viet Cong should be eliminated daily; and with an Air Cavalry Troop and an Assault Helicopter Company 13.6 Viet Cong should be eliminated daily.

The table below indicates the brigade days of available assets for the period December 1968 through May 1969.

There was little increase in assets between July 1968 and December 1968 when we had Air Cavalry Troops *48 days a month* and Assault Helicopter Companies *53 days a month*. However, as explained above, this changed dramatically in January 1969 with

TABLE 11—BRIGADE-DAYS WITH AIRCRAFT ASSETS, THEORETICAL
COMPUTATION OF VIET CONG ELIMINATED

Assets	Factor, VC Eliminated per brigade per day	Brigade-Days Month						
		Jul 68	Dec 68	Jan 69	Feb 69	Mar 69	Apr 69	May 69
Air Cavalry Troop & AHC	13.6	48	48	81	87	90	70	65
Assault Helicopter Company Only ..	6.0	5	5	0	0	0	20	20
Air Cavalry Troop Only	5.1	0	0	19	37	60	43	60
No Assets	1.6	37	37	9	3	0	0	5
Computation of VC Eliminated		742	742	1213	1377	1530	1291	1318

the addition of 1 Air Cavalry Troop and 1 Assault Helicopter
Company. In the months of February and March we improved our
aircraft availablity so that we could fill the stand-down gap of the
Air Cavalry Troops and Assault Helicopter Companies with organic
aviation. Additionally, we were flying an average of 20 night missions per brigade. In April we lost an air cavalry troop and this
began to have its effect on combat effectiveness. The Viet Cong
eliminated shown in the total at the bottom of table 11 was computed by multiplying the brigade-days by the factors shown.

The actual Viet Cong eliminated per month in combat operations involving day cavalry, night cavalry, and day infantry is shown
in table 12. These were the only type operations that were directly
affected by aviation assets. The Sniper Program, night infantry, and
artillery were not influenced to any appreciable degree by aviation
assets.   `

Note that for the months of July 1968, December 1968, January
1969, and February 1969, the enemy losses computed were roughly
the same as the actual enemy losses attributable to those operations
utilizing aircraft. The exceptions were the sizable improvements

TABLE 12—ACTUAL VIET CONG ELIMINATED

U.S. Units	Jul 68	Dec 68	Jan 69	Feb 69	Mar 69	Apr 69	May 69
Night Cavalry ...	—	34	143	391	580	355	266
Day Cavalry	—	398	341	337	572	429	516
Day Infantry	735	396	539	726	1138	1293	1034
TOTAL	735	828	1023	1454	2290	2077	1816

over the calculated figure for the months of March and April 1969. In these two months everything jelled for the division. The Viet Cong apparatus became unglued and we capitalized on their shock at being taken apart both day and night. After two months of intensive nighttime operations the Viet Cong reacted and partially turned us off and we were never as effective as we were during the initial period of our stepped up night operations.

One might presume that with our improved tactical innovations and optimized flying hour utilization that there should have been a greater improvement in tactical success; yet, except for the exploitations in March and April, the increase in Viet Cong eliminated was directly proportional to the assets available.

But there was in fact a larger payoff. It came in the savings of American lives. (*See Table 13 and Chart 6.*)

While the enemy eliminated remained directly proportional to our aviation assets, our exchange ratio—the ratio of enemy eliminated to U.S. killed—increased dramatically, reaching its peak also during March and April 1969 when the Division-wide ratio was over 80 to 1. This compares to a ratio of around 16 to 1 prior to honing our airmobile techniques. Although we were pleased with our increased efficiency in eliminating the enemy it was this dramatic reduction in the relative (and absolute) loss of our own personnel that was the most satisfying aspect of our improved utilization of aviation assets (and improved tactics).

Optimizing Support Facilities

In the Spring of 1968 the three brigades of the division were located in the Delta area: the 3rd Brigade was located in Long An Province in the III Corps Tactical Zone, a very rich province south of Saigon; the 2d Brigade (Riverine Force) was located primarily aboard ship but was headquartered at Dong Tam with its primary focus toward Kien Hoa Province, IV Corps Tactical Zone, long a Viet Cong stronghold; and the 1st Brigade was located in Dinh Tuong Province, IV Corps Tactical Zone, with the job of keeping open Highway 4, the critical life line for food supplies between the delta and Saigon. On the other hand, the Division Headquarters with the majority of the Support Command and almost all of the

TABLE 13—COMBAT EFFICIENCY EXCHANGE RATIO OF TOTAL ENEMY ELIMINATED TO U.S. KILLED IN ACTION

Jul 1968	Dec 1968	Jan 1969	Feb 1969	Mar 1969	Apr 1969	May 1969
13.6:1	18.6:1	15.6:1	33.0:1	80.9:1	84.8:1	43.4:1

CHART 6–Comparison Actual vs Computed (Base Period March–
August 1968) Viet Cong Eliminated in Airmobile Operations
December 1968 thru May 1969

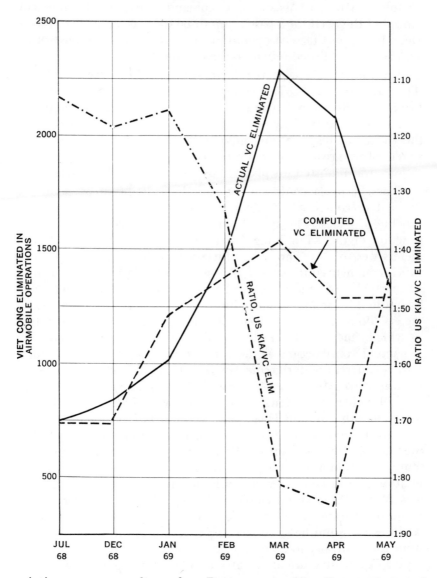

aviation assets were located at Bearcat some 15 miles northeast of
Saigon. This presented major difficulties. The overland supply
route between Bearcat and Dong Tam took 5 to 6 hours since all
vehicles were required to go through Saigon. Even by air it was a
45 minute helicopter flight. Thus our logistical and support op-

erations were very inefficient in that we were operating on anything but interior lines.

In the summer of 1966, long before the 9th Division arrived in Vietnam, Military Assistance Command, Vietnam, became convinced of the need for a base camp to be established in the Mekong Delta to support tactical operations in order to deny the use of the area as an established refuge to the enemy.

Specific criteria with regard to site selection were established. The base camp had to be deep within Viet Cong territory to allow maximum disruption of enemy operations. The land, about 600 acres, had to be sparsely populated so as to be readily available to the United States with minimum resettlement. Ready access to the system of waterways, which are the Delta's major lines of communications, was required for planned use by the Riverine Forces.

These criteria could not be met by existing areas, so it was decided to construct an adequate area by hydraulic fill utilizing pipeline dredges. The site chosen was a rice paddy located at the junction of the Kinh Xang Canal and the Song My Tho, 8 kilometers west of My Tho. The objectives of the dredging operation which commenced in August 1966 were to dredge a 54 acre turning basin capable of handling up to LST type naval craft and to provide hydraulic fill capable of elevating the 600 acre tract an average 2.8 meters. Both of these requirements were met by 29 November 1967 by which time 17 million cubic yards of fill had been dredged.

Actual construction of the cantonment area began in January 1967 concurrent with the construction of a 1500 foot stabilized earth landing strip. After *Tet* 1968, everything was accelerated so that by July 1968 there was enough construction available at Dong Tam to move the 9th Division Headquarters from Bearcat.

The move of the division from Bearcat to Dong Tam took place over a two month period. Each step was well planned, with sound programming techniques to insure that operations at both locations could be carried on without any loss of combat effectiveness. When the division closed at Dong Tam in July 1968, a new phase of operations was heralded. By October, when the heliport facilities were finished, we were able to operate almost completely from this centrally located base. No longer were the Assault Helicopter Companies and air cavalry units wasting approximately two hours a day flying to and from Bearcat in order to conduct combat operations in the delta. The construction of the port facilities enabled ammunition, petroleum and other supplies to be brought directly to the Division Support Command and 1st Logistical Command units supporting the division at Dong Tam. Army and Navy

DONG TAM BEFORE AND DONG TAM AFTER

logistical back-up in the same area enabled better communications and enhanced Riverine Operations. This relocation to Dong Tam, as much as anything else, enhanced the division's combat posture.

The port facilities initially consisting of the turning basin project, started in March 1967 and completed in December of the same year, were expanded by 1969 to include a sheet pile seawall, a LST ramp, a LCU ramp, a pontoon barge finger pier, and storage facilities.

Equally as important as the port facilities was the construction of the huge helicopter facility which included 21,000 square yards of maintenance apron; 351,000 gallons of fuel storage with a 595 gallon pump feeding 24 refueling points, fully capable of handling two Assault Helicopter Companies at once; and 174 helicopter revetments sufficient to park two Assault Helicopter Companies and two Air Cavalry Troops. The most important aspect of the new heliport was the five large hangars which enabled our around the clock maintenance to be performed. Considering the 2700-hour 30-day Assault Helicopter Companies limitations imposed by higher headquarters, the move to Dong Tam resulted in an 18 percent increase in flying hours available for combat operations.

The 12,500-man Dong Tam cantonment area was officially completed on 15 June 1969. The total expenditure by Army and Navy construction agencies involved approximately $8,000,000. The majority of the vertical construction was done by the combat troops themselves who, during the period, expended 572,148 man hours to complete 1,005,600 square feet of buildings while at the same time carrying on extensive combat missions. The more complex buildings and storage facilities were constructed by Army Engineers who also installed a 6,000 kilowatt hardened power plant and distribution system, a 27,000 gallon per hour water purification plant and distribution system a protected Medical Unit Self-Contained Transportable (MUST) hospital facility and 13.5 miles of cement stabilized roadways.

The farsightedness of General Westmoreland, who personally decided to construct this base camp and helped choose the site as well as the name Dong Tam which means "Friendship" in Vietnamese, materially assisted the 9th Division in its efforts to help pacify the Upper Delta Region.

CHAPTER IV

General Background For Battlefield Analysis

We have mentioned earlier that analytical techniques are useful to sub-optimize elements of operations. For example, one cannot readily describe the major functions involved in planning and executing a daylight company reconnaissance. This would require pages of checklists and if done would probably result in a mechanical operation. However, one could idealize and simplify the actual contact and sub-optimize that particular sub-program. As one begins to move up the scale and improve an operation as large and complex as the operations of a reinforced division one has to concentrate on essentials or the effort becomes so diffused that progress is slow and erratic.

The rough rule we used was to concentrate on matters that improved operations, tactics, and intelligence and to let other matters go at their own speed. This concentration was pursued with considerable intensity. We also insisted on rapid results. If an area needed improvement we would quick fix it on the basis of available information and as our data and understanding increased kept recycling the operation and analysis until we were satisfied. This resulted in a rapid surge of improvement that was very encouraging. This was somewhat comparable to painting a moving train—instead of stabilizing a problem for analysis we would analyze it dynamically. The Operation Safe Step research program previously discussed was a good example in that we were able to compress several years of normal sequential experimentation and research into a period of months by means of multiple approaches and plowing partial knowledge back into the project.

This is a subtle process but most profitable when one gets the hang of it. It depends on *focus* and *speed*—which in our case meant emphasis on operations and tactics, pursuing them with intensity and in a timely manner.

Of course there is an ever present danger that the analytic approach may stifle innovation. It is inherently a structured approach which tends to keep thinking and alternatives within certain frameworks. One can only attempt to keep an open mind on the one hand while closing in on the more specific problems through analysis.

This was what we attempted to do as we strove to increase our combat efficiency. We wanted to optimize our results by providing maximum security within our area of operations at the least cost in lives and equipment to the soldiers of the division. These efforts directed towards making our fighting men in the field as efficient as possible in the performance of their missions depended upon our intelligence, tactics, combat operations, and pacification efforts.

The Problem

As mentioned earlier, in the big unit period of the Vietnamese War (1965–1967), the North Vietnamese (and to a lesser extent the Viet Cong) evidently felt that they could defeat United States and South Vietnamese units in face-to-face combat under favorable conditions. During this period, while it was not easy to bring the enemy to combat on our terms, it was a manageable problem. In mid- or late-1967, the Communists went to ground and began to rebuild their units for the *Tet* offensive. This resulted in "evasive" tactics by which the Communists devoted the bulk of their energies to avoiding contact, accepting combat only when cornered or when the odds looked extremely favorable. During this period the tactics which had worked well for U.S. units for several years became less effective. This "evasive" period appeared to end with the *Tet* attacks. However, it became apparent later on after *Tet* that the enemy had adopted a "high point" policy which called for weeks or months of "evasion" followed by a short "high point" of attacks. It became more and more evident that this enemy tactic or strategy called for a change in tactics by the friendly troops.

In January of 1968, orientation courses at Forts Benning, Sill, and Rucker still featured battalion-sized operations, clover leaf patrols,[1] heavy firepower, digging in every night, large (10 to 20 ship) airmobile assaults, and so on. It was recognized that changes were due but there was no coherent doctrine nor overall concept for changing to a more delicate approach. Upon arrival in Vietnam in the Spring of 1968 we intuitively sensed that we should change our doctrine, but had no clear-cut idea of what to do. In February and March, the enemy was still trying to capitalize on the *Tet* attacks, so it was relatively easy to come to grips with him. There was another high point in May and June, but thereafter (south of Saigon at least) the enemy emphasized evasive tactics even more,

---

[1] A type of patrol used in jungle growth which featured a clover leaf pattern for searching out the enemy and ensuring thorough coverage of the terrain.

and it became most difficult to maintain contact with him. With this as a backdrop, the 9th Infantry Division went into the spring and summer of 1968 looking for a solution—how to bring the enemy to battle on *our* terms rather than on *his* terms. We were willing to try anything within the limits of common sense and sound military judgment.

If one studied the enemy situation pessimistically and realistically, one could theorize that it would take several years to defeat the enemy badly enough to render him unable to threaten the security of the Vietnamese people. This phenomenon was most apparent in the 9th Division area in Long An Province. Here, U.S. units had been weakening the enemy modestly for several years. During *Tet* of 1968, however, the enemy was able to attack the province capital. Although enemy losses were fairly high and the damage to the capital minimal, he still had the psychological advantage of having been able to mount an attack. In March and April of 1968 he avoided contact, rebuilt his units to some degree and in May put elements of four or five battalions into the Mini-*Tet* attacks on Saigon. His casualties were again quite heavy, and in late May and June he avoided contact again, controlled his losses, and started to rebuild. We obviously had a real problem—unless we could get hold of and damage the enemy, he would come out of hiding every six months or so and achieve some successes—hopefully only psychological but successes none the less.

The Solution

The solution arrived at, which took months of trial-and-error experimentation, was to find, encircle, and heavily damage the enemy main force and provincial battalions. The enemy reacted by dispersing into company and platoon sized elements. These were then dealt with by lowering the scale of friendly operations to company and platoon size and attacking these small enemy units on a continuous basis. This dispersed style of combat led to frequent day and night engagements. By stressing light infantry tactics and techniques, it was possible to inflict heavy cumulative losses on these small enemy units with low friendly casualties. This favorable exchange ratio became more pronounced as the enemy lost experienced leaders. An unexpected by-product of the dispersed style and the constant pressure was that enemy units at all levels were weakened, thus reducing their ability to generate replacements from local guerrilla units. As a result of the constant heavy military pressure, rallier (Chieu Hoi) rates also skyrocketed—thus further weakening the enemy forces. As the pacification program advanced, the Communists progressively lost control of the people. South Vietnamese territorial forces also became more aggressive. The cumulative effect of all these interacting defeats was that the enemy lost strength and combat effectiveness geometrically rather than arithmetically.

All of the above sounds very simple but was achieved only by a concerted application of hard work, professional skill, tight management, lots of guts, and some luck. It took from six to nine months of tight management to get the infantry companies in top fighting shape. Optimum utilization of aviation assets required about six months to develop. Aggressive and effective small unit operations required two months of on-the-job retraining and so on. The two major breakthroughs were the result of sheer professional artistry. The rapid breaking down of the enemy battalions was the result of the perfection of both the Jitterbug and the seal-and-pile-on technique (the rapid build-up of combat power to surround and destroy an enemy force) by Colonel Henry E. "Hank" Emerson. These highly complex tactics, in the hands of a master, shattered many large enemy units. The effective use of aggressive small unit operations was demonstarted as feasible by Captain Michael Peck Jr., an infantry company commander. By capitalizing on his example, we were able to break the enemy companies down. Thereafter, by close observation and analysis of results, we were able to vary our tactics and techniques and continue to put heavy pressure on the enemy.

The Constant Pressure Concept

When one first observes the fighting in Vietnam, there is a tendency to assume that the current tactics are about right and that previous tactics were rather uninspired if not wrong. The first conclusion is probably correct, the second is probably wrong. For example, one hears much criticism of the Search and Destroy Operations which were extensively used in 1967 and before. However, if one looks at the situation then existing and what was actually done, the tactics were pretty well chosen and did the job. Any reasonably effective commander, after observing the enemy operate a while, can cope with him reasonably well. The difficult task was to decide how the enemy was going to change his operations, to anticipate his change, and then keep driving him down, and thereby preserve the initiative. This requires very clear thinking, some risk-taking, and a flexible approach.

Our experience in the 9th Division illustrates the process well. When our units were first introduced into the delta, the practice (for a variety of sound reasons) was to make strong battalion or multi-battalion sweeps followed by periods of lower level friendly activity. The enemy was pretty cocky and would attempt to block these sweeps into his long-time base areas and suffered heavy losses in the process. By the spring of 1968, he had decided to evade such sweeps whenever possible and as a result became more difficult to bring to battle. However, by a process of vigorous reconnaissance through both Jitterbugging and ground patrolling, we were able to find these evading units, encircle them, and deal them very damaging blows.

While the division was spread out over a large area and largely made up of three company battalions, each encirclement required a peaking of effort (with all available companies committed) followed by a stand-down period to rest and refit. This allowed the enemy to regroup somewhat, and his losses were damaging but manageable from his viewpoint. To put it differently, while his losses in trained personnel were damaging, he was able to replace a sizable proportion of his losses with new recruits. On the other hand, as he dispersed his units, his command and control mechanism was reduced in efficiency, and resupply became more difficult.

When the division reached its full strength, it was possible to put the pressure on the enemy continuously and conduct small encirclements with troops on hand. This resulted in many small contacts and a constant drain on the enemy, both in quality and quantity with which he could not cope. The loss of leaders was particu-

Encirclement

larly crippling. Eventually, the enemy became so disorganized that small friendly units could just overrun the enemy and encirclements were no longer necessary. [For some unknown reason, enemy artillery (mortar) units were much more difficult to neutralize than the infantry.]

This process sounds rather mechanical; however, the decision to break down to company and platoon level operations took real courage. One ran the risk of having a company overrun occasionally by an enemy battalion. However, luckily for us, by the time the enemy realized what was happening to him, he had been too badly damaged to do anything but break down further into platoons and ultimately into squads.

CHART 7—PATTERN OF ENEMY LOSSES RESULTING FROM SWEEPS

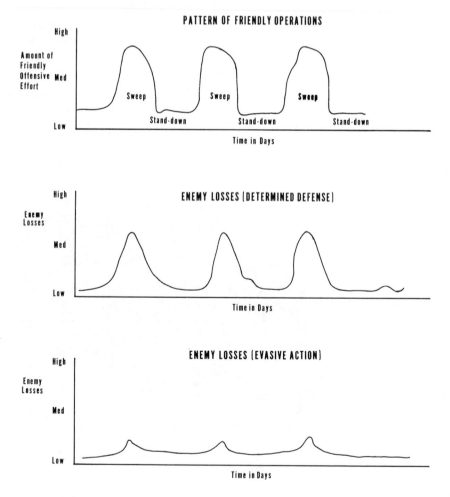

PATTERN OF FRIENDLY OPERATIONS

High

Amount of Friendly Offensive Effort Med

Sweep   Sweep   Sweep

Low   Stand-down   Stand-down   Stand-down

Time in Days

High   ENEMY LOSSES (DETERMINED DEFENSE)

Enemy Losses

Med

Low

Time in Days

ENEMY LOSSES (EVASIVE ACTION)

High

Enemy Losses

Med

Low

Time in Days

This process is graphically portrayed in Charts 7 and 8. The first chart indicates the friendly offensive effort associated with large sweeps. Because of the large numbers of troops participating in a sweep, there were periods of intense activity followed by prolonged stand-down periods. If during a sweep the enemy chose to stand and fight, his losses could be high. Naturally enemy losses would fall off during the periods of stand-down. If the enemy chose to evade, he

CHART 8—Pattern of Enemy Losses Resulting from
Reconnaissance Mode

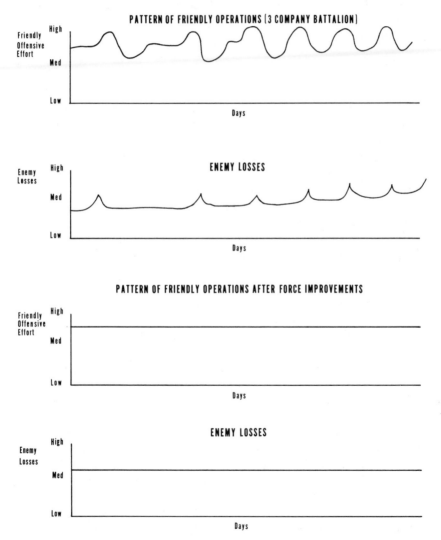

normally could side-step large unit operations and his losses even at the peak of the sweep would not be very high. On the other hand, when we went to the reconnaissance mode of operations (*Chart 8*), covering large areas on a daily basis, friendly offensive efforts were generally maintained at a medium intensity, although from time to time in an encirclement the level of activity peaked. The enemy's losses were also about medium level. As we refined our tactical operations, fighting night and day, and gained our full strength through force improvements, the level of friendly offensive effort became constantly high with few perturbations. As a consequence, the level of the enemy losses went even higher and they were constant, damaging the enemy so rapidly that his units deteriorated steadily and could not recover.

The Theoretical Basis of the Constant Pressure Concept

The Constant Pressure Concept paid off in cold results; however, in retrospect, its real strength was that it largely disrupted a Communist concept of operations which had proven successful since the early days of the Indochinese War.

The classic method of operating for a Communist unit (North Vietnamese Army or Viet Cong) was to take refuge in a relatively secure base area and spend some weeks reorganizing, retraining, and replacing losses of men, matériel and supplies. During this period, it would carefully plan a set-piece attack on a government unit or objective and then execute the attack with the actual movement to the attack, the attack itself, and the withdrawal taking place in a short period of three or four nights or less. If the attack, due to this careful preparation or other reasons, was reasonably successful, the government strength and confidence dropped and the more confident enemy recycled the whole procedure.

With the Constant Pressure Concept, friendly units upset this enemy timetable. By means of constant reconnaissance, small engagements with enemy units and pressure on their bases, the Communists were no longer able to rest 25 days a month; they could not refit and retrain and eventually could not even plan new attacks very well, much less execute them.

This process is very difficult to measure in any finite way. However, as a rough estimate, if the friendly forces (all types) in an area can diminish the enemy about 5 percent a month and achieve a friendly-initiated to enemy-initiated contact ratio of 3 to 1, the friendlies have the initiative and the enemy slowly goes down hill. In this situation, pacification proceeds and compounds the enemy's difficulties by separating him from the people who had previously helped him (willingly or unwillingly) by furnishing recruits, food, labor, information, etc.

The best performance ever seen to my knowledge was in Long An Province where in 1969 and 1970 the friendly forces were able, months on end, to weaken the enemy about 10 to 15 percent a month and achieve a contact ratio of about 6 to 1. This paralyzed and eventually almost disintegrated the enemy, even though the Cambodian sanctuaries were nearby. This military pressure, coupled with a dynamic and most effective pacification program led by Colonel Le Van Tu, a superb province chief, brought Long An from a highly contested to a relatively pacified area in about two years. This was the perfect strategy—excruciating direct military pressure coupled with strong pacification hitting the enemy from the rear. The Cambodian operation, by denying the enemy a secure base, was the *coup de grace*.

Thus, by adopting tactics which not only bled the enemy, but worked against his classic method of operating, one could make impressive gains. This approach, while very obvious in retrospect, was not clearly seen at the time and was arrived at by trial and error. It required a high degree of tactical skill by the regular units (U.S. or South Vietnamese). When coupled with a substantial increase in Regional Force and Popular Force units to maintain reasonable and continuous local territorial control and security, the Communists steadily lost ground.

In all fairness it should be admitted that we rather backed into this solution. Prior to our beginning to keep detailed statistics on combat results, we thought that our larger engagements were the payoff and the smaller just a bonus. However, as one observed the statistics closely, it became apparent that the aggregate results from small contacts were quite important. Once we began to stress small unit operations, it was established that the great majority of the enemy losses (80 percent to 90 percent) came in very small contacts with medium or large contacts amounting to a smaller percentage (20 percent to 10 percent). We then began to realize that the supermarket approach of large turnover with small unit profit paid off much more than the old neighborhood grocery approach of small turnover with a large markup. This particular solution was even more necessary in the upper delta than might have been the case elsewhere, as the enemy was constantly in motion over the open terrain rather than hidden in large jungle-covered secret base areas. This made constant pressure a necessity.

It is interesting to observe the South Vietnamese experience by way of contrast. The South Vietnamese were rather cautious (with good reason—they and the Viet Cong had historically taken turns decimating a battalion or two every six months or so). They planned big multi-battalion sweeps and coordinated them with all agencies. As a result the Viet Cong not only had general knowledge of their plans due to leaks, but the tactical plan was usually a highly stylized attack of the French staff school variety. As a result the Viet Cong could usually sidestep the operation. (We sometimes obtained moderate returns by sending units along the edges of a South Vietnamese operation to pick up the evading Viet Cong units.) We avoided similar security problems by obtaining large operational areas for periods of time and telling no one what we had in mind. Once a South Vietnamese unit changed to a looser style and minimized leaks, its effectiveness rose perceptibly.

A more fundamental reason for the success of the Constant Pressure Concept plus pacification was that it upset the entire Maoist method of organizing the "masses" and if done well over time forced them to reverse the traditional Maoist three phase concept.

If one looks at Chart 9 of the Communist structure, one can visualize the way in which the Viet Cong made the people (the so-called masses) support the bulk of the war effort. The people were forced to do all the work, furnish the food, intelligence, labor, and the raw recruits. Each Communist level supported the one above, and if a lower level unit such as a district company was in trouble, a larger and higher level unit was brought in to rectify the situation.

Historically, after 1954, the Communists organized the people, went into guerrilla war, and in 1964 and 1965 went into the open warfare stage and with North Vietnamese help were making real progress until U.S. units were introduced and began regularly to defeat the Viet Cong and North Vietnamese Army main forces. In an effort to stop this series of defeats, the enemy attacked the cities in *Tet* of 1968. The *Tet* battles were supported in many areas by drawing heavily on the lower levels for replacements for main force units. The heavy losses incurred seriously weakened the underlying structure.

By using the Constant Pressure Concept to inflict losses throughout this weakened structure, Communist ability to upgrade units and personnel was hampered. The heavy military pressure generated hundreds of ralliers (Chieu Hoi) who primarily came from the linking layers of local (village and hamlet) guerrillas and sympathizers and helpers. The linking mechanism then began to fray. As the pacification program went into high gear (in 1969) and provided more constant local security, the people in general were

CHART 9—The Communist Structure

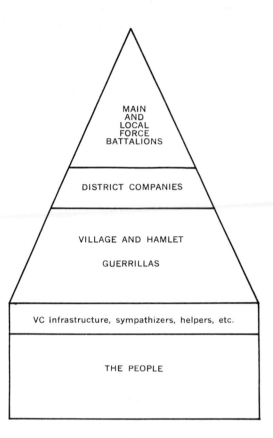

MAIN
AND
LOCAL
FORCE
BATTALIONS

DISTRICT COMPANIES

VILLAGE AND HAMLET

GUERRILLAS

VC infrastructure, sympathizers, helpers, etc.

THE PEOPLE

able to draw away from the Viet Cong or in the case of traditional Communist areas were prevented from helping them. This was a drastic shift from the Communist point of view. Whereas previously the Communist units only rested, trained and fought, they now had to support themselves. This resulted in a serious drop in their combat capability. If military pressure was heavy and pacification dynamic at the same time, the enemy structure underwent a collapsing effect. If the pressure was maintained for a year or two, the structure almost disintegrated. It took considerable skill and patience to bring this development about.

The first sign of enemy trouble was the introduction of North Vietnamese Army fillers into Viet Cong battalions; large numbers of ralliers was another sign of trouble, friendly pacification progress another, and rapid erosion of all units was a very bad sign. Central Office of South Vietnam Resolution Number 9 which stressed a return to low-level operations (terror, anti-pacification, etc.) was the formal admission by the North Vietnamese High Command that they were in real trouble, as it reversed the Maoist doctrine.

Many Westerners cannot understand why the South Vienamese situation should have been greatly different in 1970 than in 1967 or 1968. However, if one assumes that the Communists controlled half the rural population, no matter how imperfectly, in 1967 and the South Vietnamese government, which was just organizing, to some extent controlled the other half—we can see that the power balance in the rural areas was fairly even. In 1970 the Communists were in some disarray and had lost control of most of the rural population. The government had made considerable strides, had gone to general mobilization, and controlled most of the rural people plus the cities reasonably well. As a result the government was some millions of people stronger and the enemy the same number weaker.

In summary, the Constant Pressure Concept while inflicting heavy damage on the enemy struck directly at the basic Communist concept of operation and at their method of organizing their entire apparatus. It thus caused many problems for the Communists when well executed.

Increasing Emphasis on Offensive Operations

It is, of course, a military truism that offensive operations are more effective than defensive operations. However, this principle was somewhat blurred during the earlier years of the Vietnamese war by the willingness of the enemy, particularly the North Vietnamese, to try to overrun fire support bases, thereby losing several hundred men in a few hours. In the delta area, however, the enemy was less prone to attack fortified positions (particularly U.S. ones), so this situation did not exist to the same extent.

After some informal checking around, it was found that the general pattern in late 1967 to early 1968 was that offensive operations produced modest results and defensive operations little, except for an occasional defense of a fire support base against a strong attack. After some thought and analysis, a very simple report was devised which allowed the division and brigade commanders to keep a running account of the number of company days and nights of effort on offensive and defensive operations. This report confirmed that about one-half or more of the combat troops in the division were on security, stand-down, training, or other missions which did not contribute positively to finding and defeating the enemy.

KEEPING THE PRESSURE ON

The night percentages of defensive effort were even higher. These results were quite understandable since the average unit was assigned, either directly or indirectly, a number of missions such as find-and-attack the enemy, guard a bridge, secure a road, protect a fire support base, rest tired troops, perform training, etc. There was a tendency to assign a reasonable force to each defensive mission to lessen the risk. As a result, the offensive missions got what was left, unless a big operation was underway. The tendency towards defensive effort was even more marked at night due to the proclivity of the Communists for night attacks. By lumping all of the missions together in a continuing report, the degradation of offensive effort became more apparent and all commanders and staffs began to work to optimize the offensive effort. Correcting this defensive tendency required deliberate defensive risks in order to increase offensive effort. An attainable goal (and floor) of 60 percent of all units committed to offensive operations was set. Units tended to float between 60 percent plus and 75 percent—66 percent being a reasonable average figure for offensive operations. After several months, this control measure was not really necessary for daytime operations but was retained to impress the concept on new commanders and to permit the night rate to be observed. The night offensive rate took much longer to bring up.

Some people thought this approach was so basic as to be ridiculous, however the technique was adopted by a division which had too few men committed to offensive operations and was having extreme difficulty in finding the enemy. At first, the division offensive rate was between 40 and 50 percent; after corrective action it rose to over 66 percent. In more concrete terms, it had previously averaged about 17 companies per day on offense and rose to about 26—an increase of 50 percent in offensive effort from the same force. Obviously, this change alone did not necessarily solve its problems but it helped.

The end result was that the rifle companies of the 9th Division spent approximately two-thirds of their time in the field on offensive operations. Everything else—security, rest, care and maintenance of equipment, training, etc.—came out of the remaining one-third. This kept the men very busy but still allowed them sufficient rest to be fresh for operations. It must be admitted that we could not confirm that this measure in itself led to better results. However, the principle involved was obviously so sound that it was retained to point us in the right direction.

Company Level Operations

In the spring of 1968 in Dinh Tuong Province, one of the companies was commanded by Captain Peck—a superb small unit tactician and leader. As he began to fragment, and the enemy battalions and contacts were more difficult to come by, he—mainly on his own initiative—started aggressive company and platoon sized operations with dramatic results. Not only did he terrorize the enemy and deal them heavy casualties, but his own casualties were quite light.

This suggested the need to expand such techniques and the results were promising. Occasionally, a company or platoon was roughly handled, but as we developed more skill and the enemy's skill level dropped, we were able to employ aggressive or even audacious small unit operations with almost total success.

By March of 1969 we never, or almost never, used battalion level sweeps or encirclements but used company or platoon level operations. This, of course, multiplied our coverage of the ground, our reconnaissance effort, and our contact possibilities by an order of magnitude of roughly 3 (1 battalion equals 3 companies on offen-

FIREFIGHT

sive effort). In addition, the enemy seemed unable to figure out this dispersed style of operations and he was never able to cope with it. If he concentrated to strike a company, we encircled him; if he dispersed, the platoons overran the small enemy elements.

Obviously, this approach was very sensitive to the level of tactical skill, and we soon found that some platoon leaders or company commanders did not do well with it. By a combination of observation and analysis, we found that the utilization of artillery was critical. The Standing Operating Procedure approach for developing a contact was to bring in artillery fire and then start a flanking maneuver. This resulted in a five to ten minute delay during which time the enemy was able to slip away. We finally hit on the idea of starting the maneuver at once (battle drill style) and then bringing in the artillery, if necessary. This very simple fix was most effective. It, in effect, reduced the enemy's escape time from five to ten minutes to two to five minutes, which was not enough for his purposes.

Enemy Night Attacks

It was customary in Vietnam, particularly in the jungle, to stop moving in mid or late afternoon, resupply, and dig in a hastily fortified position. We noted relatively few night attacks in the delta, and it was almost impossible to dig in due to the high water table, so we changed. We either did not resupply or did it in late afternoon, kept going until dark, and shifted to night ambushes after dark. This simple trick eliminated enemy night mortar attacks and almost all night attacks. In a few tough areas, it did not work quite as well until we guessed the enemy was tailing our units. After we made sure to shake or kill the tails by stay-behind ambushes, this stopped.

Load of the Soldier

It was apparent that an infantryman in the delta mud and heat suffered terribly from both heat and fatigue. The flak jacket was a primary cause. After analyzing wound data and flak jacket saves, we determined we were not saving many casualties by their use and, as a result, made the wearing of flak jackets optional. Some experts felt that the gain in mobility paid off in better results with few consequent casualties although this was never clearly established. Even in heavily booby-trapped areas, one could get by with using jackets on lead men only. By rotating lead men, the fatigue element could be held down. We did not direct the abandonment of flak jackets, however, as some people derived considerable psychological assurance from them. Due to the fact that our men were only out two days and could usually be resupplied easily, we also reduced the individual load to a bare minimum by reducing ammunition loads and other paraphenalia. The theory was to get the men to the battle fresh. Perhaps not all individual riflemen would agree.

LOAD OF THE SOLDIER

We also reduced the unit loads somewhat. Due to the muddy delta terrain, the heavier crew-served weapons were very difficult to utilize and actually were not really necessary as artillery support was almost always available. Eventually, we did away almost entirely with 4.2-inch (107-mm) mortars and 81-mm mortars. This made the foot elements more mobile and freed heavy weapons men for other missions—usually as members of a reconnaissance unit.

Preparation of Landing Zones

It has been customary in Vietnam for some time to deliver heavy preparatory fires on the vegetation cover around a landing zone in order to reduce the amount of enemy fire at the choppers and at the troops. This practice was essential in some places, desirable in others, and questionable elsewhere. The preparation might involve gunships, tactical air, and artillery and took from five to fifteen minutes, depending on the amount considered necessary and the complexity of the fire plan. As our contacts began to drop in 1967 and 1968, we examined this practice critically. We finally judged that the enemy had very few .50 caliber machine guns in any case and intuitively guessed that the time used for the "prep" was alerting the enemy and allowing him to evade. So we cautiously experimented with airmobile operations without using preps. After finding we received very little fire, we changed the Standing Operating Procedure 180°. No preps were used unless the commander felt the situation demanded it. This worked well—we had to go back to standard preps only in one place—a very tough area where we had one whole lift shot up due to a sloppy light prep. Not only did the no-prep policy increase our element of surprise, but it saved artillery ammunition, air strikes, and gunships for more lucrative targets. The biggest bonus was to relieve the air cavalry gunships so they could work with their parent troop. The lift ship gunships initially overwatched the insertion so they could intervene if necessary. After some weeks, we noticed that the enemy was "leaking" out of the area as soon as the lift ships began to land. We then shifted the gunships to watch the outside rather than the inside of the insertion area. This not only cost the enemy casualties, but held them in place. As a result we had, over a period of months, essentially turned the landing zone preparation around.

Insertion Distance

The original approach in open delta terrain had been to land our assault helicopter lifts 600 to 1,000 meters from the objective in order to minimize the effect of direct fire on aircraft and infantry. This meant that it took the troops an appreciable time and physical effort to make their way through the rice paddies to the objective. After observing the low incidence of enemy .50 caliber machine guns, we cut the distance to 500 to 600 meters and observed no problems. After a few weeks, we reduced it to 300 meters (based on effective rifle fire and light machine gun range) and had few problems. This reduced the approach march time by two-thirds to one-half and increased surprise. By the combination of eliminating preps and reducing the standoff distance, we increased surprise and lessened troop fatigue.

Later on in 1969 the 3d Brigade of the 9th Division in Long An reduced their standoff distance to as little as 15 meters. The enemy by that time had little but AK–47 rifles to work with. This short distance was ideal, as surprise was almost total and only one or two enemy could fire at a particular chopper. Usually, they elected to hide instead.

Discussion

Why did it take us so long to decide on variations that were obviously such good ideas? The situation was not crystal clear at the time. To begin with, the previous Standing Operating Procedure (liberal prepping and substantial stand off distance) was adopted during a period when the enemy response to an airmobile assault was a withering hail of fire from all weapons, and a vigorous defense until nightfall, when he made good his escape. When the enemy changed to evasive tactics, he began to lie doggo and try to avoid contact with a view to escaping in daylight or at night depending on the amount of concealment available. If the friendly unit made contact, the enemy opened fire at very close ranges (perhaps 15 feet) which usually led to a costly, difficult, and time-consuming organization of an attack from a different direction. An examination of exchange ratios during the spring and summer of 1968, ratios which were around 10 to 1, shows that we were having difficulty with these enemy tactics. If one drove head on into a heavily bunkered position, friendly casualties were high; and if one maneuvered, the enemy slipped away. Fortunately, at this juncture, the Jitterbug technique, which had a high success rate in finding enemy units, and the seal and pile-on tactic which prevented escape and inflicted crippling losses on enemy units were perfected. The overall result was that the enemy units began to fragment. At that point, the changes in landing zone prepping and insertion distance began to be more advantageous and paid off in increased enemy eliminations and higher exchange ratios. So, as we have stated earlier, the solution to a tactical problem was not necessarily simple or straightforward.

One difficulty encountered in analyzing such complex operations was that one did not understand the critical points involved. The whole desired effect of changing the prepping and standoff Standing Operating Procedures was to increase surprise and consequently the closure rate. If one assumed that the total closure time was sixty minutes originally and was able to reduce it to thirty minutes—nothing in particular happened. What was overlooked was that the enemy only needed an escape envelope of ten to fifteen minutes. It was not until we achieved the technical skill and took the risks to effect lightning fast frontal attacks that the critical envelope was penetrated and the success ratio climbed to high levels. There were many other factors involved, discussion of which must be omitted due to length.

Summary

The foregoing general discussion gives you some feel of the problems faced, some of the solutions, and our thinking behind these actions. To summarize succinctly the 9th Division evolved differing tactics and techniques which basically involved the theory of constant pressure through offensive actions using small units operating night and day.

The key to ground tactical success was breaking down into small unit operations, particularly at night. We passed on this formula to the 7th ARVN Division which operated with us in the delta. It proved at that time to be a shot in the arm for their combat efficiency also although they were more reluctant to break down into small units because of some bitter experiences earlier in the war. Finally, the key to all of our tactical success was good intelligence, without which even the most refined techniques would have been substantially less productive.

In all of our operations we applied as best we could the analytical approach to our problems. The technique employed was to isolate those pieces of the problem which could be analyzed. The remainder had to be attacked primarily by means of professional skill, experience, judgment and often intuition. The overall integration always had to be done on this basis. Even in areas such as small unit techniques which on the surface responded well to analysis, the actual cause and effect relationships could not be traced with any real confidence. However, as has been mentioned earlier, the Vietnamese War was, and is rather complex, murky, and difficult to understand. It should also be recognized that many aspects of the war are too complex to be susceptible to operations analysis. Field force, division, brigade and battalion operations, for example, are just too complex to completely comprehend by analytical methods. These comments should not discourage attempts to improve operations by analysis or otherwise; we merely make the obvious point that the human mind can grasp large problems by some means which are difficult or impossible to duplicate on paper.

Straightforward collection of statistics has its pitfalls also. This approach leads toward optimizing the operation being studied. While this is obviously desirable as a rule, it may tend to stifle innovation and unconventional thinking. For example, one good way to improve the effectiveness of daylight operations is to improve night operations. The theory is that the enemy is thereby forced to operate more frequently in the daytime. However, this cannot be proven. In defending against booby traps one rapidly gets up in the flat portion of the learning curve. A good way to finesse the problem was to rely heavily on night ambushes. The overall outcome was better results with less booby trap casualties. However, this alternative obviously did not stem from a close analysis of the bobby trap problem. A similar turn around of interest was the reversal of roles of airmobile operations and ground operations. In mid 1968 the Jitterbug (intensive small unit airmobile reconnaissance) was driving daylight operations with ground patrolling a poor second. However, by early 1969, ground patrolling became more and more important and the Jitterbug less so. Similarly, the air cavalry role switched from one of finding targets for the Jitterbug to that of attacking targets flushed out by the ground patrols. It is theorized that the Jitterbug became so feared that the enemy would never break cover unless physically contacted whereas the ground patrol was so unexpected (and more thorough) that he could not accommodate to it.

To give a better insight into our approaches to improving operational efficiency through analysis, we will subsequently discuss several of our fundamental building blocks, i.e., intelligence, tactical innovations and operational reviews.

CHAPTER V

The Intelligence Function

Our tactical operations were at all times oriented on the enemy, his political as well as his military organizations, with less emphasis on terrain or geographical considerations. To maintain this orientation all division tactical operations were undertaken with intelligence operating as the pivotal point. Intelligence was and remained the chief targeting device for the employment of combat assets.

This concept had two major salutary effects: first, the application of unremitting military and psychological pressure on the enemy at all levels; and second, the economical employment of limited tactical assets on enemy units without dissipating them on a mechanical area coverage basis.

Within the division the intelligence theme initially was the centralization and control of all intelligence assets followed subsequently by decentralization to the lowest echelon capable of operating the asset. Initial control of these assets at division level was necessary to bring a particular intelligence source into operating harmony with the division concept. Once this was accomplished the source was turned over to the appropriate brigade or battalion. In all cases a requirement was maintained for rapid and accurate reporting up and down the intelligence chain.

Intelligence Support

External intelligence support for the division was received from the South Vietnamese Army and U.S. intelligence units in III and IV Corps Tactical Zone, depending on the area in which these units provided dedicated coverage. External sources while plentiful in number and diverse in nature were, in many cases, not co-ordinated in their activities and not always oriented toward satisfying the intelligence needs of tactical units. The reason for this problem was that the systems in use were not initially designed for passing "real time" intelligence but rather for reporting enemy activity which was hours and even days old. (*Chart 10*) The thrust of the division intelligence effort became one of co-ordinating and managing all of these sources to respond to the tactical requirements of the

CHART 10—TIMELINESS OF INTELLIGENCE REPORTS

(Average Hours Elapsed from Event to Receipt of Report)

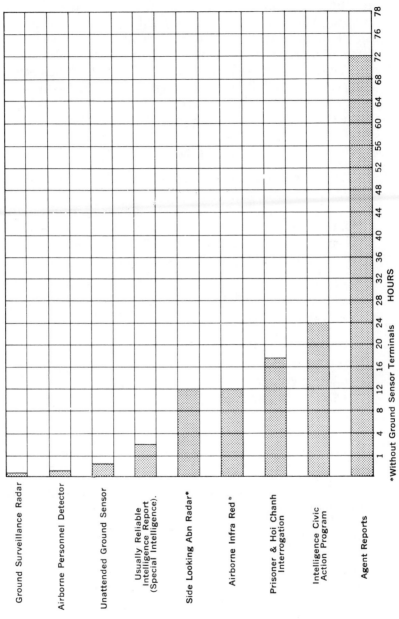

division and to pass their highly perishable intelligence as close to real time as possible, enabling the division to operate against valid targets. Although these efforts resulted in substantial improvements in the system, they were never completely successful. The large number of intelligence units involved made complete coordination a nearly impossible task. (*Table 14*) The detection and compression of intelligence time lags through analysis is much more important than generally realized. Unquestionably, real time intelligence information really pays off.

The Division Intelligence Function

One of the best tools for orchestrating the intelligence and operational functions of the division was the daily Command and Staff Briefing. The briefing, conducted twice daily at 0700 and 1700, consisted of a graphic and oral presentation of all divisional activities which had occurred during the previous period. Present during the briefings were the Commanding General, the two As-

TABLE 14—PARTIAL LIST OF EXTERNAL INTELLIGENCE SOURCES

South Vietnamese Army	U.S.
G-2/Senior Advisor G-2 IV Corps Tactical Zone	G-2, II Field Force, Vietnam
G-2, 7th South Vietnamese Army Division 25th South Vietnamese Army Division	G-2, Capital Military Assistance Command
S-2, Province: Long An Dinh Tuong Kien Hoa Go Cong	G-2, 25th Division S-2, 199th Brigade CO, 3rd Combat Intelligence Battalion III Corps Tactical Zone
S-2/District Intelligence Operations Co-ordination Centers	CO, 4th Combat Intelligence Battalion IV Corps Tactical Zone
Phung Huong/Phoenix Committees for each Province. (4)	CO, 73d Surveillance Aviation Company (Mohawk), III Corps Tactical Zone
Province Chieu Hoi Centers (4)	CO, 244th Surveillance Aviation Company (Mohawk) IV Corps Tactical Zone
Province Interrogation Centers (4)	Military Assistance Command, Vietnam, J304 (Unattended Ground Sensors)
Province National Field Police (4)	Combined Intelligence Center Vietnam
Chief Military Security Service, III & IV Corps Tactical Zone	Combined Military Interrogation Center
S-2, 44th Special Tactical Zone	Combined Document Exploitation Center

sistant Division Commanders, Chief of Staff, principal staff officers and selected members of the special staff. The intelligence portion of the briefing consisted of significant friendly and enemy activity in all Corps Tactical Zones with particular emphasis devoted to highlighting patterns of enemy activity such as "high points" of his offensive campaigns and his current methods of tactical employment. This was followed by a presentation of all reported enemy activity within the division operational area and in peripheral areas. Intelligence reports presented were evaluated as to their validity. A large 1:50,000 map display was used for graphic portrayal of all enemy activities and reports. The map contained a resume of the past 72 hours of reported activity, divided into three 24 hour periods. Each 24 hour period was keyed to a color; red, amber or green. Each source of intelligence such as Side Looking Airborne Radar, Airborne Infra Red, Agent Reports, radars, etc., was designated by a distinctive symbol in the proper color to denote the appropriate time period in which the event took place. The map was maintained on an hourly basis as information was received and evaluated. It was in essence an intelligence watch over the area and was a major tool for achieving a totally integrated intelligence and operational effort for the division. This system made enemy patterns of activity more discernible thereby facilitating timely operational decisions for the allocation of assets against targets with a fair degree of assurance of gaining contact with the enemy. The only intelligence source not covered during the open briefings was Special Intelligence which was presented to a selected group following the morning general briefing. The Special Intelligence briefing was presented with regard to those areas which dovetailed with other intelligence sources.

The dissemination of intelligence was not restricted to the formal briefing but was passed continuously as the information and situation warranted. The G–2 and G–3, working in close proximity to each other, coordinated and assessed intelligence targets as they developed. This coordination was absolutely essential and evolved into a system whereby each brigade was assigned a minimum of one intelligence target per day from division with the G–3 recommending the allocation of available tactical resources in accordance with the weight or evaluation of the overall intelligence picture. The system of assigning intelligence targets increased the number of contacts with the enemy on a division scale. The increased contacts in turn resulted in improved intelligence due to the captured prisoners and documents and these in turn produced more targets. An example was the apprehension of five North Vietnamese Army prisoners and some documents taken from the lead element of a large enemy unit initially targeted by agent reports. The prisoners and documents disclosed the size, strength and assigned operational areas for a North Vietnamese Army unit infiltrating from Cambodia to Long An Province. This information enabled the division to gain additional and almost continuous contact with other elements of the North Vietnamese Army unit resulting in heavy losses and final dispersal of the enemy. The same rule also applied to the Viet Cong infrastructure. The apprehension of a courier or minor village functionary often permitted a roll up operation on a portion of the local infrastructure. These are but a few examples of the maxim that the more contacts you get the more you improve your intelligence and therefore improve your chances of finding the enemy. However, even information gained in this manner is highly perishable and must be reacted to immediately or it is lost. An unusual feature of the Vietnamese War was that most of the Communist prisoners of war or defectors (Hoi Chanh) "sang like birds." They almost seemed to heave a sigh of relief at being captured alive and decided that the more information they could disclose the better off for everyone. The Communist doctrine taught that one fought until death and that the enemy (U.S. and South Vietnamese) would slaughter any prisoners. (In fact, at the tactical level, the Communists themselves ignored the Geneva Conventions.) Due to the lack of indoctrination on the realities of the situation, the average Communist prisoner was so overwhelmed by the considerate treatment he received that presumably he lost all sense of restraint.

Summarizing, we operated on a three phase intelligence cycle: reviewing operations and intelligence inputs in the evening; re-evaluating again early on the morning of operations; and finally reacting to new intelligence as operations progressed. This kept our commanders finely tuned to enemy activities and our operations were executed utilizing real time intelligence to the maximum extent possible.

Use of Internal Resources

The lack of agent coverage by other intelligence organizations in certain critical areas such as eastern Long An Province and all of Kien Hoa Province was a shortcoming that required much innovation on the part of the division to remedy. Normal close-in early warning nets were expanded into collection nets and targeted on these and other lightly covered areas. The building of agent nets, not normally a division function, was a slow process with an equal number of successes and failures; however, coverage was provided in areas previously not covered. The division nets had one major advantage over other agent operations—the ability of the division to target these nets on specific missions. The nets also gave us the advantage of having a finger on the pulse of the population. For example, we had a report from one net that the Cai Be City Viet Cong Intelligence Section Chief would attempt to infiltrate one of the division nets. Within two weeks this individual offered his services through a principal agent who in turn notified his U.S. handler. A decision was made at division to recruit the Viet Cong agent to determine his target and detect his agents if possible. He was operated in isolation from other agent nets. He soon offered information that he had uncovered a number of Viet Cong who wished to Chieu Hoi. The U.S. handler received nine of these Chieu Hois one at a time over the next two weeks; however, instead of taking them to the Chieu Hoi Center he delivered them to the Division Prisoner Collection Point where interrogation disclosed that their mission was to infiltrate the Province Chieu Hoi Center and later be recruited into the South Vietnamese Army and the Kit Carson (Tiger Scout) program. When the Cai Be Viet Cong agent complained that he was unable to see his friends at the center he was taken into custody and confessed to the whole scheme which included ascertaining the identity of members of the division net which the Viet Cong Province Chief wanted to destroy. He also disclosed the names of agents of the Viet Cong net operating in central Dinh Tuong Province which the Phung Huaong ("Phoe-

VIET CONG INFRASTRUCTURE

nix") Committee was delighted to receive. (The Phoenix Committee was a Vietnamese agency which worked to identify and eliminate the Viet Cong infrastructure.)

South Vietnamese Army Sources

Essential to successful intelligence operations was the maintenance of close and continuous contact with the Vietnamese forces operating in the area. They had a thorough and detailed knowledge of the enemy forces. The reluctance of District and Province organizations to pass intelligence was overcome when they realized that the dissemination of information was a two way street. When the Phung Huaong (Phoenix) Committees and District Intelligence Operations and Coordination Centers realized that the division would react rapidly to targets which they developed, they "tried harder" to develop better targets for the division. One excellent means of establishing rapport was to require each brigade to station a liaison team with the Province Intelligence Operations Coordination Center with which they were operating and to have our battalions do the same at the District level. Liaison of this sort provided ready access to target information and permitted closer cooperation with the government forces responsible for the area.

Operational Analysis

We subjected our intelligence resources to constant analysis and appraisal to determine their effectiveness and reliability. As stated earlier the key to the use of intelligence was lightning quick operational reactions. Without the immediate tie-in of intelligence to operations and the built-in flexibility of the operational system to react to new intelligence at any time—day or night, the 9th Division could not have improved its combat efficiency so markedly. One of the most unusual studies concerning intelligence that came out of the Vietnamese conflict at a divisional level was one conducted during the period 1 March through 30 April 1969. During this period the total quantity of intelligence reports received in each of the brigade areas was logged and the number of reactions to these intelligence reports was noted and confirmations of the correctness of the intelligence were listed. From all sources during this two month period there were 8,172 intelligence reports—an astonishing number—of which 2,559 were reacted to and 709 were confirmed. Confirmation is defined as tangible evidence indicating the validity of the report. Generally confirmation was interpreted as contact with the enemy but we also included documents, caches, and in the case of unattended ground sensors, trail activity.

Concomitant with our study, Lieutenant Colonel Leonard A. Spirito, the G–2, made an analysis of the timeliness of our normal intelligence resources. We found that there was a tremendous spread, from an average of 72 hours for agent reports to not more than one-half hour for reports of the People Sniffer, ground surveillance radars and sensor fields. The reports of ground surveillance radars, which would have added another 20 to 30 daily sightings, were not included in our overall intelligence analysis.

Over 30 percent of all intelligence reports were reacted to and almost 30 percent of those reacted to were confirmed. Consequently, it is no wonder that once we got the ball rolling the momentum carried the division forward. This high level of intelligence activity was reached during the months of March and April when the division obtained its highest number of enemy eliminated–240 Prisoners of War taken and 6,621 Viet Cong killed. Naturally the two phenomena go hand in hand. As the enemy unravelled we had more intelligence, more contacts, etc. The process fed on itself.

Analysis indicated the relative reliability of intelligence information obtained from personnel in the field (Prisoners of War, Chieu Hois, friendly villagers) compared to the intelligence obtained by machines. The overall confirmation from Agent Reports (15 percent), Prisoners of War and Hoi Chanhs (11.4 percent) and Integrated Civic Action Programs (19 percent) were much higher than those received from Side Looking Airborne Radar (4.5 percent),[1] Infrared Emissions (4.4 percent)[1] and Usually Reliable Reports (7.0 percent). Because of their increased reliability the division continued to emphasize the necessity for prisoners and Hoi Chanhs. On the other hand, even though the reliability of personnel reports was appreciably higher than the intelligence obtained from sensors, the quantity of sensor data was so much greater that the number of confirmed personnel reports (237) was only half of the number of confirmed sensor reports (472). (Table 15.)

The most reliable source of intelligence in the 9th Division was the People Sniffer, wherein over 33 percent of all significant readings were confirmed. Without question, the reason for this high rate was the fact that People Sniffer readings were obtained in *real time*, with air cavalry on the spot and infantry resources on the pad available to react within the hour. The importance of real time intelligence cannot be overemphasized and we feel that steps must

---

[1] These figures indicate rather small returns from Side Looking Airborne Radar and Infrared. Unfortunately the discrimination of the equipment and the built-in time lags of the reporting systems were not suited to the small, soft, and elusive targets that were presented.

be taken to insure that ground sensor terminals for Side Looking Airborne Radar, infrared, and other devices are available to the combat commander in order to make possible rapid readouts and real time reactions.

One last generality which may be of interest is the fact that intelligence gathered from friendly personnel generally was worthwhile in static situations only. Thus these sources rarely enabled the division troops to chalk up major contacts. On the other hand the sensors often unearthed targets of opportunity and frequently led to major contacts where a large number of the enemy could be fixed, surrounded, and badly cut up. However, the importance of many small contacts must not be underestimated. The trade off between many small contacts versus a few large contacts has been discussed elsewhere. It was also apparent from studying the analysis that some brigade commanders neglected useful sources of information.

TABLE 15—RELIABILITY OF SELECTED INTELLIGENCE RESOURCES DIVISION AGGREGATE TOTALS FOR PERIOD 1 MARCH–30 APRIL 1969

Source	Quantity Received	Number of Reactions (percent)		Confirmations (percent)[a]		Overall Confirmations (percent)
Agent Reports [b]	885	357	(40)	135	(38)	15
Usually Reliable Intelligence Reports	1368	193	(14)	98	(51)	7
Prisoner of War Interrogation & Hoi Chanh Reports	367	110	(30)	42	(38)	11
Integrated Civic Action Program Reports [c]	318	147	(46)	60	(41)	19

[a] Confirmation Criteria: Tangible evidence that confirms the validity of the report, that is, contact, Prisoners of War, documents, caches, trail activity, and so forth.

[b] Figure degraded because one brigade used contacts only for information.

[c] See section on pacification for description of Integrated Civic Action Program.

In retrospect we did not realize until late in the game the advantages to be realized by the systematic evaluation of all intelligence modes as to their effectiveness and pay-offs. This was one of our major failures. Unquestionably, the key to intelligence utilization is to obtain the reports on a real time basis and to react immediately and vigorously.

The Intuitive Leader

Never did commanders have more intelligence sources going for them than they did in Vietnam. On the other hand, since the

American Revolution the Army had not been engaged in the type of conflict where the enemy was all around, sometimes hiding among the local inhabitants. The situation was further complicated by the very difficult language barrier. It should not be construed that all the literally thousands of contacts made by the 9th Division during this period resulted from intelligence reports. On the contrary, many of the most lucrative results came about as the result of a commander's intuition. Several of our more gifted commanders had the ability to "feel" the enemy. Some of our junior leaders could literally smell the enemy. Our major contact in the 1968 Viet Cong Fall Offensive on Saigon at Phouc Lam, where we engaged three enemy battalions for three days in a battle that decimated two of those battalions, resulted from a gut feeling. Thus, although it is important that tactical commanders react quickly to intelligence reports, it is also necessary to give a good commander his head because intuitive leaders will find the enemy regardless of the situation. What was termed intuition usually resulted from a very thorough knowledge of the situation.

Summary of Intelligence Operations

The intelligence function of the 9th Division was primarily one of managing the diverse indigenous and U.S. sources in such a way as to cause them to operate in support of the division mission. Constant management was applied to these sources to speed up their dissemination of information to overcome the perishability factor. Stress was placed on the value of obtaining prisoners as important sources of information. The more contacts, the more prisoners; the more prisoners, the more valid the intelligence.[1] All intelligence sources were subjected to constant analysis and appraisal to determine their effectiveness and reliability. Close and continuous liaison with South Vietnamese forces was necessary for maintaining a continuous flow of information and in instilling trust and confidence for the U.S. on the part of Vietnamese agencies. The total integration of intelligence and operations was a major key to success.

There is an unavoidable tendency to view intelligence and operations as separate activities. If one can develop a "closed loop concept" in which information leads to combat action immediately, the overall efficiency of the operation increases manyfold.

---

[1] A separate system, quite different from the prisoner of war evacuation system, was set up for screening and processing civilians. The civilian system has not been covered since it is outside the scope of this monograph.

CHAPTER VI

Tactical Refinements And Innovations

As discussed previously, in the spring and summer of 1968 we were looking for ways to bring the enemy to battle on our terms and were willing to try anything within the limits of common sense and sound military judgment. To do this we adapted known tactical techniques to the unique delta environment, resulting in some tactical innovations which proved highly successful. The first of these, involving the use of airmobile assets, was the Jitterbug. About the same time, to complement our daytime airmobile activities, we adapted the ground tactical "Bushmaster" and "Checkerboard" techniques. Later when the enemy broke down into smaller units rendering our daytime operations less effective, we turned, of necessity, to nighttime techniques including the "Night Hunter," the "Night Search" and the "Night Raid."

Throughout the period we were perfecting sniper techniques and as a result of their great success, we turned to a "quick kill" method of combat. Subsequently we will discuss each of these tactical innovations. Our discussions of the Jitterbug techniques are more detailed to bring out the interplay of intelligence and the great amount of coordination required to achieve tactical success on the Vietnamese battlefield. The discussion also includes examples of the Viet Cong reaction to our new techniques, providing an insight into the requirements for continued analysis of operations if a unit is to stay on top of the situation.

Jitterbugging

The dense population and the broad expanse of inundated flatlands in the Mekong Delta dictated an adaptation of conventional airmobile infantry operations developed elsewhere in Vietnam. Viet Cong units dispersed and blended very effectively with people in the numerous villages and hamlets, greatly complicating reconnaissance difficulties and problems of fire control. Flooded rice paddies severely inhibited our ground mobility. The maze of canals and streams, generally bordered with dense nipa palm growth, presented formidable obstacles, while at the same time affording the Viet Cong a convenient network of very strong defense positions.

On the other hand, the open country permitted virtually unrestricted access by airmobile forces. Landing zones were readily available and could be selected to conform to the enemy situation; extensive preparation of an LZ with its inherent loss of surprise was usually unnecessary. Enemy bunker complexes were normally linear, with canals and open rice paddies bordering the long axis. While these obstacles deny approaches in two directions, they also channeled Viet Cong escape from the bunker complex. As a result, it was technically possible to surround a Viet Cong unit by cutting the canal and woodlines leading out of the bunker complex and interdicting the canals and rice paddies by fire and aerial observation.

The environmental characteristics of the delta thus placed a premium on two particular aspects of tactical doctrine: reconnaissance and encirclement. Intensive, rapid reconnaissance in the delta required skilled orchestration of the capabilities of local intelligence, electronic and chemical sensors, air cavalry, and airmobile infantry. This process appeared complex and frenetic to the uninitiated, and hence was aptly nicknamed "Jitterbugging." When most successful it provided an opportunity for airmobile encirclement of a Viet Cong battalion or company. The rapid build-up of combat power to surround and destroy an enemy force was known variously as "piling-on" or establishing a "seal."

Command decisions at every stage of Jitterbug and seal operations required a sensitive feel for Viet Cong tactics and patterns and the capabilities of the intelligence system. Therefore, it was vital that commanders at every level immerse themselves in the details of the intelligence process to insure a thorough understanding of enemy movements and pattern of operations.

Brigades generally rotated the assignment of air assets among subordinate battalions. The day before an impending operation the designated battalion had already been alerted to its mission and the assets expected to be available, normally an Assault Helicopter Company and an Air Cavalry Troop. The brigade commander usually withheld his selection of specific targets until the evening before the operation in order to make use of the most recent intelligence. His decisions resulted in instructions assigning five to seven tentative targets with priorities to the assault battalion. Planning at this stage was very flexible, because the targets were frequently changed the following morning on the basis of new intelligence. The brigade staff made arrangements for night visual

JITTERBUGGING

reconnaissance, Side Looking Airborne Radar, Red Haze (IR), Long Range Reconnaissance Patrol and radar coverage of the target areas that night. Tactical air strikes were planned for the next day on likely targets. If the objective areas were outside existing artillery fans, arrangements were made for movement of firing batteries (either before or during operations) to new fire support bases by air, barge, or overland. Chinook sorties were requested for movement of artillery (CH–54 for 155-mm batteries) and logistic resupply. New Areas of Operation were cleared with the Government of Vietnam and South Vietnamese Army authorities, if necessary. Provision was made for establishing forward aviation fueling and rearming points if needed. Finally, liaison was established with the supporting air cavalry troop and assault helicopter company.

At the battalion base camp, targets were analyzed in conjunction with aerial photos, photomaps, and pictomaps to determine specific areas to be searched by aerial and ground reconnaissance. Detailed information about the area and Viet Cong operations was secured from the District Chief and Tiger Scouts familiar with the locale. The concept of the operation was developed and expanded and orders were issued to the two assault companies (the remainder of the battalion was usually engaged in Checkerboard, Night Ambush, or local security missions). All preparations were completed the night before the operation.

The air cavalry troop "target detection package" was comprised of light observation helicopters (LOH's), AH-1G's (Cobras), and Manpacked or Airborne Personnel Detectors (People Sniffers) as well as E–158 CS Canister Clusters. The People Sniffer and CS canisters were carried in the Command and Control of the Air Cavalry Troop. Once a hot People Sniffer reading was obtained, gas was dropped to assist in verifying the Sniffer reading by flushing the Viet Cong out of hiding. The LOH's attempted to pick up the slightest indication of movement while the Cobras circled above to provide immediately responsive firepower should the Sniffer or LOH's draw fire. Once again, the use of CS gas in a target confirmation role increased the probability of developing a good contact before troops were inserted.

As mentioned previously, the technique of insertion was the key to the success of the Jitterbug—and insertions took a great amount of tactical judgment on the part of the commander, in fact it separated the true tactician from the commonplace one. The 2d Battalion, 60th Infantry became quite skilled in Jitterbug operations. Usually the Jitterbug in conjunction with our intelligence paid off well, resulting in enemy contacts. However, one day the 2d

Battalion 60th Infantry dry-holed it all day long (most unusual for this hard hitting outfit), and at the end of the day Lieutenant Colonel Jim Lindsay had made 16 insertions on suspected targets, sweeping each target. This was a peak in smooth, rapid operating and the command and control of troops. It gives an indication of the great number of targets in a large area that could be covered by one battalion utilizing airmobile assets. His successor, Lieutenant Colonel Fred Mahaffey, was equally skilled in the use of airmobile assets and refined the operations of the battalion until in Long An Province insertions were made no farther from the target than 100 meters and in some instances as close as 15 meters. This was pushing the balance of the risk of a hot landing zone against the achievement of total surprise to its limit. However, the technique paid off as during the period of a year no lift ships were lost. Over 90 percent of the 2d Battalion 60th Infantry contacts were over within 10 to 30 minutes as a result of the speed of the operation and the aggressive attitude of the troops. On the other hand when a reconnaissance developed a larger enemy force, the battalion was prepared to exploit to the maximum with classic pile-on tactics.

Once a large contact was developed the encirclement phase began with a rapid build-up of combat power or piling-on of all available brigade resources. The aim was to completely encircle or seal the enemy force as rapidly as possible, then destroy it through firepower rather than frontal assault. In this manner we assured ourselves of minimum troop casualties while inflicting tremendous punishment on the enemy.

Artillery fire was registered by the aerial observer, and the company commander employed artillery as necessary to support movement of his elements toward enemy-occupied tree lines and nipa palm groves. The Air Cavalry Troop screened the general area of contact and provided responsive fire support to the battalion commander. As the situation developed, the battalion commander usually moved a second company to a convenient pickup zone and prepared to insert it in a position to cut off enemy escape from the point of contact.

At that time Viet Cong tactics called for delaying action by guerrilla or light security forces to allow the main force to escape before it was engaged. For this reason additional troops were inserted as rapidly as possible after a sizable enemy contact had developed. Flight routes were carefully planned to prevent unnecessary check fires and excessive delays in insertions. If the engagement looked promising, the battalion commander also alerted the base camp to prepare another company for commitment, if possible. If the situation was beyond the capability of the battalion, the brigade commander assumed direction of the operation and established the seal with additional brigade units.

The brigade commander had to be fully abreast of time and space factors in controlling the air movement of additional infantry units, the shifting of artillery resources, aircraft refueling and rearming, and logistical support. The ultimate goal of the Jitterbug was the entrapment of the Viet Cong. For a large enemy unit this required commitment of most or all of the brigade's resources. The secret to successful encirclement of an engaged enemy force lay in the accurate positioning of sufficient rifle companies to cordon off all routes of escape from the area of contact. A gap of as little as 20 meters in heavy cover would permit the enemy battalion to escape almost as soon as night fell. The premium therefore was in an early decision to commit forces sufficient for encirclement and the rapid accumulation of the means to feed major forces into the area of contact and provide them with a continuous, heavy volume of fire support. Battalion commanders occasionally made conservative estimates of the force confronting them and as a result developed an encirclement that was too small or added reinforcements incrementally at the point of contact. The brigade commander had to be alert to these possibilities and be prepared to take over control of the operation early enough to allow commitment of additional forces in a large seal. That was always a tough decision, for no one wanted to commit two battalions to destroy a small enemy force.

Initially artillery fire was brought to bear as needed by the companies and battalions, to fill in gaps in Air Cavalry and Tactical Air coverage and to seal enemy avenues of escape. Once the ring was tightened by converging infantrymen, fire control was centrally supervised to avoid casualties to friendly troops. Once night fell and if adequate artillery support was available, the Air Cavalry Troop was released (although a division Light Fire Team remained on call) and throughout the night the encircled enemy was pounded with artillery. Canals and rivers were sealed with concertina wire stretched from one bank to the other on a rope. Troops on each bank had to know each other's positions exactly. This was accomplished with small strobe lights. Hand grenades were thrown into streams every five to ten mintes to discourage swimmers from infiltrating through U.S. lines. Rear security was established (normally listening posts only) and the artillery periodically fired on likely avenues of approach outside the ring to prevent reinforcement or attack from Viet Cong units not encircled. CS was dropped into the interior of the ring from time to time. After several hours of bombardment during daylight, all fire was halted for five to ten minutes, and Tiger Scouts (or Hoi Chanh's, if any materialized) appealed over airborne and hand-held loudspeakers to the Viet Cong to surrender. Pre-prepared appeals keyed to possible platoon tactical situations, and designed to reach individual Viet Cong soldiers temporarily separated from their superiors were broadcast by hand-held loudspeakers (AN–PIQ5A's) . After a brief pause to allow the Viet Cong to "rally" the artillery bombardment would be resumed. This denied enemy commanders the opportunity to maneuver their units away from areas under fire. The possibility always existed that the encircled enemy would attempt to break out through the thin U.S. lines. If the enemy knew how tenuous our "seals" sometimes were they could have broken out easily.

The Jitterbug, seal, and pile-on techniques were most effective in the hands of a skillful commander and reasonably effective with the average commander. However, they required an integration of details that was hard to bring off. For example, the People Sniffer had to work well mechanically. This was often a problem with the early sniffer equipment. However, by using two sets simultaneously

TIGER SCOUT PERSUADING THE ENEMY

ON A "SEAL" OPERATION

(which reduced complete outages), by having a backup reserve pool, and by improving our preventive and regular maintenance, we reduced on-the-job down time to essentially zero. This increased confidence and operator skill.

With targets of battalion size and during wet weather, the sniffer worked well. However, as target size reduced due to enemy fragmentation, readings became progressively more unreliable. We then conducted a series of tests (discussed subsequently) which allowed us to improve flight tactics, operator skill and reliability.

Next, the air cavalry had to work smoothly. It had been customary, due to its great utility, to fragment the troop. This made it difficult for it to operate effectively as real cavalry. We reassembled our air cavalry and it developed a complicated technique of taking targets from the sniffer, locating the exact spot, dropping CS in the cover to flush the enemy from bunkers and then hovering at low altitude to blow the vegetation about and uncover any enemy scuttling away. If the air cavalry and ground commanders felt there was a valid target, an insertion was started.

The seal and pile-on required very precise infantry and artillery techniques to insure an air-tight seal and "danger close" artillery support.[1] The seal also required courage and stamina as the troops had to hang on all night in order to insure destruction of the enemy.

Of equal importance, the three-cycle intelligence approach (mentioned earlier) maximized the possibilities of the sniffer detecting enemy troops.

Chart 11 shows the sequential nature of a Jitterbug. Its strength lay in the fact that seven of the operations tended to increase the possibilities of a contact. One can theorize that this increase was on the order of 12 times. The difficulty of the technique was that poor performance at any one point could break the chain. For this reason the technique required a high level of skill and tight supervision. Once the enemy target size became fine grain, the overall technique was not worth the effort and simpler techniques were indicated.

We also discovered that some batteries had great difficulty with this precision work. By means of rigorous tests we discovered that some were inaccurate due to sheer wear and tear on their howitzers after months of shooting and others just hadn't mastered the techniques involved. By systematically replacing worn out parts and retraining batteries, we were able to gain optimum accuracy in most batteries.

The enemy described our Jitterbug as "Hawk Tactics." As far as he was concerned this was probably most descriptive because in reality we were sweeping down and scooping him up. We began to perfect our Jitterbug tactics in July 1968 and it did not take the Viet Cong long to catch on. In the latter part of September 1968 we captured a Viet Cong letter from Headquarters Military Region II to its subordinate regiments written in late July. This letter covered the employment of "Hawk Tactics" by our forces. It admitted that these tactics had been successful in locating and destroying base camps and inflicting casualties "in the corridor area." Interestingly, the letter pointed out several weaknesses in U.S. techniques which subordinate Viet Cong regiments should exploit. It stated: first, operations were generally conducted from 0900

---

[1] The mention of very close-in artillery fire brings out two modest but interesting examples of analysis. In a close seal one could receive two or three casualties from friendly artillery fire. However, the constant artillery fire was instrumental in attaining heavy enemy casualties. By comparing the enemy and friendly losses due to artillery with the loss pattern in normal meeting engagements, we gained a fairly clear picture that lessened our overall casualties by accepting the penalty of small losses due to artillery. The breaking up of a sizeable enemy unit was the bonus that made this penalty doubly worthwhile.

CHART 11—Simplified Jitterbug Flow Chart

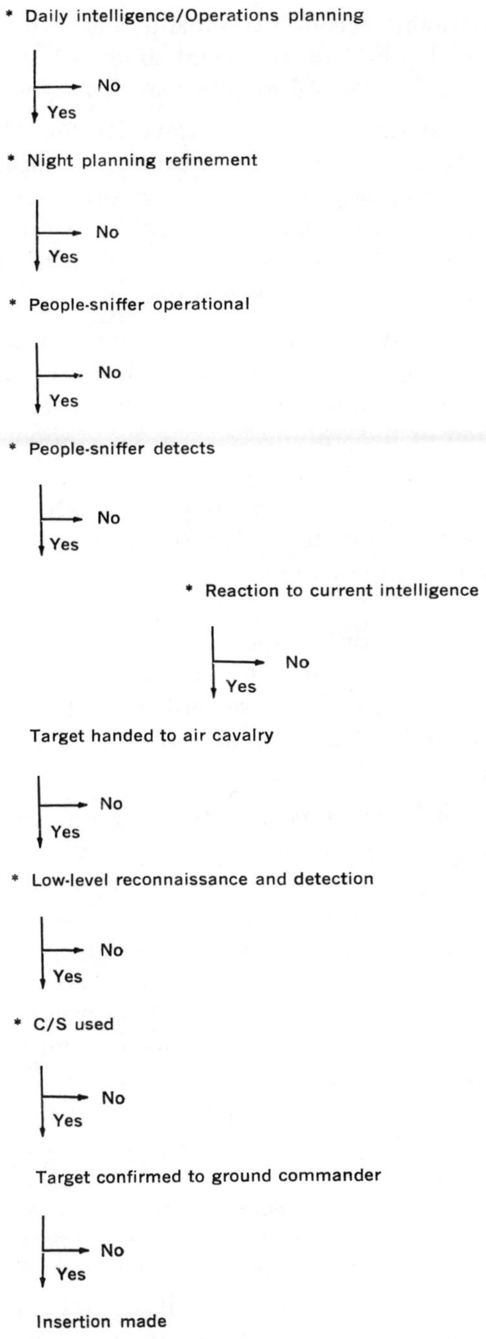

* Daily intelligence/Operations planning

    → No
    ↓ Yes

* Night planning refinement

    → No
    ↓ Yes

* People-sniffer operational

    → No
    ↓ Yes

* People-sniffer detects

    → No
    ↓ Yes

        * Reaction to current intelligence

        → No
        ↓ Yes

Target handed to air cavalry

    → No
    ↓ Yes

* Low-level reconnaissance and detection

    → No
    ↓ Yes

* C/S used

    → No
    ↓ Yes

Target confirmed to ground commander

    → No
    ↓ Yes

Insertion made

*Increases possibility of a contact

until late afternoon; second, command and control helicopters circled suspected landing zones several times before insertion; and third, the landing force was normally a small unit without support.

The letter also directed the Military Region II regiments to select several landing zones ambush squads for training. Each squad, armed with one automatic rifle, one claymore, three to four AK–47's, and one sniping rifle would then link up with local guerrillas and set up ambushes "in the areas where the enemy has frequently landed." The instructions to these squads were fairly explicit:

1. If the enemy drops his troops close to the edge of a village and the choppers have not quite landed, we will concentrate maximum firepower to destroy the enemy force immediately. The function of the sniping cell will be to shoot down the CP chopper.

2. If the enemy drops his troops away from the edge of the village, we will deploy in combat formations and wait for them. When they are three or four meters from our positions, we open fire.

3. If the enemy drops troops on our position, our efforts depend on the situation. After we have destroyed the enemy force and cleared the battlefield, we will move to another location 300–500 meters from the contact area and deploy again, ready to fight.

An analysis of helicopters shot down or hit while entering or leaving landing zones in support of the 9th Division during the time period July through December 1968 seems to indicate that the Viet Cong were most effective in their anti-hawk tactics during the months of July and August. In this two month period, supporting Assault Helicopter Companies had 31 helicopters shot down, 74 hit by hostile fire, with 131 rounds received. However, we learned to react quickly to Viet Cong tactics. We stopped reconnoitering landing zones with both the Command & Control and Air Cavalry elements. We improved the use of our People Sniffer so that we had good verification whether to expect Viet Cong or not and we were rarely caught by surprise. The LOH's replaced the OH-23's and every time a Viet Cong fired his weapon, unless he was in a bunkered position, he signed his own death warrant because the LOH's picked him right off. As a result, the Viet Cong went almost completely defensive and avoided contact at all costs. Table 16 shows the statistics of aircraft shot down for the period July through December 1968. Less than half the aircraft shot down were totally destroyed.

TABLE 16—AIRCRAFT DAMAGED BY HOSTILE FIRE
1968

Damage	July	August	September	October	November	December
Aircraft Shot Down ..	11	20	8	5	2	1
Aircraft Hit	31	43	26	36	25	41
Rounds Received	50	81	84	61	43	86

The aforementioned should give a feel as to the capabilities of the Viet Cong to "turn us off" once they grasped our tactics. We found much evidence of Viet Cong analysis of our tactics, including map studies of actual operations wherein they analyzed our encirclement tactics. Once they caught on to our new techniques they dispatched operational immediate messages to all their units describing our tactics and their proposed countermeasures. Consequently, we had to be alert to the need for changes in our operational approach to keep on top of the situation. This required a systematic analytical study of combat operations subsequently described.

Bushmaster and Checkerboard Operations

The Jitterbug is an airmobile operation. However, in the summer of 1968 our brigades received the support of an Air Cavalry Troop and Assault Helicopter Companies only a little over one half the time. Jitterbug tactics required at a maximum one battalion when a good size contact was made. Most of our battalions, then, were engaged in ground mobile tactics and we were constantly trying to improve our techniques.

Colonel Henry E. Emerson, drawing upon his earlier experience in Vietnam, began experimenting with "Bushmaster" and "Checkerboard" tactics to supplement the Jitterbug. These proved very successful and were implemented division-wide. We continuously adjusted and adapted these tactics to the terrain and the enemy of the delta.

Bushmaster Operations.

Bushmaster operations involved an infantry company broken into platoon sized elements. The Bushmaster was used in areas where the enemy was strong, and where breaking down into less than platoon sized elements risked heavy losses. The Bushmaster was normally used to interdict known enemy communications-liaison routes, and the primary ingredient of the Bushmaster was valid intelligence. Once the area had been chosen and the approximate sites of ambush determined, the Bushmaster force was usually inserted using helicopters during the last two hours of daylight. It was inserted directly into its area of operations or adjacent to it, infiltrating the remaining distance on foot. Under either situation, the final positions were not occupied until after dark. Once in the area of operations, a small command group set up a command post. The platoons were spread out and, if possible, units were made mutually supporting, located at a distance whereby they could reinforce in less than one-half hour. In the rice paddies this distance was not over 750 meters, so that a company sized Bushmaster normally covered an area three-fourths of a kilometer square. The Bushmaster, although primarily a night time operation, was also effective during daylight. However, during daylight, much more stealth, cunning, ingenuity, and planning were required.

Checkerboard Operations.

The Checkerboard concept was an outgrowth of the Bushmaster, and often times it paid off to use the Bushmaster one night, completely familiarizing the troops with the area and then breaking up into a Checkerboard on the second day of a two-day operation. Whereas in the Bushmaster a company was broken-down into platoon sized elements, the Checkerboard was configured in squad sized elements. These elements had fixed areas of operations comparable to the squares of a checkerboard, and once in these areas of operations they moved continuously from one terrain feature to another in order to interdict the enemy. Checkerboard personnel must have increased communications capability and must be highly mobile. Therefore, they were lightly equipped and carried only basic ammuntion and rations, preferably long range reconnaissance patrol type. The Checkerboard was an offensive operation and aggressively sought to establish contact in order to find and fix enemy positions. The Checkerboard was also a precursor of the "pile-on" because once the enemy was found, other troops were brought in to encircle and destroy him. Since the Bushmaster and Checkerboard generally were conducted at night, the operations were kept within artillery range and a Light Fire Team was kept available on standby. Checkerboard patrols were also mutually supporting and, because they were broken into small units, 500 meters between patrols was the normal distance in the delta. Fifteen slick loads of personnel broken down into 10 to 12 man units could easily cover an area $1\frac{1}{2}$ kilometers square, or 4 times that of a Bushmaster.

Both the Checkerboard and Bushmaster techniques were excellent training vehicles for young company commanders. After the brigade or battalion headquarters had picked the general area of operations the company commander could plan the location of his unit, the method of movement, and the control required. When inserted and left on his own, a company commander took intense pride in insuring that his troops were trained and disciplined enough to establish a contact. The key to success on a Checkerboard was small unit leadership, flexibility, stealth, and aggressiveness. Like ourselves, the enemy had to move to get his resupply, his replacements, and to deliver his non-electronic messages. The Checkerboard was ideally suited to interdict these activities since it covered a substantial amount of terrain. A 48-hour Checkerboard could cover an area three kilometers square. In a two-day operation, troops were rested during daylight so that they were ready to operate at maximum potential during the night. Checkerboards were not conducted in enemy base areas with known large size operating units. Such base areas were better handled by Bushmaster or Jitterbug operations.

Ambushes

The importance of keeping constant pressure on the Viet Cong was discussed previously. By constantly disrupting his supply and personnel infiltration routes, both by air and ground maneuver, we strangled his much needed support. One of our best tactical examples of constant pressure were the ambushes conducted by the Riverine Brigade in Kien Hoa Province. Traditionally the Riverine Brigade had lived aboard ship—foraying out on Reconnaissance in Force missions and upon completion of their operations withdrawing to the large APL's. In the fall of 1968, the 3d Battalion, 47th Infantry broke with tradition and established a base camp in a coconut grove astride the main highway and canal arteries of Kien Hoa Province. The results were instantaneous and dramatic. Because they were on the ground the intelligence picture got better as the result of constant liaison with the District Chiefs, and others. They started running more Integrated Civic Action Programs and established radar and sensor fields.

Armed with better intelligence, the men of the 3d Battalion 47th Infantry under the leadership of Lieutenant Colonel Ismael Pack went to extraordinary lengths to set up and spring ambushes. The ambushes were planned to coincide with Viet Cong movement times and routes. The ambushes were augmented with snipers and pink lights and were tied into the radar and sensor nets.

The 3d Battalion 47th Infantry after initial successes had enough confidence to allow the advance Viet Cong elements in a unit to pass through the ambush so that their traps were usually sprung against Viet Cong main bodies. They built their fire power around claymore mines and M–79's. When the Viet Cong entered the killing area, the ambush was initiated by the detonation of the claymore belts and the area was sealed with M–79 fire augmented by direct fire weapons. Artillery fires were adjusted into the area of contact and along likely avenues of escape. Terrain permitting, the infantry moved forward to establish contact. At the conclusion of the ambush new troop positions were occupied in the contact area to ambush the enemy anew as he attempted to retrieve his dead.

During the period January through March 1969 the Division conducted over 6,500 ambushes. (*Table 17*) This table is activity oriented indicating only the level of activity reached; this averaged 70 ambushes per night in early 1969. The success rate of the ambushes increased even more. Of course the availability of night vision devices gave our friendly troops a major technical advantage. Trained snipers provided expertise not previously available and gave the infantrymen a new confidence in their weapons and capabilities. Thus, using intelligence, stealth, cunning, and aggressive tactics the 3d Battalion 47th Infantry and other battalions in the division were able to take the night away from the Viet Cong by interdicting his route of communications thus upsetting his time schedule, his flow of supplies, and his personnel.

TABLE 17—9TH INFANTRY DIVISION TOTAL AMBUSHES CONDUCTED

Quarter	Number
3d Qtr 1968	4,461
4th Qtr 1968	5,957
1st Qtr 1969	6,430

Sniper Program

In the Spring of 1969 our most successful ambush tactic was the sniper mode. Our sniper program was initiated in the States and was set in motion as result of a visit to Fort Benning in January 1968. The Army Marksmanship Unit cooperated with us to the fullest extent, and funds were made available to increase the accuracy of fifty-five M–14 rifles and to provide sniper-scopes. The idea was to get an outstanding training team from the Marksmanship Unit to train our soldiers in Vietnam in sniper tactics.

The Army Marksmanship Unit team led by Major Willis L. Powell and consisting of seven non-commissioned officers arrived in Vietnam in June 1968. Upon arrival in the country they revamped the M–16 training methods at our division training establishment, the Reliable Academy. Subsequently they supervised the construction of a 500 yard range at Dong Tam and periodically accompanied ambush patrols to assimilate the delta tactics. Progress was slow. Brigadier General James S. Timothy was given the task of getting the sniper program off the ground in early August. This gave it the needed boost. Eventually the more accurate M–14 rifles arrived as well as special national match ammunition. Our first hand picked group of volunteers from each battalion graduated in early November 1968 and the first sniper kill was registered on 19 November 1968 north of Binh Phuoc in Long An Province. The second group of snipers graduated in early December, giving us a full complement of 72 snipers, six per battalion and four per brigade. Notwithstanding all the personal attention that had been given to the sniper program, the early performance was ragged with only eight kills in November and eleven in December. This was clearly a dismal performance, considering the large number of men and the effort that had gone into the program.

Therefore, we set about analyzing our equipment, personnel, methods and tactics. We hit upon the flaw in the system, and while the solution was extremely simple, it had an immediate effect. Initially snipers had been parcelled out by the battalions on the basis of two per line company. The company commanders, then, had the responsibility for the snipers and most company commanders could not care less. They used snipers just as any other rifleman. This was the reason we were not getting results. Consequently, we directed assignment of the snipers to the battalion headquarters and held the battalion commanders responsible for their proper utilization and for emphasis on the program. Once the battalion commanders learned to assign the sniper teams to the companies going on night operations the problem was solved. Snipers reported directly to company commanders, received a briefing on proposed tactics, picked the platoon and the area where they thought they could be most effective, and waited for a target. The nighttime sniper teams normally consisted of two snipers and two additional infantrymen armed with an M–79 and an M–16 and carrying a radio. Snipers worked in pairs to offset the eye fatigue which set in after long periods of peering through a starlight scope.

Once the snipers began to get personal attention and could handpick their assignments and fit their talents to the mission,

CHART 12—Sniper Kills, 9th Infantry Division,
November 1968–July 1969

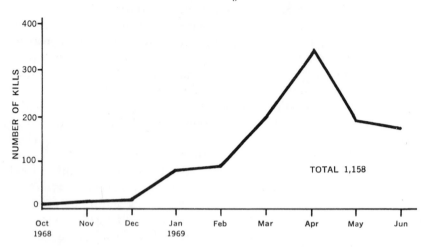

the results were extraordinary. Chart 12 shows the steady improvement in sniper results, culminating in 346 enemy killed in the
month of April and leveling off at about 200 kills per month. It
was a flat learning curve initially but it soon steepened up.

After the snipers began to gain confidence and unit commanders saw that they were a great boon to the unit, the whole
nighttime pace increased. To be quite frank, things went slowly
initially because the ambush units were fearful of drawing attention
to themselves as the result of snipers engaging the Viet Cong. However, our units soon became more confident and aggressive in
night operations, primarily as a result of the sniper program—
a large unexpected bonus that we had not considered.

One of the unusual night sniper employments resulted from the
6th Battalion, 31st Infantry operating from riverine boats along the
Mekong River. In this case, the snipers working in pairs positioned
themselves on the helicopter landing pad of Tango boats. The
Tango boats travelled at speeds of 2 to 4 knots moving about 100
to 150 meters from and parallel to the shore. Often they would
anchor for periods of a half-hour before moving to a new location.
As the Viet Cong moved along the shoreline the snipers after positive identification of the enemy, that is detection of a weapon, would
open fire. During the period 12 April to 9 May 1969 snipers of the
6th Battalion, 31st Infantry killed 39 Viet Cong. About 1.7 Viet
Cong were killed per engagement. The average distance to the
target was 148 meters and it took 6 rounds per kill. The average
time of engagement was 0040 hours.

As an interesting war story, our most successful sniper was Sergeant Adelbert F. Waldron, III, who had 109 confirmed kills to his credit. One afternoon he was riding along the Mekong River on a Tango boat when an enemy sniper on shore pecked away at the boat. While everyone else on board strained to find the antagonist, who was firing from the shoreline over 900 meters away, Sergeant Waldron took up his sniper rifle and picked off the Viet Cong out of the top of a coconut tree with one shot (this from a moving platform). Such was the capability of our best sniper. We had others, too, with his matchless vision and expert marksmanship. Sergeant Waldron earned two Distinguished Service Crosses for his outstanding skill and bravery.

Space does not permit us to recount many of the ingenious methods that were used in our sniper program. One of the most effective was the use of pink filtered searchlights during periods of limited ambient illumination. Another was the effective use by the 4th Battalion, 39th Infantry of daytime sniper operations. They would insert snipers in the early morning along known trails and infiltration routes likely to be used by the enemy. They used six-man teams—highly trained individuals capable of remaining in the field for several hours without moving a muscle when the situation required.

The sniper program of the 9th Infantry Division was one of the most successful programs that we undertook. It took over a year from its inception in the States to its peak of performance in Vietnam. It also took plenty of hard work and belief in the concept and in our snipers. But more than anything it restored the faith of the infantryman in his rifle and in his own capabilities. Fighting alone at night without the usually available combined arms team, the "rice paddy" soldier was more than a match for the enemy.

The 15-Second War

When snipers came into their own, it became apparent that aimed rifle fire was killing Viet Cong. In thinking about this, the thought occurred that the Viet Cong basically could not shoot and our men could. By that time (December 1968) the Viet Cong were beginning to fragment and we had many contacts which were essentially meeting engagements between small groups of men. By polling the commanders, it was found that the contact ranges were much closer than we had imagined in such open terrain—on the order of 10 to 25 meters.

We then decided, more on faith than conviction, that we would go for aimed shot kills rather than fire superiority. We devised a

SNIPER AT WORK (SGT WALDRON)

very simple training drill to teach men to shoot under these conditions:

a. Quick kill technique
b. Short range
c. Single aimed shots (quick kill)
d. No full automatic mode
e. Quick reaction (seconds)

The battalion commander, after an informal poll of riflemen, would determine what his normal opening range was and how quickly a soldier must fire to beat the enemy to the draw. We will say that a battalion commander set 25 meters and 8 seconds as his criteria. Each company, every third or fourth day during stand-down, would have the riflemen shoot at anything (tin cans, targets, whatever) until they could get a first round hit at 25 meters in 8 seconds. By repetition, this became an automatic reflex action. This one idea in combination with good night ambushes made it possible for our small rifle units to wreak heavy damage on the enemy with low friendly casualties. One reason it worked so well was that the average Communist soldier was not trained to shoot and could not afford to expend the ammunition necessary to learn. Actually this concept which was formulated at division level received more or less attention and implementation at lower levels, depending upon the commanders involved. However, there appeared to be some key element which was helpful. Nevertheless, it is one of the best examples we can think of which combined an analytical approach, military judgment, training, execution and substantial results. This idea has been termed the "15-Second War." Chart 13 shows why.

It seemed absolutely incomprehensible that some hundreds of riflemen wandering around could inflict heavy losses on a Communist enemy and seldom use the artillery, bombs, and so forth that were necessary in more formal warfare. (Naturally, if one hit a bunkered position, one shifted to heavy firepower.) However, this idea paid off manyfold on the battlefield in the Upper Delta and III Corps area during all of 1969.

What's Best

During March, when all of our tactics seemed to be paying off, we questioned ourselves as to what were the best methods of operations in the daytime and nighttime environments. Since we normally monitored brigade operations by type, size and whether the operation was conducted during the day or night, we decided to

15-Second War

CHART 13—FIRE POWER VERSUS TIME CONCEPTION

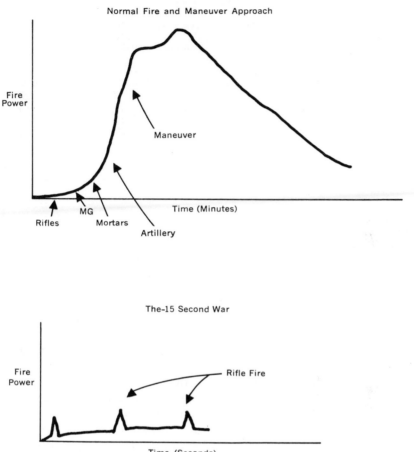

Normal Fire and Maneuver Approach

The-15 Second War

keep tabs on their results and to analyze our operations in order to be able to reinforce success. These statistics are shown in Table 18.

Daytime Operations.

Checkerboard and Bushmaster operations yielded 0.27 and 0.22 contacts per operation respectively. Thus, the choice of these ground mobile modes was pretty much a toss-up. On the other hand company-sized airmobile Jitterbug operations produced 1.80 contacts per operation as compared with platoon reconnaissances in force which produced only 0.08 contacts per operation. We concluded that daytime company-sized operations paid off, undoubtedly due to the better command and control provided by the company command section.

TABLE 18—COMPARISON OF TACTICAL RESULTS CONTACTS PER OPERATION
APRIL 1969

DAYTIME OPERATIONS

Type of Operation	Number of Operations/Contacts		
	Squad	Platoon	Company
Jitterbug		640/51	335/603
Bushmaster			111/ 25
Checkerboard			93/ 25
Ambush			
Total		640/51	539/653

NIGHTTIME OPERATIONS

Type of Operation	Number of Operations/Contact		
	Squad	Platoon	Company
Jitterbug			
Bushmaster			269/88
Checkerboard			65/26
Ambush	1080/37	654/123	
Total	1080/37	654/123	334/114

Nighttime Operations.

Nighttime operations had a few surprises. The Checkerboard and Bushmaster operations yielded 0.40 and 0.33 contacts per operation respectively. This was exactly 50 percent more contacts per operation than in the daytime. So again the choice between type was pretty much up to the unit commander. However, it can be seen that over four times as many Bushmasters were conducted than Checkerboards. This was because the Checkerboard required much greater control and much tighter leadership than was required with a Bushmaster and few of our battalions felt confident enough to conduct Checkerboards. Although the company-sized operations produced more contacts per operation on a percentage basis than did the platoon-size ambushes, for the number of troops involved the platoon ambushes were 60 percent more effective than the company-size Bushmasters and Checkerboards. Squad ambushes did not produce significant results, again probably because of the security problems involved with a small number of personnel. We concluded that squad operations did not pay off; whereas platoon ambushes were effective. Since the results of the Checkerboards and Bushmasters were almost identical, it appeared to be sounder to conduct Bushmasters at night because the chance of being overrun by the enemy was much less.

The number of enemy eliminated in April resulting from daytime infantry tactics (1768) was about twice those eliminated during nighttime infantry operations (847) . However, when the enemy eliminated per contact was computed it was most startling to find that the average nighttime contact resulted in 3.1 enemy losses compared to 2.5 in the daytime. A comparison of equivalent platoon days during the month of April shows that the number of troops in the field was almost identical daytime versus nighttime averaging 75 platoons per period. Therefore, the daytime effectiveness per infantryman was double the nighttime effectiveness even though the enemy losses per contact at night were greater.

By April we had come to rely on the fact that a great number of small contacts over a large area literally bled the enemy to death. Our units had quit looking for the "big contact" because by then the Viet Cong were entirely fragmented and in hiding, generally without ammunition and food and avoiding contact at all costs. We concluded that the answer to "What's Best?", was more of the same.

Night Hunter

In the fall of 1968 when the Viet Cong throughout our tactical area of operations were directed to break down into small groups and ordered to avoid combat at all costs, it became much more difficult to find the enemy. The effectiveness of Jitterbugging declined and commanders frantically sought better methods of employment. About this time we received permission to break down into five slick insertions for our reconnaissance-in-force to meet the reduced level of enemy activity and to cover a much broader area more thoroughly. In Long An Province, Colonel John P. Geraci of the 1st Brigade turned to night operations since the daytime targets had dried up. Up until this time our radar sightings were engaged with unobserved artillery fire and we had no follow-up target damage assessment during the hours of darkness. It was assumed that Viet Cong were being killed but we were unable to confirm that assumption. Consequently, our radar sightings were of value mainly as intelligence information since we had no way of assessing the artillery results.

In an attempt to solve his reduced daytime contacts and the unknown effect of our engagements on radar sightings, Colonel Geraci developed what he called his "Night Hunter" technique. Night Hunter was a very complex tactical maneuver utilizing radar vectored air cavalry. The Night Hunter task force was comprised of three essential elements: a ground surveillance radar, air cavalry gunships, and a direct support artillery element. Initially we used a ground reaction force also. The maneuver worked something like this. Our AN/TPS-25 radar was monitored by the command and control group. When they found a major sighting of 20 or more Viet Cong they monitored it for some time and when they were assured that it was, in fact, enemy personnel they started the Night Hunter in motion. The artillery prepared to place a battery volley, shell high explosive, fuze variable time, on the target as well as two rounds of shell illuminating with a 200 meter height of burst. Both the high explosive and illuminating rounds had to arrive on target simultaneously. Data were also computed to follow up the initial illumination with continuous illuminating rounds with a 600 meter height of burst.

The air cavalry commander scrambled his gunships and they orbited some 5 to 10 kilometers away from the target. Ground elements were dispatched to blocking positions. As the Time on Target approached the air cavalry commander vectored his gunships toward the target on a flight path generally perpendicular to the artillery-gun target line and at an altitude below the burst height of illumination. Through precise coordination, the artillery fire burst over the target as the gunships rolled in to exploit the shock effect of the combined attack. If the target was large enough the ground troops were brought up.

It is amazing that this highly complex tactical maneuver worked at all—but it did. The first Night Hunter resulted in 22 enemy being killed, completely surprising a major enemy unit. We tried three or four subsequent operations, all of which were successful with an average enemy eliminated of about 25. However, this was a costly maneuver, requiring great judgment on the part of the commander. It needed an air cavalry standby which on many nights was never scrambled due to lack of lucrative radar sightings. In other words, we were tied to the black box, thus limiting the area coverage and the number of targets that could be engaged. However, from this interesting maneuver, the most complex that we know of in the Vietnamese environment, we proved conclusively that the air cavalry could operate effectively at night. The Night Hunter was the precursor to our very successful Night Search operations which were developed because of the foregoing limitations of the Night Hunter. Once the Night Search was implemented the Night Hunter technique was abandoned.

Night Search

Night Search operations evolved from the Night Hunter in early December 1968 for the reasons just mentioned. The Night Search was a pure nighttime air cavalry operation with a great many twists in techniques. The assets required were minimal—a Command and Control Copter and two Cobras. The operation was not hampered by anything except weather. The key to our Night Search operations was again good intelligence plus highly trained personnel.

Operational areas were selected predicated upon enemy movements and current intelligence. Search patterns were organized primarily focusing on canals and waterways because this was the main method of Viet Cong supply in the delta. The operation was led by the Command and Control chopper flying 300–500 feet over the target area. Our spotters in the Command and Control copter initially used starlight scopes to scan the ground area below the flight pattern of the aircraft. Since spotters were the key to the operation, we ultimately went to our trained snipers for this duty. Once they identified a target they engaged it with a burst of full tracer fire. This enabled the gunships flying close to the Command and Control copter at about 1500 feet to zoom in for the contact. As the Cobras attacked the Command and Control copter patrolled areas adjacent to the target to observe the results and to permit the snipers to engage any enemy fleeing the area. This simple technique resulted in over 1,800 enemy kills in a six month period. Not only did it weaken the enemy but it completely disrupted his normal pattern of nighttime movement.

We encountered some skeptics concerning the efficacy of such a simple operation. The J–3 of the South Vietnamese Joint Staff, Colonel Tho, visited us one night to observe the technique in operation. Upon his return to Dong Tam he somewhat excitingly exclaimed: "We killed 18 of them. You could see them as clear as day."

The key was in identifying the enemy. To illustrate how small things make the difference, our heliborne snipers easily tired of scanning the ground through sniperscopes. We then introduced the Night Observation Device to identify targets, but it vibrated so much that it wasn't particularly effective. Some enterprising soldier suggested that we suspend it from the chopper doorframe with a rubber cord spring. Once we did this, we had a stable platform that literally turned night into day. Although we pioneered this operation our techniques were chewing gum and bailing wire modifications. The Night Search techniques reached their perfection later on in the 25th Infantry Division and 1st Air Cavalry Division who developed much improved hardware.

Another innovative method of finding the enemy was developed for periods when there was no moon to activate the Night Observation Device. In such cases, we would patrol a waterway as far as 10 kilometers distance from our actual target area, covering it with artillery illumination. We were certain the Viet Cong under the artillery illumination dug in; but we also knew that the Viet Cong in outlying areas relaxed. As they relaxed our Night Search team barrelled in, using the flares to activate the night vision device. We always racked up a good number during those no-moon periods which normally were considered nonoperational times.

But good hunting doesn't last forever. The Viet Cong soon caught on and took countermeasures. Table 19 highlights the operations of the 1st Brigade, which initiated and perfected our Night Search operations, as well as the division totals. The efficiency of the operations built up and peaked for the 1st Brigade in March 1969. Thereafter results tapered off greatly as the Viet Cong learned to cope with this technique (or possibly reduced their night movement).

As our spotter teams became more skilled, the spotters not only could mark the area for the Cobras but were actually successful in killing the enemy with rifle fire from the aircraft. Approximately 15 percent of the total kills of the night search operation was attributed to sniper fire. If one has not flown in a chopper at night over the delta it is hard to describe how lonely and difficult it is to keep your bearings and to operate. All our night activities took a tremendous amount of guts and those on the Night Search had their quota of them.

Night Raid

The most daring of all our tactics was the Night Raid. In late February 1969 our liaison with Government of Vietnam authorities was hitting on all cylinders and we were obtaining much more

TABLE 19—9TH INFANTRY DIVISION RESULTS OF NIGHT SEARCH OPERATIONS

| | 1969 | | | | | | |
	JAN	FEB	MAR	APR	MAY	JUN	TOTAL
1ST BRIGADE							
Total Operations..	12	24	20	23	23	17	119
Total VC Killed ..	134	324	407	219	155	38	1,277
Kills/Operation ..	11.2	13.5	20.4	9.5	6.7	2.2	10.7
DIVISION TOTAL							
Total Operations..	19	37	60	43	60	50	269
Total VC Killed ..	134	373	477	388	300	141	1,813
Kills/Operation ..	7.0	10.1	7.9	9.0	5.0	2.8	6.7

information about the Viet Cong. The 2d Battalion, 39th Infantry, first under one of our most outstanding battalion commanders, Lieutenant Colonel Donald B. Schroeder (who was killed by enemy fire in early 1969), and subsequently under Lieutenant Colonel Robert A. Sullivan, had a particularly good intelligence section. This battalion was located along Highway 4 north of the District Headquarters of Cai Be in Dinh Thuong Province. Their S–2, Captain Joseph W. Hudson, (later killed by hostile fire on 17 March 1969) had noted that the enemy dispersed during daytime but in the evening they reassembled in small isolated groups of abandoned houses throughout the District area. Whenever U.S. troops set ambushes, even though we would pick off one or two enemy, they remained generally dispersed and did not concentrate. Captain Hudson suggested that it was too bad we could not raid some houses, and so the concept of the Night Raid was initiated. The Night Raid combined the techniques associated with the Night Hunter and the Night Search into a dramatically daring attack on an enemy stronghold. The operational team consisted of a Command and Control copter, two Cobras, and two slicks carrying six combat infantrymen each. The operation unfolded something like this.

About midnight when we were sure the Viet Cong had settled down for the evening the aircraft would become airborne. At a prearranged time artillery would fire illuminating rounds lighting up the target huts. The Cobras would swing in and strafe the peripheral areas and the Command and Control copter would follow the Cobras and mark the landing zone with a flare. The two Hueys protected by the Cobras would land, deposit the troops, and circle again. After the initial illumination the Command and Control copter normally provided additional flares but the artillery would remain on call if needed for high explosive or illuminating rounds. The troops on the ground were prebriefed as to layout of the area, the buildings to be searched and what they expected to find. Each man had his job and upon hitting the landing zone they set out to accomplish it in a period of 5 to 10 minutes at the most. So sudden was the element of surprise gained on these raids that we have killed Viet Cong guards sitting up against a tree reaching for their rifles in order to combat the U.S. attack. Most of the times the Viet Cong were caught asleep so that we could capture prisoners giving tremendous intelligence bonuses. The attack ended as fast as it had begun, with the Hueys coming in to the pick-up zone to pick up the troops and depart rapidly. These raids were so successful that in the dozens which occurred in the midst of Viet Cong strongholds with

100 or more Viet Cong on hand we suffered only two U.S. soldiers killed.

The decision to conduct the Night Raids was one of our toughest decisions. In most people's minds we stood a good chance to lose two choppers and twelve infantrymen. As it turned out we never lost an aircraft, had minimum casualties and maximum returns. The shock to the Viet Cong who realized that they were not safe even in the middle of the night in far off areas was more than they could stand. This helped to keep them off balance and when considered with all of the other day and night operations that were going on was one of the keystones of our constant pressure technique.

Day or Night?

Many have asked whether all the planning, training, scheduling, maintenance and time that went into night operations were worth the pay off. After the mini-*Tet* in May 1968 the total enemy losses (Viet Cong, killed in action, Prisoners of War, Hoi Chanhs and V.C. Infrastructure) for the period June through December 1968 averaged approximately 983 a month. At the same time the ratio of Viet Cong eliminated to U.S. Killed in Action was about 13.7 to 1. (*Table 20*) Throughout this period we had conducted continuing

TABLE 20—RATIO OF VIET CONG ELIMINATED TO U.S. KILLED, JUNE 1968–JUNE 1969

DATE	VC KIA	PW	HC	VCI[a]	TOTAL VC ELIMINATED	U.S. KIA	VC ELIMINATED U.S. KIA
Jun 68	888	69	7	—	964	113	8.5:1
Jul	646	84	5	—	735	54	13.6:1
Aug	968	108	9	—	1085	101	10.7:1
Sep	735	104	12	—	851	67	12.7:1
Oct	901	92	25	—	1018	66	15.4:1
Nov	961	140	22	—	1123	44	25.5:1
Dec	968	101	26	13/ (11)	1108	59	18.8:1
			Sub-Total Avg		983	72	13.7:1
Jan 69	1292	95	24	24/ (10)	1435	92	15.6:1
Feb	1799	82	42	26/ (8)	1949	59	33.0:1
Mar	3504	124	75	20/ (21)	3723	46	80.9:1
Apr	3117	116	71	6/ (15)	3310	39	84.9:1
May	2677	122	37	11/ (24)	2847	65	43.8:1
Jun	1792	127	55	7/ (20)	1981	45	44.0:1
			Sub-Total Avg		2541	58	43.8:1

[a] Numbers to left of slash mark represent civilians held for trial by South Vietnamese authorities. Numbers in parentheses indicate military personnel killed or held as prisoners of war.

night operations but not on the scale that occurred in 1969. Our night cavalry tactics commenced in earnest in January 1969, but in that month we only had 19 Night Search operations. Our Night Raids didn't get started until late February and our snipers didn't begin to be productive until January. The influence the snipers had in making our nighttime ambushes more aggressive was not really felt until February or March. Considering the fact that we really didn't get moving in nighttime operations until February there was a tremendous change in the statistics between the last half of 1968 and the first half of 1969. It must be remembered that in July of 1969 the division was alerted for withdrawal and combat operations dropped off sharply as the troops prepared to relocate to the Continental U.S. If the month of December 1968 is any criteria of the nighttime activities for the last half of 1968 the ratio of nighttime enemy eliminated to total enemy eliminated during the month was 17 percent. (*Table 21*) This compares to an average of 35 percent eliminated during night operations in the first half of 1969. In other words, the percentage of enemy losses due to night operations in 1969 was twice that in 1968. Moreover, the absolute increase in enemy losses was most impressive. During January—June 1969 the average monthly number of enemy eliminated jumped from the 983 previously discussed to 2,541 while at the same time the average monthly exchange ratio more than tripled to 43.8 to 1. (*Table 20*)

TABLE 21—9TH INFANTRY DIVISION VIET CONG ELIMINATED DAY—NIGHT OPERATIONS

	DEC 68	JAN 69	FEB 69	MAR 69	APR 69	MAY 69	JUN 69	JUL 69
Day Air Cavalry	398	341	337	572	429	516	564	209
Day Infantry	396	539	726	1138	1293	1034	724	174
Others	124	146	157	377	340	485	145	121
Total Daytime	918	1026	1220	2087	2062	2035	1433	504
Night Air Cavalry	34	143	391	580	355	266	113	12
Night Infantry	145	193	245	845	547	346	275	175
Snipers	11	73	93	211	346	200	160	56
Total Nighttime	190	409	729	1636	1248	812	548	243
Total	1108	1435	1949	3723	3310	2847	1981	747
Ratio, Night/Total	.17	.28	.37	.44	.38	.29	.28	.33

While greatly increasing enemy losses we had reduced U.S. casualties relatively and absolutely.

There is no question that by breaking down into small units and applying continuous pressure day and night, the two building blocks of our tactical innovations, we were able to get the Viet Cong on the run and really clobber him. His apparatus fell apart. The Viet Cong lost his leaders, his followers, his ammunition, and his food. In short he became unglued, resulting in additional enemy eliminated. We decimated four or five of his best battalions.

In our opinion, our tactical innovations, particularly those at night, were the key to the division's success.

These innovations came about as a result of improved support and an analytical approach to combat operations. To answer the question, Day or Night?, we can only reply, "Day *and* Night."

Mines and Booby Traps

As the war wound down in Vietnam the number of friendly casualties due to mines and booby traps became more pronounced or at least more obvious. Whether this was due to more enemy effort in this area or due to less direct combat casualties overall or both was not determined.

However, all units felt compelled to study this problem and hold it under control. One approach was to try to teach the riflemen as much about mines and booby traps as possible. The 9th Division took the opposite approach; by analyzing the types and setups in depth it was determined that about two types of devices and three or four setups covered the great majority of engagements. By concentrating on these it was possible to teach all of the men most of what was necessary to know to detect booby traps and to minimize casualties. The men who demonstrated a flair for detection were given more training and used as on-the-job-training instructors. Statistical records were kept which could be studied by every commander so that he, in his own way, could seek means to reduce losses by enemy booby traps and mines. Our analytical approach allowed us to come up with many changes that helped reduce casualties. Highlights of our analysis are discussed subsequently.

How Detected.

Almost all of the booby traps not detonated were detected visually. (*Table 22*) Very few—less than one percent—were detected as a result of informants or scout dogs. Therefore, men must constantly be on the alert, eyes focused and searching ahead of the line of march. In this respect, as mentioned above, training was of vital

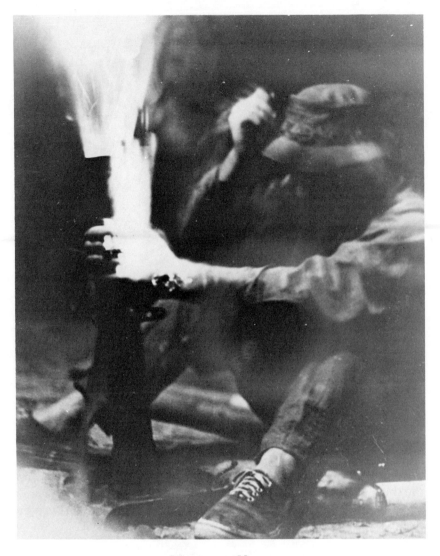

MORTAR AT NIGHT

importance to new men in-country prior to gaining the experience that comes only with being in the rice paddies.

When Detected.

We found that the peak of booby trap detection occurred at 1100 in the morning when the troops were fresh and alert. The average peak of detonations on the other hand occurred at 1600 hours, when the troops were tired and not as alert. (*Chart 14*)

MINE DETECTION, THE HARD WAY

The majority of all casualties from booby traps occurred on recon-naissance in force missions. When a soldier plodded through a rice paddy up to his waist in water for several hours in the hot humid atmosphere he became terribly fatigued, his ability to concentrate was low and he was an easy mark for a Viet Cong booby trap. Just the simple fact that the commanders were told to rotate units as well as lead personnel as the day progressed in order to always have alert troops as point men cut our booby trap casualties greatly.

TABLE 22—METHOD OF DETECTION OF ENEMY MINES AND BOOBY TRAPS

Method	Number	Percent
Visual	503	66.4
Detonation	221	29.2
Mine Detector	13	1.7
VC Mine Marker	4	0.5
Scout Dog	4	0.5
Informant	3	0.4
Other	10	1.3
Total	758	100.0

CHART 14—TIME DISTRIBUTION OF BOOBYTRAP INCIDENTS,
9TH INFANTRY DIVISION, 1–30 APRIL 1969

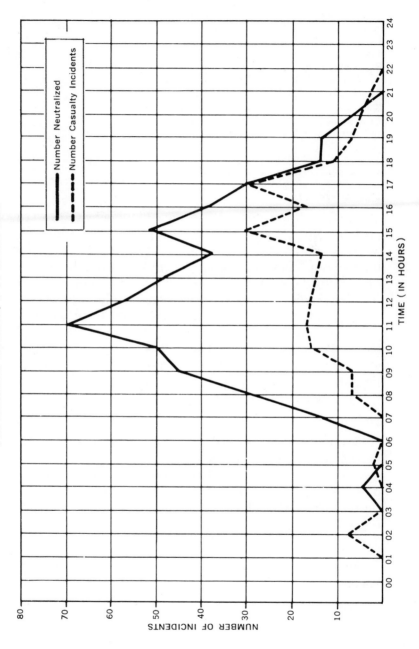

TABLE 23—LOCATION OF ENEMY DEVICES

Location	Number	Percent
Jungle	274	36.1
Trail	154	20.3
Rice Paddy Dike	101	13.3
Canal or Stream Bank	83	11.0
Rice Paddy	71	9.4
Road	35	4.6
Open Field	21	2.8
Intersection of 2, 3, 4, or 6	10	1.3
Structure	9	1.2
Total	758	100.0

Where Detected.

We found that about 34 percent of all booby traps were located predominantly along trails and rice paddy dikes while 36 percent were located in the jungle growth. *(Table 23)* At first this was thought surprising but, then, when Viet Cong tactics were considered this booby trap pattern appeared plausible. Prisoner interrogations indicated that the Viet Cong employed booby traps as a defensive measure around perimeters of bunkered positions. Their booby trap fields were normally one or two strings in depth. Consequently, our infantrymen had to be alert for booby traps throughout the complete perimeter of nipa palm or built-up enemy positions.

Disarming of Booby Traps.

We found that approximately three-fourths of all devices were trip-wires attached to a grenade. *(Table 24)* Generally these were detected visually and activated by heavy objects thrown ahead and dragged over the ground. We concluded that every squad going into the field should have some type of drag device and found

TABLE 24—TYPE FIRING DEVICE

Type	Number	Percent
Tripwire	549	72.4
Pressure	124	16.3
Unknown	27	3.6
Cmd Electric	24	3.2
Press/Electric	8	1.1
Cmd Pull	1	0.1
Other	25	3.3
Total	758	100.0

that 155mm shipping plugs made excellent dragging devices. Interestingly, 94 percent of all the booby traps and mines encountered were not covered by fire. This did not mean that Viet Cong were not in the vicinity, but most probably indicated that the Viet Cong used them as a measure to keep Allied troops away from defensive positions. They relied heavily on the detonation of the booby traps to divert our movement. Since mines and booby traps were not covered by fire, troops could take their time to neutralize the booby traps as they come upon them. In addition to the trip-wire booby traps, most of the other (16 percent) were pressure activated. One might believe that pressure activated booby traps would be located almost completely along dikes and trails. Unfortunately, this was not true; only 35 percent were located along travelled ways, with the rest dispersed in jungle, open fields, rice paddies, and structures. We recommended that all mines and booby traps should normally be blown in place.

Origin of Booby Traps.

The majority of all booby traps were made from Chinese Communist grenades, although 19 percent of the mines and booby traps were from U.S. munitions. (*Table 25*) Chicom grenades were small, easily assembled, and in plentiful supply, so troops had to expect them anywhere within the tactical area of interest.

Multiple Casualties.

Forty-six percent of all mines and booby traps detonated resulted in multiple casualties. (*Table 26*) This was caused by the bunching up of troops as they walked closed up in single file instead of walking as skirmishers with the proper distance between elements. A prisoner of war commented on this state of U.S. discipline when he said:

U.S. troops were moving fast, so I knew they did not have any idea the booby traps were there. Suddenly I heard some booby traps explode.

TABLE 25—ORIGIN OF MANUFACTURE OF BOOBY TRAPS

Origin	Number	Percent
Chicom	425	56.1
U.S.	145	19.1
VC Local	54	7.1
USSR	3	0.4
Other	9	1.2
Unknown	122	16.1
Total	758	100.0

THE DEADLY ENEMY BOOBY TRAP

Five U.S. soldiers in the front element went down and were wounded or dead. Then the entire U.S. element stopped, laid down for five minutes and started advancing again. I think U.S. troops were staying too close together during movement. U.S. troops move single file, too close together, causing many booby trap casualties.

We could not tolerate this sloppy field discipline and really put the pressure on commanders to get better control. We concluded

TABLE 26—9TH INFANTRY DIVISION MINE AND BOOBY TRAP CASUALTY STATISTICS 1–30 APRIL 1969

Battalion	No. Detonated	No. Detonated Causing Casualties	Casualty		Casualties/ Detonation	No. of Multiple Casualty Incidents	Percent of Multiple Incidents	No. of Multiple Casualties	Average Casualties per Multiple Incident
			KIA	WIA					
6–31 Inf	40	34	3	57	1.5	20	50	46	2.3
2–39 Inf	30	29	0	43	1.4	9	30	23	2.6
3–39 Inf	8	7	0	10	1.2	2	25	5	2.5
4–39 Inf	16	16	1	32	2.1	9	56	26	2.9
3–47 Inf	10	10	0	16	1.6	4	40	10	2.3
3–60 Inf	18	18	4	41	2.5	9	50	36	4.0
4–47 Inf	28	24	2	49	1.8	19	68	46	2.4
5–60 Inf	12	12	1	28	2.4	5	42	22	4.4
2–60 Inf	25	25	1	46	1.9	11	44	33	3.0
2–47 Inf	28	23	1	56	2.0	13	46	47	3.6
15th Engr	10	4	1	6	0.7	2	20	5	2.5
Others	5	4	2	10	2.4	3	60	11	3.7
Total	230	206	16	394	1.8	106	46	310	2.9

that a casualty rate of over two per incident indicated bunching, a casualty rate over about 1.5 indicated reduced distances or interval, etc. The advantages of an analytical approach are demonstrated by setting optimum distances between men based on simple field tests with the most frequent types of traps. If this distance was maintained, multiple casualties were infrequent.

The 25th Division elaborated upon this type of analysis by placing the data on their computer, thus giving them the capability to present and study the problem with minimum clerical effort.

We found that the mine and booby trap tactics of the enemy varied seasonally. For example, when rice planting time came around at the beginning of the wet season the enemy did not rig booby traps in the rice paddies so as to avoid casualties among the farmers tending to their livelihood. Because of the variations by the Viet Cong, divisions in Vietnam had to resort to analytical approaches to stay on top of this most important problem. For us, the analytical approach paid off. In a short period of time our booby trap neutralization rate increased from less than 50 percent to over 70 percent. Not only did we increase the percentage of mines and booby traps detected without detonation, but by emphasizing proper ground formations we were able to reduce the number of casualties per detonation, thereby protecting our most important asset—the soldier.

All of the significant information resulting from our analysis of mine and booby trap data was published in a Monthly Mine and Booby Trap Report. Included in the report was a handout entitled "The Story of a Booby Trap Casualty" which was disseminated to all infantry soldiers. This handout related cold statistics to reality and we hoped it would help to prevent booby trap casualties.

The Story of a Booby Trap Casualty

The battalion has the assault helicopter assets today and members of the 2d Platoon Alpha Company are on the PZ waiting for the "slicks." Amongst the 1st Squad is PFC Jones, infantryman, in-country for six weeks. The assault helicopters arrive and the 2d Platoon fills five slicks. As they lift off the PZ the day's reconnaissance in force has started. About 20 minutes later the 30 combat infantrymen are inserted 400 meters from a nipa line along a canal on the edge of the Plain of Reeds. Upon insertion the men hit the ground behind a paddy dike, but it is a cold LZ. The platoon leader is now issuing instructions to move to the north and check the nipa line. It is about 1100 hours in the morning as the men are closing in toward some dense underbrush in the tall coconut trees. So far there has been no fire; however, they can see bunkers interspersed amongst the edge of the foliage. The Tiger Scout who is walking point raises his hand, indicating something suspicious. Every-

MEDEVAC

one halts, and the squad leader comes forward to see what's up. A visual inspection indicates a trip-wire grenade booby trap carefully camouflaged amongst the foliage.

(The majority of all booby traps are detected in the early morning when troops are fresh. Many of the booby traps are detected by the several hundred Tiger Scouts, former VC themselves with an intimate knowledge of VC tactics and techniques, which the 9th Infantry Division has operating with the troops in the field. 70% of all booby traps encountered are detected. 72% are trip-wire grenade types. 36% of all booby traps encountered are in the jungle. Only 6% of these booby traps are covered by VC fire; that is, 94% have no one covering them, or if the VC are covering them, they don't fire. The majority of all grenade booby traps are Chicom.)

Having seen that the pin is still in the Chicom grenade, the squad leader instructs the Tiger Scout to cut the trip-wire, rendering the grenade safe. This having been done, they destroy the grenade and the platoon moves forward again and, encountering no more booby traps, they check the bunkers. Finding no VC, they blow the biggest bunkers and return to the rice paddies and a new PZ, ready for pickup and additional airmobile insertions elswhere.

Two more insertions follow, one of which results in an enemy contact. The troops are proud of their two VC bodycount and the one AK–47 captured. Towards the end of the day, at 1600 hours, they are inserted again, this time approximately 500 meters from another nipa line along another canal where intelligence has indicated there may be VC. Again they are instructed to move out and check the nipa for VC activity. By now the point man has changed three times, and PFC Jones is walking point. He is tired. Although during the dry season there is not any water in the rice paddies, Jones nevertheless is walking along the rice paddy dike where the movement is quicker, because during the dry season the paddies are broken and the footing is difficult. His buddies are in the same frame of mind and instead of walking as skirmishers they follow in a single line. They are bunched up, too, as they move forward. They really don't expect anything and everyone is as relaxed as you can get in the rice paddies—which isn't very relaxed. About 100 meters from the nipa line, Jones hears a POP. He realizes that he has set off a booby trap. But Jones freezes; he can't move; he can't speak. The booby trap goes off and Jones and two buddies just behind him are hit by fragments.

(9th Division statistics show that 40% of all casualties occur to soldiers in-country less than two months. 30% of all booby traps encountered during the month of April were inadvertently detonated. 34% of all booby traps found were on trails and rice paddy dikes. 16% of these booby traps were pressure type. 36% were buried in the ground.)

Jones has been seriously wounded. His foot is torn up; he has fragments in the gut. God! how it hurts! Dustoff is called immediately and it arrives 20 minutes later, taking Jones and his two buddies to the hospital at Dong Tam. One of his buddies was lucky. He is treated and released. Jones is sent immediately to the operating room.

(During the month of April 75% of all men wounded by booby traps were hospitalized. 46% of all the detonated booby traps resulted in multiple casualties. An average of 2.9 men were wounded per multiple incident.)

Jones, back from the operating room, has had a lot of time to think it over. The doctors hope to save his foot, but right now he is awfully glad just to be alive. He relives that terrible moment in the paddy. And now, too late, he realizes he should not have walked on the paddy dike. But he was tired, and he was not paying attention to where he put his feet. Brown, the other man hospitalized, a veteran of eight months in the paddies, knows he should not have been walking so close to the point man. However, the detonation came without any warning to Brown. So as they lay convalescing in their hospital beds, he asks Jones why he did not holler. Jones admits that he froze when he heard the pop of the booby trap. Jones feels badly because if he had hollered the other men probably would not have been wounded.

(All troops entering the Reliable Academy are given instructions 'to holler "HIT IT" and to hit the ground immediately upon hearing the pop of a booby trap. Yet, surveys show that when confronted with reality inexperienced soldiers sometimes just don't react.)

And so it goes, even though A Company had a two VC bodycount for the day, three men had been wounded, two seriously.

(In April 1969 41% of the 9th Division soldiers killed in action, and 63% of those wounded were casualties from booby traps. Booby traps are the single most important casualty producer in the 9th Division area.)

This, then, is the story of a booby trap casualty. The patterns, types, locations and enemy reactions are all predictable. To prevent such incidents the 9th Division collects the most detailed statistics, disseminates vital tactical information, teaches refresher courses, follows up with reaction tests, and constantly exhorts troops to utilize proper combat formations and distances between soldiers. Notwithstanding, in the last analysis it is the action of the individual soldier that will detect enemy booby traps and insure his and his buddies' safety.

REMEMBER!

Be alert

Utilize the expertise of the Tiger Scouts

Don't walk on trails and rice paddy dikes
   if you can help it

Probe jungle foliage carefully

Watch where you step

Change point men often when you are tired

Use artificial drag lines

Don't bunch up

And when the above don't work and you
   hear a booby trap "pop", holler
   "HIT IT" and hit the ground

You, the rice paddy soldier, are the most important asset the 9th Division has. Don't be a booby trap casualty.

The People Sniffer

As discussed earlier one of our most reliable sources of intelligence was the Airborne Personnel Detector (People Sniffer). Over 33 percent of all significant readings were confirmed by operational contacts. This high success rate was directly associated with the real time readout of information. The device was normally mounted in a UH–1 aircraft and connected by a flexible hose to an airscoop mounted to the underside of the aircraft. Air passing through the People Sniffer was sampled for the presence of carbon and ammonia, emitted by man and other sources, and compound sigma, an emission peculiar solely to man. Readings on a graduated dial could indicate the presence of personnel in an area. It should be noted that the Airborne Personnel Detector was much superior in every way to earlier models and improvisations. It automatically produced better results.

Although we had great success with the People Sniffer the turnover of personnel had been such that in the Spring of 1969 the newer commanders were not completely familiar with its capabilities and were not utilizing it to its fullest extent. Therefore, we found it worthwhile to re-emphasize the tactical importance of this valuable sensor. To insure that we refined our tactics to the utmost we did a great amount of field experimentation which gave us a much better insight into the preferred use of the People Sniffer. The utilization and effectiveness of the People Sniffer was influenced by many variables, such as the flight pattern and altitude of the aircraft, local climate, wind and precipitation, time of day, population, and the numbers and dispersion of enemy personnel.

Other Influences.

From time to time pundits have claimed that the People Sniffer was influenced by water buffaloes or other animals. However, repeated structured tests have shown that most animals do not exude a scent which is detectable on the People Sniffer. A Viet Cong practice of arraying various human excreta produced an only minor and predictable effect on the People Sniffer, and it was not widely encountered.

Drawing upon past experience and fortified with new experimental information we were able to provide our commanders with ideas to assist units in improving the results obtained by the People Sniffer. It, like any other intelligence source, required careful employment and proper interpretation to obtain maximum benefits. We provided information concerning the employment of aircraft, the employment of personnel and the pattern and time of searches. However, the most important fallout of our experimentation was in the field analysis of read outs.

The crux of the situation was the ability to differentiate between actual enemy on the ground and residual scents. We relied heavily on the air cavalry to sort out our readings. The LOH's would hover over areas of significant readings seeking visual information. The LOH's also employed CS gas extensively in attempts to flush out the enemy. However, in bunkered areas most of the time the air cavalry could not tell whether the enemy remained or whether the bunkers were indeed emptly. However, we set up a system where, by on-the-spot analysis of read outs, we could differentiate between residual scents and actual enemy, thus giving a high rate of assurance that when our units reacted to People Sniffer readings they would find some enemy. During the months of March and April over one half of all significant readings to which we reacted resulted in contacts.

It is of interest to note that our best test and analysis of this device took place in the Spring of 1969 which was pretty late in the game. Ideally it should have been done months earlier. We would have then gained maximum benefits from it.

It should be mentioned that this discussion is primarily oriented towards the technique of handling the sniffer. It is somewhat handicapped by the security classification of this study. More importantly, however, it does not do justice to the importance of having the capability to react at once to favorable reports. People Sniffer readings as intelligence were of academic interest. Readings, leading to quick contacts were of real importance.

CHAPTER VII

The Analytical Approach

In any military operation one tries to get hold of what is happening by many standard devices—command and staff visits, briefings, reports, statistics, and so forth. In Vietnam the operations tended to be so repetitive, so far flung, and at such a low tactical level that statistics became unusually important.

In 1968 in the 9th Division these statistics were largely *activity* oriented: that is, we conducted so many operations, fired so much artillery, and so forth. There was also a tendency to lump results, going from daily reports to total results over periods as long as weeks or months.

When the enemy began to evade, the relationship between *activity* and *results* changed so radically that the previous statistics comparisons lost much of their pertinence. We therefore hit on the idea of results (or output) oriented statistics. For example, we would record:

Activity level (input) as related to ———→ results (output). This tended to place activity in a useful context as it obviously was most meaningful if the outcome was a tangible result.

The next step was to measure efficiency in a gross way as results per unit of input. Results (output) divided by Activity level (input) equals efficiency (results per unit of input). This, of course, normalized the statistics and made it easier to deduce a rough standard of efficiency by comparison with an accepted norm.

The final step was to target the enemy and to measure his condition. This gave a rough measure of the total and final effect on the enemy:

Activity (U.S.) ———→ output (U.S.) ——→ efficiency (U.S.)
Activity (ARVN) ——→ output (ARVN) —→ efficiency (ARVN)   overall status
Activity (RF/PF) ——→ output (RF/PF) —→ efficiency (RF/PF)   → of enemy units
Activity (Other) ——→ output (other) ——→ efficiency (other)

All of this was a rather painful process initially as only final results really counted. The big talker and little doer took a rather dim view of this approach. However, after a while it became obvious that these statistics helped each echelon of command get a grasp on their operations, and gradually acceptance of the approach became fairly general.

Another refinement was to keep statistics on a daily, weekly and monthly basis. This enabled commanders to keep close tabs on developing trends in operations—both friendly and enemy. If a particular type of activity began to pay off, more effort could be put into it. If an activity or area began to slump, more attention could be given to it to determine why.

On the other hand, there were areas where we did not pay much attention to statistics. For example, once it became obvious that our vehicle deadline rates were so low that active operations were not affected, we only looked at these monthly. However, we looked at bulldozer and generator rates (which were historically poor) weekly.

As an aside, some observers of the Vietnamese war have been critical of the use of statistics on various grounds. What they have overlooked is that the conditions of combat in Vietnam were such that it was difficult, if not impossible, for higher commanders to get down and personally observe the details of combat and straighten things out as was done in World War II, for example. Also, progress was rarely seen in climactic victories, but rather in the cumulative effect of hundreds of thousands of small scale engagements. Statistics, if properly used, in conjunction with more traditional techniques, helped one to get hold of and evaluate these small combat events.

We also tried to keep out of the area of diminishing returns. For example, we used highly simplified training approaches. The art was to determine a small number of skills that could be taught in a short period of time and obtain reasonable results. This tended to keep training on the productive area of the learning curve and minimize gold-plating. It was particularly suited to the rapid turnover generated by a twelve month tour plus normal attrition.

Ideally, and this was hard to do, the statistics should relate directly to the overall mission, operational concept, the tactics and technique of the unit concerned. Then as one traced through the statistics, one measured results and corrected shortfalls within the framework of the command system and the operational concept.

In summary, a good general rule was to concentrate on measuring activities that culminated in meaningful results, to measure them periodically, and to stay in high efficiency areas.

All of these added up to what might be termed the analytical approach—an insistence on results and reasonable efficiency.

Performance Orientation

The tremendous surge in results experienced by the 9th Division in early 1969 aroused considerable interest and, it might be added, some criticism in Vietnam. It was difficult to explain to someone that this surge was the cumulative result of many improvements and innovations implemented over a period of months. It was also due to a complete concentration on getting results.

This insistence on results was sometimes hard on a brigade or battalion commander. If he was in an area where the enemy was tough and wily, it was difficult to avoid "skating over the top of the enemy." To break through this defensive skill on the part of the enemy—it was almost like a layer of armor plate—took tremendous ingenuity and sheer will power. Some people interpreted this determination to close with the enemy as an over-emphasis on "body count." It was nothing of the sort—it was an insistence on bringing the enemy to battle and breaking his units up. Occasionally when a battalion was in a real "dry hole," the consequent lack of results had to be accepted as a fact of life and hopefully the battalion could be shifted to a more profitable area later on.

The proper approach was to work for good performance. If a unit was dry-holing, one could only ask it to do better. We used the Vince Lombardi technique more or less—hard tackling, hard blocking and good fundamentals would win. Of course, there was no doubt that the end result was very hard on the Communists—that was our job. However, one had to insist on fair play in combat operations and on restraint and care to avoid civilian casualties and property damage. The record speaks for itself. Any really professional outfit tends to steer clear of the practices that one reads about in the more sensational accounts. If one is really concentrating on the enemy, combat, while inherently dangerous, tends to end up as a rather clean cut affair.

Statistical Review

As we began to get our operations under control, we initiated statistical reviews. The guts of our review was a series of "operations" charts. Although they varied, in general they listed the normal categories of operations: ambush, reconnaissance in force, Checkerboard, Bushmaster, pile-on, patrol, raid, cordon and search, installation defense, and so forth. They also showed the level of operation (squad, platoon, company and battalion), the level of effort—that is, how many units, the number of contacts, and the results (Hoi Chanhs, enemy captured, killed, and so forth.)

These very busy charts were difficult for the newcomer to grasp. After using them for a while, however, the division, brigade, and battalion commanders could determine quickly and objectively which operations were getting results and which operations were not. For example, if night operations were not working, one could assume that technique was poor and do some retraining. One could also determine efficiency in a rough way as the charts also indicated what level of operation was most efficient. For example, our subjective judgment was that platoon level operations would be more efficient than company level. However, for much of this time, platoons operating under company control in daytime gave results over ten times as good contact-wise as separate platoon operations. When the enemy was completely cut up, the platoon operations began to pay off.

One could also use these charts to guide night versus daytime effort. If the enemy was having difficulty in the daytime, he would sometimes shift to night movement. By readjusting effort, one could drive him back into the daytime where operations were about twice as efficient manpower and effort-wise.

Most importantly, the charts stimulated skill in the various standard operations. It became obvious to the battalion commanders that they needed units that were skillful in a spectrum of operations Over-concentration on one type might produce results for a short time but would eventually prove unproductive. A variety of operations gave the Communists problems as they found it very difficult to decide how to react or even protect themselves.

Moreover, the enemy deteriorated by phases under heavy pressure. When the pressure was put on initially, he reacted very well until attrition ate into his junior leaders; then his units began to react in an unprofessional way; this was followed by a detectable collapse when the enemy lost unit integrity and reacted in a disjointed manner like a flock of chickens followed by mass fragmentation to squad level or lower, with the main effort devoted to hiding and staying alive. Mopping up these fragments was a long tiresome process requiring very skillful operations and a vigorous pacification effort.

Weekly Operational Review and Analysis

Once we had our military operations under control we began to edge into the integration of military operations and pacification. We were anxious to pull all of the relevant data and key people involved in our efforts into a systematic, recurring process of analysis and consultation to insure a cross-fertilization of tactical and pacification concepts and ideas, not only among U.S. unit commanders (brigade and battalion) but also between ourselves and the U.S. advisory and South Vietnamese Army officials representing the four provinces and the South Vietnamese Army units. To do this we established a weekly meeting attended by brigade commanders and province senior advisors which we called our "Weekly Operational Review and Analysis." This simple procedure provided the statistical base line and the coordination mechanism that were to prove central to the division operations from October 1968 onward.

About the time we were getting a handle on our personnel strengths, aircraft maintenance, intelligence inputs and new tactical concepts, two new campaigns were initiated from on high—the Military Assistance Command, Vietnam—South Vietnamese Armed Forces Accelerated Pacification Campaign and the IV Corps Dry Weather Campaign. We mentioned earlier that the initiation of the Dry Weather Campaign gave us much needed additional air assets. Additionally, the clear-cut objectives of the Accelerated Pacification Campaign proved to be a vehicle for much closer ties with the Vietnamese civil authorities and the Vietnamese military, resulting in more integrated operational plans. We combined combat operations and Government of Vietnam pacification efforts from the very beginning of our Weekly Operational Review and Analysis. Let us face it, the security of an area is the key to pacification for without it no lasting overall progress can be made.

Therefore, the combat operations of the South Vietnamese Army and Regional and Popular Forces were almost as important to us as our own U.S. operations. We realized early that we could not accurately estimate the strength of the enemy unless we took into consideration the combined effectiveness of all Allied efforts in our tactical area of operations. Our accomplishments were only important in the totality of events. For example, it made little difference whether the Viet Cong rallied to a South Vietnamese Army unit or to a U.S. unit—the important thing was to get as many of the enemy to defect as possible thus reducing the capabilities of the enemy and enhancing the strength and prestige of the South Vietnamese Government.

The requirement to integrate the totality of operations in our area resulted in the briefing, discussion and analysis of 18 different statistical operational summaries during each of our weekly sessions. By this means we and the province representatives were able to keep our fingers on the pulse of those operations that were paying off best in a particular area. We also were able to compare the relative performance of each brigade within the division, of U.S. units versus South Vietnamese Army units, and of Regional Force and Popular Force units vis-a-vis both U.S. and South Vietnamese Army outfits. Most importantly, our nonproductive efforts stuck out and we could take coordinated action to improve or de-emphasize them.

Through evolutionary changes we streamlined our data collection, refined our charts, and systematized the presentation to provide an unusual analytical process highlighting the effectiveness and the efficiency of both our combat operations and pacification efforts.

Combat Operations.

A statistical operational summary, an example of which is shown on the following page, was prepared for the U.S., South Vietnamese Army and Regional and Popular Forces contingents operating in each of the four provinces of our tactical area of operational responsibility.

By way of explanation, the data on the U.S. forces was maintained by the G–3 and G–5 and was derived from daily situation reports and intelligence summaries. Data on the South Vietnamese Army forces was obtained from the senior U.S. advisers to the 7th South Vietnamese Army and 25th South Vietnamese Army Divisions and data on the Regional Force and Popular Force forces and provincial pacification activities was obtained from the Military Assistance Command, Vietnam Advisory Teams. For comparative purposes all operational efforts were reduced to equivalent company days. The company days available were the maximum number of company days which could have been utilized by a unit operating in both the nighttime and daytime phases of a 24 hour period. Thus each 24 hour period contained two potential company days for a company sized unit. As an example a brigade with three battalions of four companies each would have 168 company days available per week.

As mentioned earlier, we expected the U.S. companies to operate three days out of four; whereas for the South Vietnamese Army and the Regional Force and Popular Force we felt it would be more reasonable if they operated every other day (one out of two). We defined "Operational Effectiveness" (for want of a better term) as the ratio of company days used to company days available; thus, the goal for Vietnamese units was an operational effectiveness of 0.50. When we initiated our statistics no Vietnamese unit in any province approached this. After several months most Vietnamese units were operational in the field 50 percent of the time. This was a doubling of the number of the units in the field and the effect on

TABLE 27—OPERATIONAL SUMMARY GO CONG PROVINCE REGIONAL FORCE AND POPULAR FORCE

Day / Night

Date	Company Days		Type of Operation			Enemy Eliminated			Weapons	
	Available	Used	Airmobile	Riverine	Foot Mobile	KIA	PW	HC	S/A	C/S
24	100	50	4 / 0	4 / 0	30 / 12	3 / 3	0 / 0	2 / 0	5	1
25	100	60	0 / 0	4 / 2	40 / 14	8 / 4	2 / 0	1 / 0	3	0
26	100	45	6 / 0	4 / 2	30 / 3	1 / 0	0 / 0	0 / 0	0	0
27	100	55	0 / 0	0 / 0	50 / 5	2 / 0	1 / 0	0 / 0	0	0
28	100	50	2 / 0	0 / 0	40 / 8	2 / 1	0 / 0	0 / 0	0	0
29	100	40	0 / 0	4 / 0	28 / 8	1 / 0	0 / 0	2 / 0	1	0
30	100	50	0 / 0	4 / 2	30 / 14	4 / 2	0 / 1	2 / 0	3	1
TOTALS	700	350	12 / 0	20 / 6	248 / 64	21 / 10	3 / 1	7 / 0	12	2
INDICES [a]	.80	.20	.50 / —	.15 / .33	.09 / .14					

Overall Operational Effectiveness Index: .50   Overall Operational Efficiency Index: .12

[a] The indices, compiled from data from several sources, summarize the enemy eliminated by type of operation, enabling an assessment of the effectiveness of the various operations.

the Viet Cong was readily apparent by the jump in enemy eliminated.

Our initial thrust, then, was to get both the U.S. units and the South Vietnamese Army units to operate more often. Once this occurred we set out to increase the operational efficiency of the units in the field. No unit likes to go for "walks in the sun"—patrolling with no results is very hard on the troop's morale. When gross eliminations or the contact success ratio of a unit was low for an extended period of time we concluded that there most likely was something basically wrong with the unit's operations. We then attempted to get a fix on the problem.

There are several methods of measuring combat outputs—gross eliminations, the elimination or exchange ratio, and the contact success ratio. However, to give us an indication of how efficient various modes of operations were (that is airmobile, riverine, or foot) as well as the total efficiency of the contingents within a province, we computed what we called our "Operational Efficiency." Quite simply it was the total number of enemy eliminated (Killed in Action, Prisoners of War, Hoi Chanhs) per company day in the field. By relating the numbers of enemy eliminated to a day's operation, we were able to normalize our statistics. It is astonishing to note that if every company in a U.S. division eliminated only one enemy each company day of operations (considering 10 battalions of four companies operating 75 percent of the time day and night), the gross eliminations per month would be 1,800. You can see that modest results under the Constant Pressure Concept added up in the aggregate. As we stated previously, the supermarket approach of a small unit profit with a large turnover could pay off handsomely.

We found for example, that as soon as we broke down into small units and started operating extensively at night that our operational efficiencies increased dramatically. The same experience translated to the South Vietnamese Army units later on. The improvement in results of the Vietnamese units in our tactical area of responsibility was quite marked. First, they generally doubled the number of company days in the field. On top of that they also improved their operational efficiency almost two fold. As a result, for many units the number of enemy eliminated per month almost quadrupled over the six month period between October 1968 and March 1969. One of the factors that gave the Vietnamese units quite a boost was the fact that we were able to help them with marksmanship training. After we had trained a sufficient number of our own snipers we established marksmanship classes attended not only by the 7th

South Vietnamese Army Division but by the Vietnamese ranger and airborne troops from other areas of the country. When the South Vietnamese snipers returned to their units and the units worked into a night operational mode the same confidence that spread through U.S. units took hold for the South Vietnamese Army and they began to get results. Overall the greatest improvements occurred in the provincial Regional Force and Popular Force units. About the time we were prodding them to get into the field more often they also received much better equipment (M–16's primarily) and they really took off.

In the example (*Table 27*) it can be seen that the Regional and Popular Forces in Go Cong Province were in the field 50 percent of the time. Almost every unit operated during the day—an Operational Effectiveness Index of .80. On the other hand only 1 out of 5 of the units operated at night—an Operational Effectiveness Index of .20. The overall Operational Efficiency Index was .12; thus, for every eight company days of operations, the Regional and Popular Forces eliminated one enemy. Their most efficient type of operation was daytime airmobile. Unfortunately the Regional and Popular Forces rarely received air assets for any operations due to shortages of lift. Both the airmobile and riverine operations were more efficient than foot operations. Also, whenever the Regional and Popular Forces operated at night they were more efficient than they were in the daytime. The problem then in this hypothetical case would be to attempt to get the Regional and Popular Forces out more at night and to raise the efficiency of the foot mobile reconnaissances-in-force. Actually, small improvements in operational efficiency could result in a large increase in gross eliminations.

Whenever the results obtained on one type of operation dropped off while another type of operation was going great guns, the brigade commanders would go about reinforcing their current successes while attempting to analyze the reasons why other efforts were drying up. Thus on a weekly basis we were able to see the results of actual changes in Viet Cong tactics. When one of our tactics began to dry up we did not always understand what was going on at first; but after several operational reviews, the trends were apparent and we generally had determined the reasons. We, in turn, revised our method of operating or cooked up new solutions in order to keep damaging the enemy. In a nutshell the statistic "company days used" was the measure of our constant pressure whereas "the enemy eliminated per unit in the field" grossed out the efficiency of our intelligence efforts, tactical innovations, individual training and leadership.[1] Our Weekly Operational Review and Analysis tended to keep our combat operations in the ball park.

Pacification Efforts

When the Accelerated Pacification Campaign was initiated, with its clear-cut objectives, we integrated our combat operations with our pacification efforts to insure the optimum support of the pacification program. Although there were many aspects of the Accelerated Pacification Campaign, the most fundamental one was to choose *key* hamlets and villages that were in a contested status with the Viet Cong, and through security and civic efforts to raise these hamlets to more secure Government of Vietnam status. The selection of key hamlets was quite properly left to the Government of Vietnam authorities and they were chosen for their economic, social and political importance to the province. In heavily contested areas, military considerations were also important. Generally speaking, the pacification of these key hamlets themselves was primarily a Government of Vietnam effort. However, there were a great number of things that the U.S. forces could do to facilitate this pacification.

Therefore in our Weekly Operational Review and Analysis we prepared a large scale map for each of the four provinces and color coded the key hamlets in accordance with their pacification classification. Around each key hamlet we drew circles with a radius of 5 kilometers (the maximum range of the enemy 82 mm mortars was 3.0 kilometers). It was our goal to eliminate the enemy in the vicinity of the key hamlets within this radius, thus improving the security of these hamlets and setting the stage for pacification. The envelope of all of these circles was the area in which we controlled all operations—combat as well as pacification. Each week, then, we plotted all the preceding weeks' activities on this map, including combat operations, civic action programs and psychological warfare operations. Thus, our pacification analysis included the total spectrum of division operational activities (A more detailed discussion of pacification activities is in Chapter VIII).

The basic document for the pacification program was the Hamlet Evaluation Survey Report. This report was prepared monthly by a Subsector Evaluator on the U.S. District Team. It included eighteen factors, nine of which pertained to security and

---

[1] The usage of the terms "effectiveness" and "efficiency" was obviously rather arbitrary and was retained only for convenience. As we improved our analytical technique, and gained more insight, we could have devised more precise terminology, but did not lest it confuse the many persons involved.

nine of which pertained to what we may generically call Civic Action aspects (Administrative and Political Activities; Health, Education and Welfare; and Economic Development). Each of these eighteen factors was rated between E and A in ascending order of the degree of Government of Vietnam control and an overall rating computed. To be quite frank, we had no faith in the Hamlet Evaluation Survey initially. It appeared to us that it could be a pencil exercise with little validity. Therefore, we undertook a detailed Hamlet Evaluation Survey for all the hamlets in one district in Dinh Tuong Province. We told our G–2 to be hard-nosed in his evaluations. At the conclusion of our survey we compared it with the Military Assistance Command, Vietnam, Advisory Team Survey. We were literally amazed to find that there was less than a 10 percent difference in evaluations. This gave us new and substantial confidence in the Hamlet Evaluation Survey. Additionally, by working closely with the evaluation worksheets we received a more complete understanding of the pacification efforts and we were in a better position to integrate our efforts in support of the Accelerated Pacification Campaign.

Every week, then, we reviewed our total operations in conjunction with the envelope of the key hamlets of the Accelerated Pacification Campaign. As a result we directed our efforts to areas where support seemed to be lacking and we measured the effectiveness of the joint U.S.-Government of Vietnam efforts. As a rule of thumb we seldom conducted combat operations within a kilometer of a key hamlet, thereby making certain that we did not interfere with Government of Vietnam pacification efforts.

Every month when the new Hamlet Evaluation Survey classifications hit the street we reviewed the progress of the pacification campaign. In those areas where the hamlets had returned to government control we slacked off on our operations and conversely in the areas which proved hard nuts to crack we increased our tempo, generally stepping up either our combat operations or civic action programs.

Thus by combining our combat operations with our pacification efforts through the Weekly Operational Review and Analysis we were able on a continuing basis to achieve a more surgical approach to tactical operations in the delta and to contribute substantially to the ultimate goal of pacification.

More often than not, units in Vietnam emphasized pacification by stressing civic action efforts. In our opinion, this was a mistake as long as the enemy retained even a modest military capability. In the 9th Division, we always stressed the military effort. While our civic action work compared favorably with that of other units, we always felt that it was a strong military effort *and* civic action *integrated* with the *Government of Vietnam pacification program* that achieved results. Later on in 1969 and 1970, while working on the broader canvas of the II Field Force Vietnam area of operations, this concept was further tested and proved sound. Most areas which achieved spectacular progress did so under cover of a strong military effort. Conversely, if an area was having difficulties pacification-wise, one invariably found a stuttering or ineffective military effort.

Pitfalls

The use of operations analysis in Vietnam was inherently a difficult task. For example, one should be able to describe a process (that is construct a model) and one should be able to know what is happening (that is get reliable data). Both of these tasks were most difficult, Some examples of difficult problems are given below.

One of our real failures was to up our prisoner intake substantially. Realizing that prisoners were one of the best sources of intelligence, we tried several elaborate programs to increase the number of prisoners. Our results were useful but hardly earth-shaking:

	Enemy Losses*	Prisoners of War/ Hoi Chanhs	Percent of Losses— Prisoners/ Hoi Chanhs
Oct 67—Mar 68	4,541	301	6.6
Oct 68—Mar 69	10,273	848	8.2
Percentile Improvement	126%	182%	24%

* Does not include Viet Cong Infrastructure

One can see that we did better in the later period and the intelligence obtained was probably worth the effort, but the improvement was modest. We theorized that the enemy's indoctrination program, plus the language and cultural barrier, was too great for a real breakthrough. Although we did well with prisoners of war the average South Vietnamese Army division did much better. The theoretical potential can be seen in the Hoi Chanh rates. In months when we took 25 to 75 ralliers, the provinces in which we operated and furnished the basic pressure aggregated overall from 500 to 1,500 ralliers. (*See Chart 15*) Obviously, ralliers and presumably Prisoners of War preferred to turn in to Vietnamese units rather than American, and equally obviously, we were unable to get hold of the critical element in this problem area.

As a sub-program of our prisoner program, we worked hard on using small loudspeakers on the battlefield. This effort, while useful in other ways, did not generate a larger percentage of prisoners.

Viet Cong infrastructure was another difficult area. While we could and did help the Government of Vietnam with their Phoenix effort, it was very difficult to do what was essentially police and detective work with American soldiers. Our results were comparable to other U.S. and South Vietnamese Army divisions but in gross numbers our returns were very modest. In sum, we were not able to break into another culture and into the Communist organization. We sensed that a quantum increase in qualified interpreters would have helped but could not prove it. Our Tiger Scouts were useful in softening these barriers but they were not decisive.

A general tendency which we could never overcome was the ability of the enemy to protect himself against damaging tactics after some months. When we first optimized our radar, it was most useful. After six months it was only another source of information. The Jitterbug and seal-and-pile-on technique dealt the enemy fits for about six months. Then it became only one way, albeit a vital one, of putting pressure on large areas. Small unit daylight patrolling had its heyday and so on. Even the Constant Pressure Concept began to lose its edge. It was quite apparent at that time that the war was slowing down. As the enemy began to disintegrate, it became more difficult to inflict crippling defeats on his remnants. Undoubtedly the people in Vietnam have developed an answer to this change, but it may be quite different from the techniques we used previously. We concluded that a smart enemy could eventually protect himself to a certain extent against damaging tactics.

The biggest pitfall to avoid was the conclusion that one could predict with confidence by any means—judgemental or analytical—where the real payoffs were and how to manage the overall effort. If one reads this study, one might conclude that we were quite successful in these regards. However, in all humility, these successes were achieved by hard work and trial and error.

Our two most combat effective and cost effective innovations were the sniper program and night air cavalry operations. However, these were proven effective in the doing, and we had no way of determining in advance that they would be so. Most of the advantages gained through analysis were due to laying out the operation and measuring efficiency. These impressions—and they were often impressions rather than hard conclusions—were then used to guide operational emphasis and corrective training.

However, if one could ever devise a really first class analytical approach to complex matters which worked, then a skillful commander could use it to achieve spectacular improvements in efficiency and results.

We are not suggesting that operations analysis is impossible in Vietnam; but only suggesting that the murkiness of the situation and the rapid changes placed a high premium on the element of military experience and know-how in guiding the application of the analytical process. Some areas clearly fell outside the scope of the analytical art at that time.

Summary

Our insistence on results and reasonable operational efficiency—the analytical approach—was not limited to operations and tactics. It was a total integrated approach, including all activities of the division—administrative, logistical, tactical and pacification. To improve these large and complex operations we had to concentrate on essentials so that our efforts were not too diffused. We zeroed in on weak points with considerable intensity and we insisted on rapid results. We tried to keep on the steep portion of the learning curve—where reasonable efforts provided major improvements. Eventually, our whole analytical system was formalized. We had weekly operational review and analysis meetings. We also had weekly administrative reviews, discussing personnel and logistical matters such as enlisted promotions and deadline rates. Each week we had an operational planning conference to bring intelligence information into perspective. We had our morning and evening briefings and relied heavily on our daily three cycle intelligence review. Yet we tried not to focus too hard on any one aspect because obviously overconcentration could lead to disjointed operations. Important factors were emphasized but coordinated. In summary, it was a total integrated approach.

In the preceding discussion, we have emphasized the central effort of conducting effective and efficient military operations. Obviously, there were many other areas which were kept under close scrutiny. To do justice to all of the areas which were examined and analyzed would be an endless task. Obviously, the more areas that could be kept on the plus side, the more rapid and substantial was overall progress.

CHAPTER VIII

Pacification

As mentioned previously, we attempted to integrate combat operations and pacification efforts in all of our planning. To do this the G–2, G–3 and G–5 worked as a well-oiled team, sharing the same space in the tactical operations center and coordinating their operations. To insure the pragmatic integration of intelligence, operations and civic action we hand picked two outstanding combat leaders to be G–5's—Lieutenant Colonel Tom Leggett and Major Bernard O. Loeffke. Our coordination paid off—there is no doubt that by keeping great pressure on the enemy we enhanced the security of the countryside thereby facilitating the pacification mission.

Our pacification efforts were well thought out and integrated as much as possible with combat operations. In addition, our pacification program had as its foundation five major civic action themes: (1) psychological operations or efforts to win the hearts and minds of the dissident people so that they would rally to the side of the Government of Vietnam, (2) assistance to the victims of the war, (3) assistance in health matters, (4) educational assistance, and (5) the repair and construction of facilities. In each of these approaches we attempted to innovate and improve our techniques in order to bring imaginative and worthwhile programs to the people of Vietnam.

It is not our intention to go into pacification in any detail. It is a whole subject in itself. Pacification became most important about July 1968 and although the efforts of the 9th Division in the subsequent years were innovative and rather broad gauge, they were not as concentrated nor as important as later efforts. Therefore, we will list only a few of our efforts in each of the aforementioned areas to provide an insight into pacification and to indicate how these efforts often tied directly into combat operations.

Psychological Operations

Psychological operations pervaded the total quiltwork of the war. They were necessary to break down the fabric of resistance of the active enemy forces as well as to encourage the villagers and others to return to the Government fold.

We urged the enemy to surrender or to rally to the side of the Government of Vietnam rather than face eventual death. We took every opportunity available through leaflets, loud speakers, and face to face contacts to induce him to give up his hopeless cause, and to rally to a more democratic and hopeful way of life.

We also tried to reach the hearts and minds of the people who had been subjected to much Communist propaganda. To do this we employed every available means of psychological warfare available to us. Psychological warfare, then, had two different aspects—destruction of the enemy's will to fight and the winning of the confidence of the civilian populace.

Prior to our arrival in Vietnam we set about procuring 100 hand-held loud speakers (AN–PIQ 5A) in hopes that the tactical situation would permit our talking major Viet Cong units into surrendering. While still in the States we even had cards made in English and Vietnamese so that our Tiger Scouts could coax the enemy out of his positions. The emphasis of the 9th Division

BREAKING THE LANGUAGE BARRIER

throughout the war had been primarily on obtaining Chieu Hois and Prisoners of War and secondarily on killing the enemy. We wanted the total enemy eliminated to be as high as possible, hopefully by taking as many prisoners as we could. The reasons for this, of course, are readily apparent. In combat operations Prisoners of War and Chieu Hois give a great amount of military intelligence. Chieu Hois can also be used to talk others into surrendering. One of the most valuable assets of the 9th Division in this connection were our Tiger Scouts. We assigned at least one Tiger Scout to each infantry platoon and later each squad. Because they were familiar with Viet Cong thinking and operations they often anticipated his moves, thereby giving us tactical advantages. They also afforded an important psychological and actual link to the civilian population. Most Tiger Scouts were intensely loyal to their American unit—there is nothing like a convert. Their conversion to the Government of Vietnam side was an obvious example to their countrymen.

We have previously described how during our "seal operations" we would fly aerial loud speaker missions to talk the enemy into surrendering. Once the seal was closed the enemy was heavily bombarded with artillery and air strikes. Subsequently, we would have a hiatus for the purpose of talking the enemy into surrendering. However, our aspirations were much greater than our results. For example, one day in Long An along the Vam Co Tay we succeeded in talking a Viet Cong soldier into surrendering during the middle of battle. He came out with his hands up and progressed no further than 30 meters from his bunker when he was shot in the back by one of his comrades. This so infuriated our troops that they laid down a withering suppressive fire and two of our soldiers rescued the hapless Viet Cong. He was evacuated and we managed to save his life. The thought is, that as long as there were a few hard core Communists in a unit it was difficult for any of the Viet Cong or North Vietnamese to rally.

Our psychological operations campaign against enemy units was relentless. After every major battle we dropped leaflets depicting their casualties by showing gravestones whose headings included the enemy unit's losses from previous battles. We sent messages over local radio stations to the effect that the Viet Cong should Chieu Hoi or they would be killed. We flew airborne loud speaker missions whose purpose was to spread dissension and unrest in the enemy ranks as they spent lonely, uncomfortable periods deep in the hot, humid and mosquito infested base camp areas. They hated these loud speaker missions so much that rather than listen to any more propaganda they would stand up and fire their weapons at the loudspeaker aircraft thus exposing themselves and their positions. We dropped millions of leaflets over Viet Cong positions inviting the enemy to rally to the Government of Vietnam. (One of our staff officers briefed one night that if all the leaflets dropped in the past three years in our tactical area of operational interest remained on the ground we would all be up to our "waists" in leaflets instead of water.) Many thought leaflets had no effect. That was not our experience. On one occasion we promised the enemy a hot meal and a hot bath if he would rally. One night a Chieu Hoi raised the dickens because he had not yet had his hot bath as promised by the leaflets.

Yet, no matter how hard we tried we did not appreciably increase the number of enemy rallying to our troops. The language barrier was too much. However, within our tactical area of operational interest as the pressure got hotter the number of ralliers (Chieu Hoi) to Government of Vietnam authorities increased greatly. (*Chart 15*) Since our interest lay in the totality of operations our own lack of results didn't matter too much.

Propaganda was not a one-way street. The Viet Cong had their campaigns too. By analyzing their themes we learned the "big impact ideas" and reversed the procedure with the Viet Cong as the targets. Their efforts were not as sophisticated as many would have you think, as evidenced by the leaflet partially reproduced below.

VC Propaganda Leaflet
(partial)
American officers and men in the US armed forces in SVN:
In Viet Nam lunar new year is old traditional custoon and habit.

The Vietnamese people desire for a peaceful and external for an enjoyment, in new year days in the happy atmosphere of their family reunion and for the holding of a mom oriental ceremony to commenorate their ancestors, is stronger than that of anybody else it is the same as the american people enjoy their merry xmas and happy solar new year in their sweet home beside their loved ones. The US warmongers and their Thieu Ky Huong puppt chique however don't want peace they not only sabotaged the SVNLF orde concoriving the suspenriou of all military attack derring a recent xmas but also rejected openly to implement the frouts solar new year truce order in the war future they will seek all means avuitable to sabotage the coming lunar new year truce by pushing you out on operation causing suffering mourning and hare hip to our people.

American serira men!

Winning the confidence of the civilian populace took integrated efforts in many areas. We broadcast literally thousands of ground loudspeaker hours (*Chart 16*) in support of pacification. However,

CHART 15—Number of Chieu Hois in 9th Division Tactical Area

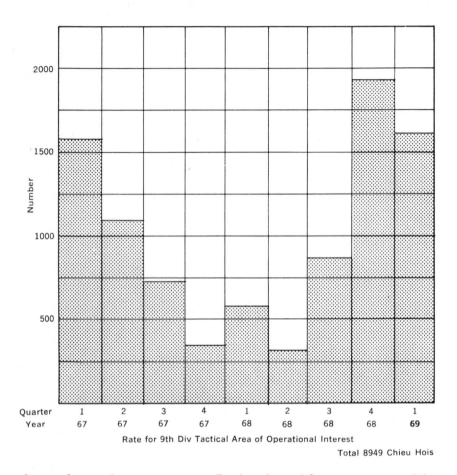

Rate for 9th Div Tactical Area of Operational Interest

Total 8949 Chieu Hois

face to face actions were more effective than airborne measures. We distributed almost two million hand-delivered leaflets through our Medical Civic Action Programs. We established games to play with the children of villages. We raffled off chickens and ducks. We gave away thousands of children's T-shirts in the colors of the Government of Vietnam. We produced cards to be passed out telling why the Americans were there. We taught our soldiers the customs of the Vietnamese so that they would not offend the local population. We went to extraordinary means to assure the Vietnamese that we were there solely to support their Government and to make a better way of life for them. The visits by U.S. medical teams with their friendly attitudes and accompanying entertainment were

CHART 16—GROUND LOUDSPEAKER HOURS

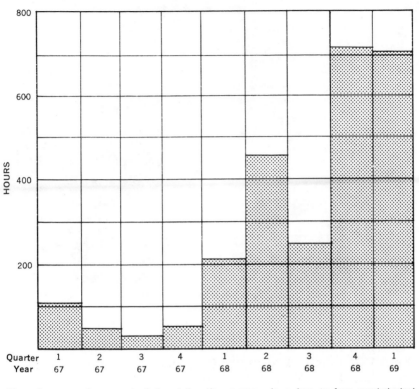

These hours are in support of the civil action program in a face to face psychological operations effort. They do not include aerial loudspeaker time.

Total time 2580 hours

events to be anticipated and remembered by many. Because of the language difficulties our attempts to win the hearts and minds of the Vietnamese were not as polished nor as fruitful as we would have liked. But in trying to reach their hearts we showed that our hearts were in the right place.

Assistance to the Victims of the War

The individual American soldier has always helped to alleviate the suffering and anguish caused by wars, and Vietnam was no exception. The 9th Division soldier was quick to volunteer with both labor and monetary contributions. We tried as much as possible to initiate cooperative programs whose objectives were to provide

CHRISTMAS WITH THE ORPHANS

assets to the Vietnamese so that they could help themselves. But the most important of all contributions was the individual soldier's willingness to assist in any manner practicable to lessen the Vietnamese citizen's plight. Orphanages, churches, leper colonies and the physically handicapped all received his warm support.

The giving of one's own time and effort is often more meaningful than gifts of money and material. As our Civic Action Programs became more organized the soldier man-days spent increased greatly so that we had on the average of 150 men daily working on construction activities, Medical Civic Action Programs and staff work in support of pacification. (*Chart 17*)

Many troops because of the pressure of combat could not personally participate in Civic Action Programs, so they dug into their pockets to help where they could. (*Chart 18*) Charlie Battery, 3d Battalion, 34th Artillery undertook to support the Ben Luc Leprosarium. Once a month on payday a collection was taken. The soldiers had a one dollar limit but participation was always 100 percent. They felt it was their leper colony and they took a personal interest in attempting to provide the patients hope for the future.

CHART 17—U.S. Labor Used on Civic Action Projects

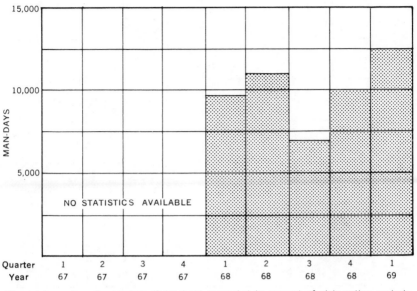

The total number of man days (8 hr days) expended in support of civic action projects, including the time expended on construction activities, MEDCAPS and staff work in support of the civic action program.

Total assistance 48,256 man days

We distributed almost two million pounds of food. As an example, the emergency relief and refugee support mission to the My Tho refugee camp stands out. We worked with the Province Minister of Social Welfare, and nearly 70,000 pounds of division furnished foodstuffs were equitably distributed to 6,000 homeless civilians and refugee families. Additionally, 3,000 gallons of potable water were delivered daily to three refugee camps, hospitals, and orphanages.

Over 16,000 pounds of clothing and a million and one-half pounds of miscellaneous supplies were also distributed by the 9th Division. The soldiers supported 89 orphanages giving them gifts of clothing, food, money, construction materials, educational and medical supplies, and recreational items. (Chart 19) Around Christmas time a Division medic, after treating one small boy for multiple cuts, presented him with a Christmas toy. The youth left, quite happy with his new toy. However, he returned a few moments later, tugged at his benefactor's trousers leg until he got his attention, then spoke to him through the interpreter, telling him, "To give you pleasure gives me pleasure." This about summarizes the

CHART 18—Monetary Gifts

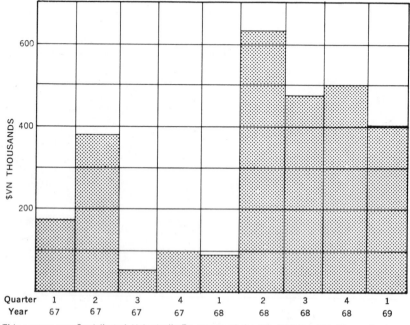

This money was **Contributed Voluntarily By** troops of the 9th Division and other voluntary organizations for distribution to churches, orphanages, and hospitals.

Total assistance 2,841,735$VN

feelings involved, the mutual satisfactions, and the increased understandings between soldiers and the civilian populace.

Every unit in Vietnam could quote chapter and verse concerning the generosity of the American fighting man. The wonder is why this steady flow of actions, so open and so discussed, has gone so unnoticed by the casual observer of the war.

Assistance in Health Matters

The medical efforts of the division in the delta just had to improve the overall health of the region appreciably.

We started at the grass roots. The 9th Medical Battalion initiated a program to train Vietnamese civilian and military personnel in basic medical skills. This increased the indigenous medical capacity as well as the villagers' confidence in the Vietnamese personnel working in local dispensaries. But more important it made the populace less dependent on U.S. aid.

Our most important thrust was the ubiquitous Medical Civic Action Program. Every day, teams comprised of medical and in-

PERSONAL PACIFICATION

fantry personnel, travelled throughout the friendly areas of the provinces to provide medical treatment to Vietnamese civilians. Over 700,000 patients were treated in a two year period. (*Chart 20*)

Dental programs were popular and well received. The need for dental care was great in the more remote areas where many of the people had never seen a dentist. Immediate treatment was given those who required it—generally extractions. However, instructions

CHART 19—ORPHANAGES ASSISTED

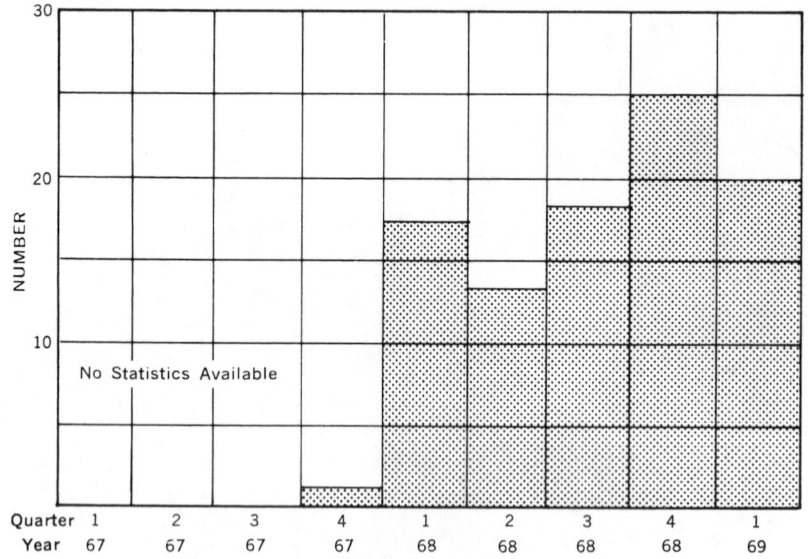

NUMBER

No Statistics Available

Quarter	1	2	3	4	1	2	3	4	1
Year	67	67	67	67	68	68	68	68	69

Assistance included distribution of clothing, food, money, construction materials, education and medical supplies and recreation items.

Total assistance 89 orphanages

in oral hygiene, including leaflets on dental care along with toothpaste and toothbrushes were distributed.

Since our medical program was so well received we reoriented it to integrate civic action with psychological operations and intelligence activities. The Integrated Civic Action Programs operated in contested and insecure areas as differentiated from Medical Civic Action Programs which operated only in secure areas. In addition to the humanitarian aspects, an objective of the Integrated Civic Action Program was to glean such intelligence as: information on the Viet Cong infrastructure; the determination of the status of security and pacification; the establishment of liaison with local leaders and officials in contested areas; and the improvement of our image. Most of the Integrated Civic Action Programs were joint operations with Regional and Popular forces and were conducted in complete coordination with Vietnamese officials, particularly the hamlet and village chiefs and other local leaders. The Integrated Civic Action Programs paid off with impressive results; some of our most meaningful intelligence was gained in this way.

With the Viet Cong on the run, our Integrated Civic Action Program teams began staying overnight, affording us the opportu-

PROVIDING AID TO THE POPULATION

nity to visit with the local farmers who were largely absent from their homes during daylight hours. It also gave the villagers a feeling of more security and enabled us to double our intelligence inputs. All of these visits were tremendously helpful to the local population because of the medical aspects and the other civic actions features, including games, lotteries, and music. The soldier guitar players and their country music were a big hit with the

CHART 20—Medcap Patients Treated

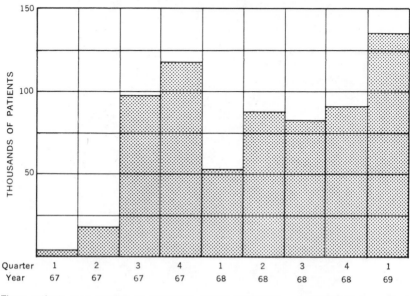

| Quarter | 1 | 2 | 3 | 4 | 1 | 2 | 3 | 4 | 1 |
| Year | 67 | 67 | 67 | 67 | 68 | 68 | 68 | 68 | 69 |

These patients were treated on MEDCAPS, ICAPS, NITECAPS and DENTCAPS by medical personnel of the 9th Division.

Total assistance 708,588 patients

Vietnamese. It was apparent that the villagers, like our young teenagers in the States, didn't have to understand the words to enjoy the music.

In summary, the medical program with all its many offshoots provided more goodwill than any other single civic action program. It reached more people in more places more frequently and with more tangible results than anything else we did.

Educational Assistance

The importance of education in the Orient cannot be over-estimated. Each head of a family worked to insure that his children obtained the best education possible. Therefore, the efforts put forth by American forces in educational assistance paid off a hundredfold in good will.

During the 9th Division's tenure we distributed 10,000 school kits consisting of paper, pencils, ink and crayons. Over 31,000 students were taught some basic English as well as crafts, skills, and other technical subjects. (*Chart 21*) We assisted over 356 schools with supplies as well as construction and repairs. By helping the

MEDICAL CIVIC ACTION PROGRAM

CHART 21—Education Classes

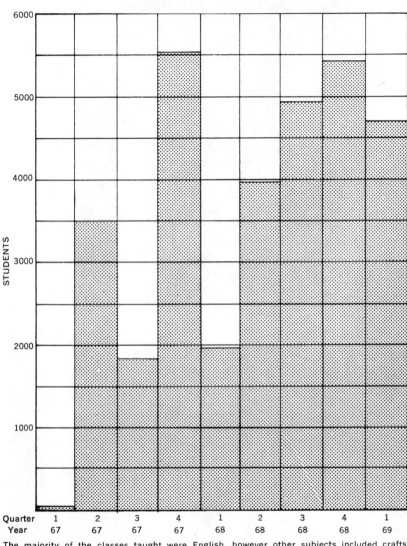

The majority of the classes taught were English, however other subjects included crafts, skills and technical subjects. Classes were usually held 2 hours per week.

Total assistance 31,717 Students

Vietnamese in their education we helped the aspirations of the Vietnamese themselves.

Repair and Construction of Facilities

The war in Vietnam has destroyed many public buildings. We

assisted in the rebuilding of 27 churches, 33 dispensaries, 37 market places and almost a thousand dwellings. We provided the Vietnamese with 1,600,000 pounds of cement, about 1,600,000 board feet of lumber and 11,500 sheets of tin to be used for roofing, thus greatly assisting the Vietnamese to assist themselves.

However, it was with our bridge repair and secondary road program that the greatest assistance was rendered. During the period 447 bridges were constructed or repaired and divisional personnel repaired over 1,100 kilometers of roads. (*Charts 22 and 23*)

CHART 22—BRIDGES CONSTRUCTED OR REPAIRED

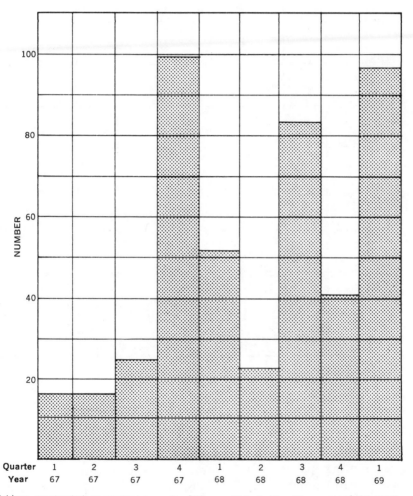

Bridges constructed or repaired were for **foot** or vehicle traffic. All were **needed to meet local civilian needs**

Total assistance 447 Bridges

CHART 23—ROADS CONSTRUCTED OR REPAIRED

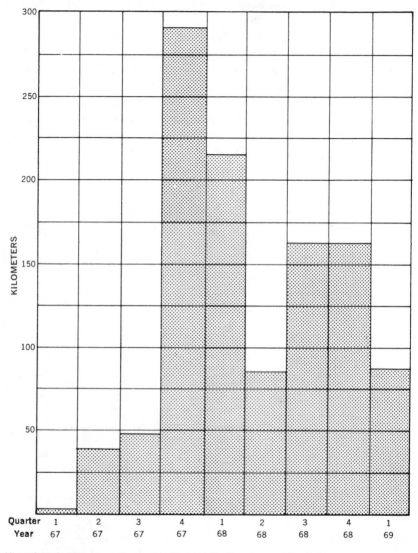

All road work **was** for civilian and military traffic thereby providing both economic and tactical advantages. Repairs do not include daily clearing of VC roadblocks

Total assistance 1107 Km of Road

An almost universal Viet Cong tactic was to cut the existing road network, particularly in rural areas, thus isolating the people in the small hamlets. The Viet Cong then went about systematically breaking up the organizational fabric of the village. They installed their own Village Chiefs and established a complete infrastructure.

It was this Viet Cong infrastructure, supported by main force and local force troops, that maintained the control of the enemy over the people. To counteract this we initiated a program to restore the road network. It was not an easy task. Inevitably, our road repair and road building efforts drew enemy fire. The Viet Cong strongly resisted any efforts to reestablish communications to the outlying villages. After we understood this we would set elaborate ambush plans and not only did we improve the roads but we took a steady toll amongst the Viet Cong units interdicting our efforts. Interestingly enough, once a road was fully established and the villagers were using it again the Viet Cong rarely recut these farm to market roads because to do so would negate the propaganda which they continuously passed out that the Viet Cong helped the people while the Government Forces did not. The reestablishment of communications with the outlying villages also enabled the Vietnamese Government Forces to erode the Viet Cong infrastructure and thus reestablish control over more of the population of the Northern Delta.

Limiting Damage and Casualties to Civilians

The foregoing civic actions were extremely positive in nature and helpful to the pacification program. However, all of the efforts put into civic actions could be undone in an area by one destructive operation. Our part of the delta, with a little over three percent of the country's land surface, had ten percent of the country's population. When we broke down into small unit operations covering large areas the possibilities for damage increased. To insure minimal possible damage and casualties to civilians we adopted urban rules of engagement as well as our own 1000 meter buffer zone around populated areas to prevent the excessive use of artillery. Although we had very heavy combat over an extended period of time in late 1968 and early 1969, we had only moderate civilian casualties and damage.

In some areas of Vietnam from time to time it has been found necessary to relocate civilians to protect them from the Communists on the one hand and to deny their services to the Communists on the other. In the delta, relocation had never been utilized much. It is really hard to say why. Some of the reasons may have been: there were too many people, the Viet Cong were everywhere, the country needed the rice, the Viet Cong tended to stay far out in deserted areas, the people generally did not like the Viet Cong and the Viet Cong did not trust the people anyway.

BRIDGE BUILDERS

We wanted to keep the people in place primarily for economic and social reasons. Since the population were kept in place we adopted an unusual style of combing through populated areas with small patrols. After some pressure, the Communists drew back away from the people and did most of their fighting from small local base areas or from the large remote base areas.[1]

---

[1] Civilians detained in the course of hostilities were presumed innocent, unless there was evidence to the contrary, and were handled separately from prisoners of war. Civilians were given good treatment and were returned to their homes expeditiously in order to generate goodwill. Amenities at the Ninth Division Civilian Center were better than in the typical peasant home, and detainees apparently appreciated the considerate treatment they received. While these civilians probably were not protected under the provisions of the Geneva Conventions, regulations governing their treatment met or exceeded the standards of the Conventions.

This afforded us the perfect setup for night ambushes, as we have discussed, since the Viet Cong had to come to the hamlets to get food, female companionship, and information. By setting up ambushes between the hamlets and the base areas we could seriously damage the enemy while breaking his line of communications. This put the Viet Cong in a state of constant tension. Then when the pacification program got into high gear and the hamlets obtained Regional or Popular Force garrisons on a permanent basis, the people were able to turn their backs on the Viet Cong.

Summary

Our pacification efforts were not hit and miss. They were well thought out and integrated with combat operations. After the initiation of the Accelerated Pacification Campaign in 1968 we focused on pacification to a larger extent, designing our combat operations to support the key hamlets and critical areas. When our efforts didn't increase the degree of Government of Vietnam control over hamlets we went directly to the evaluation sheets looking for soft spots and then we zeroed in with great precision. We felt that by placing emphasis on pacification we were shortening the war.

The success we had in integrating combat operations and pacification is best illustrated by a ceremony that took place on a hot June day in 1969 at Dong Tam. General Cao Van Vien, the Chairman of the Vietnamese Joint General Staff, had come from Saigon to present to Major General Harris W. Hollis, the fourth of the 9th Infantry Division Commanding Generals in Vietnam (others were Major General George S. Eckhardt, Major General George G. O'Connor, and Major General Julian J. Ewell), the Division's second Vietnam Presidential Cross of Gallantry Award and at the same time to present to the Division the Vietnam Civic Action Unit Award. To a casual observer the two awards did not seem to be compatible. Yet, to the soldiers participating there was no problem because they had long since learned that combat operations and civic actions were part of the same cloth. Never before that time, we were told, had a military unit been presented a Civic Action Medal. It was understood that the Vietnamese Government had previously presented the Civic Action Unit Award to the two hospital ships that had served the early casualties of the war. Here for the first time a major unit was receiving an award for humanitarian interest in the Vietnamese people while at the same time being cited for gallantry in inflicting over 10,000 casualties on the enemy during a four month period. It was no dichotomy because in our total integrated analytical approach, combat operations and pacification went hand in hand.

CHAPTER IX

Division Wrap-Up

In January of 1969 the 9th Division experienced an impressive surge in most areas of performance which lasted six months, after which time the Division began to redeploy. It is difficult to pin down the exact reasons for this surge. However, some of the factors involved are set forth below.

In the late fall of 1968, our various management improvements began to bear fruit and the Division began to firm up across the board. The most important of these was that all of our rifle companies were up to strength and we had more rifle companies operating in the field on a daily basis. Our battalions for the first time were organized on the normal square table of organization and equipment. In January we finally received three assault helicopter companies and two air cavalry troops on what was in effect an attachment basis (permanent or semi-permanent assignment and control). For the first time we had the total assets to go into high gear.

We had experienced considerable success in breaking down to company level operations in areas where the enemy had been badly cut up. As can be seen in Chart 24 our overall eliminations began to drift up while our friendly losses went down, thus improving our exchange ratio. As a result we decided to stress small unit operations particularly at night. The results were encouraging but not all good. We had several small tactical defeats which under investigation showed that our night ambushes and daylight patrols in some cases were pretty sloppy.

We therefore tried to quick-fix this by very simple, repetitive on-the-job training in night ambushes, daylight patrolling, combat shooting, and booby traps. After about a month this program took effect and the results were dramatic. Starting in late January 1969 everything began to click, and the enemy losses and the exchange ratios skyrocketed and friendly losses went down. For a period of five months the monthly gross enemy losses were from 200 percent to 300 percent over the average of the previous period, and the exchange ratios were from 150 percent to 500 percent over the previous average. In other words, enemy losses were appreciably greater while friendly losses were reduced. (*See Table 20.*)

CHART 24—ACTIVITY LEVELS—9TH DIVISION, AUGUST 1968–JUNE 1969

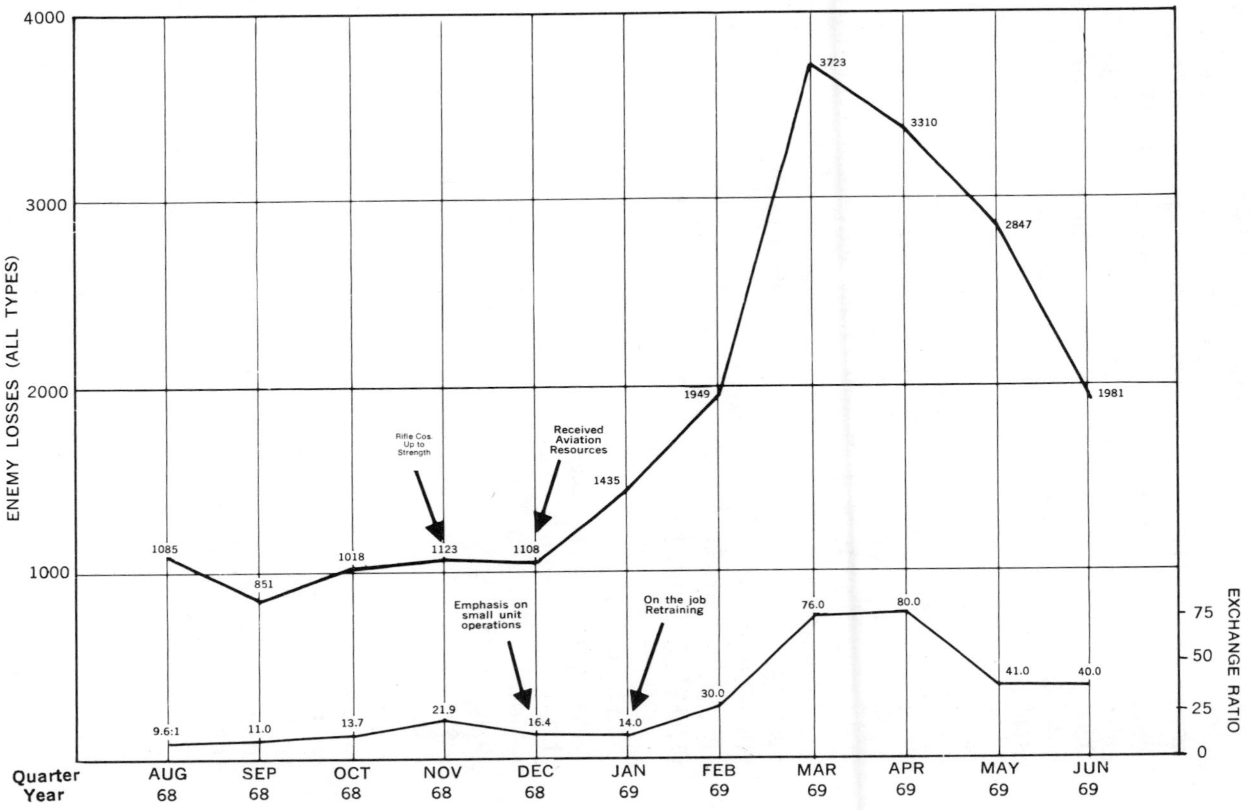

One must give the enemy some credit for this upsurge. They had planned an offensive in the winter of 1969 and it ran head on into our peaking of effort. Most probably the enemy started his offensive in late December or early January as our exchange ratio dropped slightly (18.8 to 15.6), although enemy losses went up 30 percent (1,108 to 1,435). It is also apparent that their losses from October 1968 through January 1969 crippled them badly which helped the effectiveness of friendly operations to surge and remain high until July 1969.

One can theorize that this peaking of results was due to a relative collapse of the enemy structure, a raising of the friendly skill level, an effective integration of our effort, a constant review and quick fixing of our operations, and possibly the achievement of tactical and technical surprise from which the enemy could not recover.

If one looks at each of the areas of major activity, the improvement rate was fairly constant but definitely weighted towards night operations. The increase in Viet Cong eliminated during night operations between January 1969 and March 1969 was 300 to 400 percent as compared to an increase of 100 percent during daytime operations. (*See Table 21.*)

The skill factor is more difficult to isolate. A sampling indicated that the infantry exchange ratio went up to about 40 to 1. However, air cavalry and sniper exchange ratios were extremely high and night infantry exchange ratios were around 100 to 1. We were unable to isolate any other sub-exchange ratios. However, it was obvious that the cumulative effect of improved friendly skill (and probably degraded enemy skill) was very large.

Although certain technical areas (for example air cavalry and snipers) did very well, it was our judgment that the basic infantry effort was central—the others revolved around it.

One might also theorize that the peaking of efficiency was due to the combined efforts of a group of first-class brigade and battalion commanders, plus the tremendous morale surge of the infantry when they realized that they were cutting the enemy to ribbons (coupled with the consequential loss of morale on the enemy side).

The most graphic example of the peaking effect was in our 2d Brigade. It had traditionally been used to clean out difficult enemy base areas with riverine operations and, as a result, had a rather heavy deliberate style (much like a Marine amphibious assault). However, by much hard work, it was able to shift over to the more open small unit style. It was put into Kien Hoa Province—a real Viet Cong bastion, taken off its boats, and buckled down to work.

PATROL

Fortunately, the enemy was numerous and overconfident and really did not realize what was happening until it was too late.

TABLE 28—2D BRIGADE STATISTICS

TIME PERIOD	VC KIA	PW	HC	VCI	TOTAL VC LOSSES	U.S. KIA	U.S. WIA
Apr–Jun 68	417	40	2	—	459	96	649
Dec	391	38	13	—	442	18	136
Jan 69	469	35	7	5	516	25	158
Feb	704	38	18	6	766	27	191
Mar	1,185	39	34	5	1,263	8	195
Apr	1,254	52	20	0	1,326	11	195
May	984	36	12	4	1,036	21	201

The figures tell the story. (*See Table 28.*) In the last half of 1968, under Colonel George E. Bland, the Brigade began to tighten up; in Jan. and Feb. 1969 it hit its stride ; and in the months of March, April and May under Colonel Rodman C. Rainville, the Brigade reached a plateau of skill and effectiveness which was really amazing. In these three months, the brigade averaged over 1000 enemy per month eliminated. Its exchange ratios were astronomical, peaking at 158 to 1, an elimination ratio which is possibly amongst the highest achieved in Vietnam. (By contrast, its elimination ratio in a somewhat comparable period in 1968 was 4.3 to 1.) This remarkable record was achieved in continuous heavy fighting as shown by the friendly wounded rate, which was around 200 per month. Turning from the figures to more general results, the effect on the enemy was dramatic. In a period of months, the Viet Cong there changed from the cockiest provincial force in Vietnam (Kien Hoa was the alleged birthplace of the Viet Cong and the site of the so-called capital of the movement) to a remnant of demoralized and panicky units. Things were so bad that North Vietnamese cadre and fillers (the best sign of severe erosion) began to be introduced and this was in the heartland of Viet Cong strength. The heaviest fighting was generally confined to a relatively few localities where the Viet Cong had established so-called "secret base areas" which they defended with great tenacity. If Kien Hoa is ever pacified, and it has been a dissident pirate area for some centuries, March, April and May 1969 were the beginning of the process.

On the negative side, it is of interest to note that our overall improvement was much less than one would expect. We increased our paddy strength and our effective aircraft effort appreciably. Yet our improvement in overall pressure on the enemy (measured by enemy losses) was only around 200 percent. One can only conclude that the enemy was doing his best to cancel out our improvements. In fact, by examining the history of contacts, it is apparent that the enemy had some success with his evasive tactics.

TABLE 29—CONTACT HISTORY

Quarter	Contacts	Elimination Ratio	Enemy Losses Per Contact	U.S. Losses Per Contact
3rd 1968	389	16.1 to 1	6.4 to 1	.57 to 1
4th 1968	883	19.1 to 1	3.7 to 1	.19 to 1
1st 1969	2723	31.1 to 1	2.6 to 1	.07 to 1
2nd 1969	2137	54.5 to 1	3.8 to 1	.07 to 1

Whether some tactical innovation could have kept the enemy loss figure per contact up is debatable. By sampling the battalion

RIVER PATROL

performance records, it would appear that as the overall enemy strength in an area declined, battalion skill levels stayed high but gross performance leveled off and then declined somewhat. This seems reasonable.

These results were somewhat sensitive to the overall capability of the commanders concerned. On the one hand, Major General Harris Hollis who took over the division in April 1969 was able to continue and improve on the approach; on the other hand, some lower level commanders had varying degrees of success with it.

Although the record of enemy eliminations per contact might not have been as high as one would like, this result was acceptable when one considered the 88 percent reduction in U.S. losses per contact. The dramatic reduction in the loss of American lives was the pay-off of all of our efforts.

In summary, one might conclude with reasonable confidence:

(1) A standard U.S. infantry division at full strength with adequate aviation support could operate very efficiently in Vietnam. An increase in infantry battalions was useful. Open terrain such as in the delta increased the relative effect of aviation support.

(2) The Constant Pressure Concept coupled with aggressive small unit tactics was an effective counter to enemy evasive tactics.

(3) Heavy military pressure and good pacification effort could defeat a solidly entrenched Communist effort over a period of time.

(4) Good management and sound military judgment were essential and could be enhanced by use of analytic techniques.

(5) There were many aspects of the war in Vietnam which resisted clearcut analysis and assessment.

(6) Top-notch leaders (U.S. or Vietnamese, military or civilian) transcended tactics, technique and other factors. Good leaders instinctively did the right thing most of the time.

(7) The average U.S. soldier was individually quite superior to the Communist soldier. With proper organization and support, this superiority was enhanced manyfold.

CHAPTER X

Corps Level Operations

In April 1969 the focus of this study shifts to II Field Force Vietnam at Long Binh, with the 9th Division portion continuing until mid-1969.

At corps level we see a much more complex problem and one inherently more difficult to manage and analyze. However, after a period of observation we slowly began to institute a simplified version of the 9th Division review and analysis system at the division and separate brigade levels. Some segments of operations were subjected to straight-on analysis with the remainder being handled by normal military decision methods but subjected to the general philosophy of the "analytic approach." While the improvements in performance were less dramatic than in the 9th, they were substantial enough to justify the added effort.

At II Field Force Vietnam level, we had the equivalent of five U.S. and Free World divisions as well as operational control of the advisory structure for eleven provinces and the equivalent of five South Vietnamese Army divisions. *(Map 2)*

Our enemy was principally North Vietnamese Army main force. What Viet Cong units were left were, in fact, North Vietnamese Army in all but name, as they survived only on the strength of North Vietnamese replacements.

The true diversity of III Corps Tactical Zone strikes one when you examine the kind of warfare experienced there. There were almost as many different wars as there were units since the military region encompassed a wide range of terrain and enemy situations. *(Map 2)*

For example, in Saigon we had what was principally a National Police and intelligence effort against the terrorists and the Viet Cong Infrastructure.

Moving out to Gia Dinh and the outskirts of Saigon, one found four Vietnamese Army regiments and three U.S. brigades engaged in screening in the relatively open terrain against rocket attacks and infiltrators into the city.

To the south, in Long An Province, the 3d Brigade, 9th Infantry Division was efficiently engaged in smoking out the Viet Cong

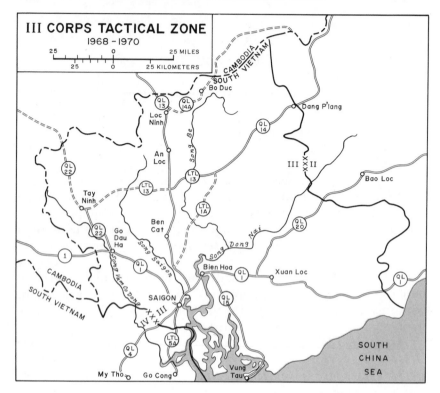

MAP 2

remnants (and 1st North Vietnamese Army Regiment) and chopping them up. This was the typical delta-type operation perfected by the 9th Division.

To the northwest of Saigon, the U.S. 25th Division faced two different wars. In Hau Nghia, a long-time citadel of the Viet Cong, one faced the combined efforts of enemy units and of a population that continued to support the Communists either through choice or necessity. The terrain was wide open—the resident Communists lived in hedgerows and spider holes. There were booby traps and mines in abundance. Principal combat was with elements of Sub-Region 1 who were based in the Boi Loi Woods and the Trapezoid.

In Tay Ninh there was an entirely different environment. Bordered on three sides by relatively heavy jungle and situated only four hours walk from the Cambodian border, it existed in a feast or famine fashion. At his choosing, the enemy moved from his sanctuaries in Cambodia to attack the populated areas. When this happened, one experienced all ranges of combat, from deep jungle to fighting in built-up areas. When the main forces withdrew to Cambodia, however, there was practically no one to fight since even the local forces based themselves in Cambodia.

The 1st Cavalry Division which spanned the northern tier of War Zone C, Binh Long and Phuoc Long had a particularly difficult situation facing it. The terrain was deep jungle and in it were elements of three Communist divisions plus the rear service groups, and Lines of Communication that passed men and supplies from the Cambodian sanctuaries to the sub-regions that ringed Saigon. (Sizeable elements of all of these were based in Cambodia). Combat here was typified by all the difficulties inherent to deep jungle and bunker warfare.

In Binh Duong to the north of Saigon, the 1st Infantry Division faced terrain that varied from deep jungle to open cultivated and built-up areas. In it, they faced local forces, several beat-up and elusive one-time Viet Cong regiments (Qyuet Thang and Dong Ngai) and parts of Sub-Region I. To a large extent, the big war had gone and left the Big Red One behind. Because of its past success in beating down the enemy, it now found little left to fight in its traditional area of operation. What enemy remained was highly elusive and consistently avoided contact.

Finally, to the east and southeast of Saigon, the Royal Thai Army Volunteer Force and the Australian Task Force faced a rough and durable assortment of one Viet Cong regiment and some battalions that habitually survived in deep jungle bases near inhabited areas. Major contacts were infrequent.

Because of this diverse and different situation, there was initially a reluctance to apply at Corps level the review and analysis techniques that had been so useful at division. Initially, the general nature of the 9th Division system was brought to the attention of the subordinate commands of II Field Force Vietnam. By so doing, we provided examples of the statistics we had collected and the practical management use derived from them. Subordinate commanders were encouraged to analyze their local situation and if they did not already have one, develop a Review and Analysis System for their own use. This effort was not limited to the tactical units. For instance, the Deputy for Civil Operations and Revolutionary Development Support worked out a system which highlighted the key measurable areas in the pacification field.

This effort started to show results almost immediately. Although the divisions in II Field Force, Vietnam had previously conducted varying types of analysis, none had kept books on an input-output or expenditure of effort versus results basis. Hence, the more adept were quickly able to obtain the benefits we had noted in the 9th Division:

(1) The ability to determine more rapidly and clearly the types of operations that were paying off with results and where.

(2) The efficiency and effectiveness of various units.

(3) An identification of unproductive expenditures of time and effort.

As has been mentioned throughout this monograph, the 25th Infantry Division employed simple operations analysis consistently. They also developed the use of computer assistance in operations analysis to a significant degree. The comments of Major General Harris W. Hollis, the 25th Division Commander in late 1969 and early 1970, are of particular interest:

> I found it was extremely important that I closely examine our operational results on a continuing basis, so that I could gain an adequate appreciation for the overall picture of how the command was progressing.
>
> I am convinced that operational analysis techniques have tremendous potential for application in future combat and particularly in the complex environment of this type of war. I saw how others had used this method with success; particularly General Ewell, when he commanded the 9th Infantry Division prior to my succession to command of that division. In no other war have we been so deluged by so many tidbits of information, for we have been accustomed to an orderliness associated with established battlelines. Here, though, we have had to make our decisions based not upon enemy regimental courses of action, but rather upon the numerous isolated actions of communist squad-sized elements. So with the scale down of the level of operations, we have had to increase our reliance on objective analysis of available information to arrive at logical courses of action.

Armed with this information, the more receptive commanders were able to optimize their efforts quickly and put their assets where they were getting better results. As they did, the II Field Force, Vietnam exchange ratio, which had averaged below 10 to 1 for the previous nine months, began to improve. For five straight months, the rate was over 20 to 1. During October 1969 the rate crested at 30.1 to 1. For the 12-month period April 1969 through March 1970, the U.S. units in II Field Force, Vietnam had an average exchange rate of 18.9 to 1. (*Table 30*) This improvement came from increased efficiency of U.S. units, who took fewer casualties to do the job while enemy eliminations gradually went down. One of the payoffs at division was the quick indication of changed enemy tactics. For example, when things got too hot for him at night, the enemy often would change to early morning or early evening resupply and so on. The new insights provided by this system of analysis showed

TABLE 30—U.S. FORCES, II FIELD FORCE, VIETNAM EXCHANGE RATIO
APRIL 1969–MARCH 1970

Date	Enemy KIA	U.S. KIA	Exchange Ratio
Apr 69	4014*	270	14.9 : 1
May	4128*	252	16.4 : 1
Jun	4655*	287	16.3 : 1
Jul	2764	180	15.4 : 1
Aug	3726	203	18.4 : 1
Sep	3371	156	21.6 : 1
Oct	2748	91	30.1 : 1
Nov	3651	148	24.7 : 1
Dec	3130	130	24.1 : 1
Jan 70	2366	111	21.4 : 1
Feb	1750	97	18.0 : 1
Mar	2383	127	18.8 : 1
Average	3224	171	18.9 : 1

* A period of heavy combat along the Cambodian border.

commanders when to adjust their tactics to compensate for enemy changes. Much greater efficiencies resulted.

As each division's data bank grew, we drew on them for certain selected summary data for Headquarters II Field Force, Vietnam. Because of the very diverse terrain and enemy situation noted above, direct comparison of division-level statistics was generally not feasible or profitable. However, these summary statistics did provide a valuable insight into what both friendly and enemy forces were doing (or not doing).

Thus, our analysis was able to confirm our suspicion that the Communists were fragmenting further after the failure of their main force attacks in the spring and summer of 1969. (*See Table 30.*) Our daily situation briefing gave us the impression of smaller contacts. Our weekly review of statistics brought the facts clearly into focus. We had not fully comprehended the damage done to the enemy during the friendly operations commanded by Generals Frederick C. Weyand and Walter T. Kerwin, Jr., in 1968 and 1969.

Further, Corps-level statistics gave the commander another indicator on potential trouble spots. When the summary statistics began to slip, it was time to pay a visit to the unit to see what the trouble was. Because of the almost unmanageable span of supervision, this tip-off feature was of great value.

However, as has been mentioned earlier, it was much more difficult to apply analytical methods to this much more complex operation. Review and analysis tended to be of the more conventional management type. If one can summarize the approach, it was to use analysis where feasible, use tight management overall, and to try to preserve the questioning, results-oriented analytical approach throughout.

Some selected examples of the various uses of analysis follow.

Working On the Enemy System

Pragmatic and cumulative experience during the Vietnam war revealed more and more clearly that one had to work on all elements of the enemy's system to achieve substantial success. This was particularly true when the Communists were operating from Cambodian sanctuaries as was the case in III Corps Tactical Zone.

This concept was crystallized and articulated by General Creighton W. Abrams. When combined with the lower level constant pressure approach it was most effective. It should be noted, however, that III Corps was unusual in that the terrain, the weather and troop availability favored the concept. We followed a highly successful program of keeping constant pressure on most elements of the enemy system although a few areas were beyond our capabilities. Geographically, this meant the Viet Cong infrastructure and local elements in the cities and surrounding populated areas, the local forces that operated around the populated areas, the subregions and their main force elements that tenanted the close-in base areas, the rear service groups that maintained the lines of communication from Cambodia, and finally the North Vietnamese Army divisions which by now clung, more and more, to the safety of the Cambodian border were all attacked simultaneously. By 1969 most enemy units were fairly well beaten down. However, from time to time, we had to drop what we were doing and turn all hands to smothering some Communist attempt at a high point. However, once the fire was put out, we immediately went back where we had left off to an overall constant pressure approach.

By September 1969 we had beaten back the final gasp effort of the North Vietnamese Army divisions to get to Saigon and Tay Ninh and their consolidation efforts against Binh Long Province. This done, we fine-tuned our efforts to insure that we had pressure on every possible element of the enemy system. In line with the improved capabilities of Regional Forces, we thinned out the regular forces protecting Saigon. In accord with the Vietnamization program, every effort was coordinated with Vietnamese forces. Fortunately, the Vietnamization program had proceeded to the point where many South Vietnamese Army units could pull their own

MAP 3

weight in good fashion. This gave us 50 to 60 more reasonably good battalions to work with.

Across the northern tier of III Corps. (*Map 3*) we deployed a coordinated force of seven U.S. and South Vietnamese brigade equivalents. They worked against the three essentially North Vietnamese Army divisions and the lines of communication that led from Cambodia into the interior of III Corps.

In War Zone C a brigade of the 1st Air Cavalry Division and a South Vietnamese airborne brigade moved in on top of the enemy line of communications that ran from the Fishhook down the Saigon River corridor to the Michelin–Trapezoid base area. They were in constant contact with and exacted a slow and steady toll on elements of the 9th North Vietnamese Army Division and on rear service elements on the line of communications.

To the east, the 11th Armored Cavalry Regiment and the 9th South Vietnamese Army Regiment worked along Highway QL 13 and west to Ton Le Cham and the Fishhook, keeping pressure on the 7th Division elements that rotated across the border and denied the enemy access to the population in the area.

Moving further east, one found a brigade of the 1st Air Cavalry Division with its battalions deployed in a linear fashion along the Song Be River infiltration route. By intensive reconnaissance it sought out the trail locations and operated along them, taking small but steady bites out of the Communist supplies and people.

Finally, at Song Be we had the remaining brigade of the 1st Air Cavalry Division and another South Vietnamese Army airborne brigade. They kept pressure on the elements of the 5th Division which were still in South Vietnam and sought out enemy logistics movements from Base Area 351 in Cambodia towards War Zone D. For several months, we achieved moderate but steady success. In the fall of 1969, air cavalry elements discovered that the Communists had established a new line of communications from Base Area 351 along the II Corps–III Corps boundary into War Zone D. (The so-called Jolley trail) Our reaction was to immediately put troops on top of the new trail to keep up the pressure and attrition. Starting from the point where this new trail crossed QL 14 northeast of Duc Phong, the cavalry and airborne leapfrogged battalions along the trail scooping up important quantities of supplies and killing rear service troops. Of equal importance this effort impaired the flow of supplies and munitions to the sub-regions around Saigon.

In summary, the combined U.S.-South Vietnamese Army effort across the northern tier was designed to accomplish two objectives. First, to erode the main force units and keep them so weak and occupied that they could not interfere with the pacification program. Second, to reduce and, if possible, choke off the flow of replacements and supplies from Cambodian sanctuary base areas into the heart of III Corps. These efforts were surprisingly successful.

In the interior of III Corps, we had a force of 18 brigade equivalents deployed in a great circle 30 to 70 kilometers out from Saigon. This force was dedicated to the tasks of maintaining pressure and attrition on the sub-regions, the close-in base areas and the lines of communications that came into the sub-regions.

Northwest of Saigon, the 25th U.S. Division and two regiments of the 25th South Vietnamese Army Division were on top of Sub-Region 1 and Sub-Region 2 keeping pressure on the main force elements and the lines of communication from the Angel's Wing. This was a particularly difficult task because of the easy Communist access to bases in nearby Cambodia.

North of Saigon, the U.S. 1st Division and two regiments of the

5th South Vietnamese Army Division were focused on Sub-Region 5 and they participated with neighboring units in a coordinated effort against Sub-Region 1.

East of Saigon, the 18th South Vietnamese Army Division, the U.S. 199th Light Infantry Brigade, the Royal Thai Army Volunteer Force and the Australian Task Force combined their efforts against Military Region 7 and Sub-Region 4. Typical of their operations was a coordinated campaign to wear down the 274th Viet Cong Regiment and drive it out of its long-term base area in the Hat Dich jungle. This involved putting troops, firebases and Rome Plows into the base area and intensive efforts to interdict resupply into the base.

In the Rung Sat Special Zone, a delta area south of Saigon, a special U.S. Navy–Vietnamese Navy effort kept continuous pressure on the water sapper elements that formerly had interdicted shipping channels. These efforts were fully coordinated with and from time to time supported by II Field Force, Vietnam.

Finally, in Long An Province, the 3d Brigade 9th Division and the 46th South Vietnamese Army Regiment combined their efforts to control Sub-Region 3 and defeat the 1st North Vietnamese Army Regiment.

This completed the middle ring. In it we kept full pressure on the organized Communist forces, eroding them, and creating an environment for pacification progress.

Gia Dinh Province and Saigon are the heart of III Corps. Because of the bitter memories of *Tet* 1968 and avowed Communist aims for 1969, we started the year with a force of four South Vietnamese Army regiments and three U.S. brigades deployed in defense of Saigon. They did their job well. Although the Communist main forces never got close, these forces kept Sub-Region 6 under a blanket. Hence, we started pulling out forces in June 1969 and completed the withdrawal of U.S. forces from Sub-Region 6 in September 1969. The airborne forces were withdrawn next and Rangers started soon after. As this occurred, the Regional and Popular Forces assumed more and more of the load—a graphic example of Vietnamization in action.

While all these actions were going on, there was a concurrent steady improvement in Regional Forces throughout III Corps. This resulted from the steps being taken to upgrade their training and equipment, the gradually improving leadership at district and province level, and the improved environment which we provided by keeping the main forces on the run and away from the populated areas. This freed the Regional Forces to work on the local Communist elements without fear of being engulfed by a main force unit.

As they enjoyed increasing success, they began to deny the enemy access to the population. The Communists were thus able to extort less and less support from the people. This, of course, put more of a burden on the already strained Communist supply system. What they could not get locally, they had to bring in from outside.

It was a vicious cycle—by keeping an unrelenting pressure and attrition on all elements of the enemy system, we pushed him closer and closer to the breaking point. He reached a point where most of his effort was devoted to his own survival. This entire operation required exquisite co-ordination and delicate emphasis.

By March of 1970 the enemy in III Corps was very weak. The Cambodian operation then destroyed his bases in the Cambodian sanctuary, dealing him a staggering blow.

We have remarked elsewhere on the positive effect of gifted commanders. It seems appropriate here to mention that an "average" or less commander during the 1969–1970 period found it difficult to do damage to the enemy in a useful way. Not only did the situation require considerable technical and tactical proficiency but also a complete determination to come to grips with the enemy.

Inventory of Communist Units

In our effort against the enemy system, we wanted to insure that we were not missing any Communist units. Hence, we made a systematic inventory of all Communist elements of any size known or suspected to be in III Corps. Next, we stratified the units by their known or suspected geographical area of operation. Against this list we arrayed the South Vietnamese and Free World Forces who operated in the area. Finally, we analyzed our past operations to determine how effectively we were doing the job.

This systematic inventory was a refinement which was initiated late in the game. It almost immediately focused our attention on an unusual problem area.

As one might expect we found out that the main force units were getting most of our attention. They were, after all, the most obvious threat and the ones who could inflict a small tragedy on us in an afternoon. The local force battalions were also systematically pursued by our side. Shifting to the very base of the Communist pyramid, the Viet Cong infrastructure was the object of a formal program designed to eliminate it. Although spotty in effectiveness, the Phoung Huang program showed promise.

However, in the middle of the pyramid (See Chart 8.) we found an entirely different picture. In many instances, local-level Viet Cong elements were existing relatively unmolested under the very noses of friendly units that were keying on bigger game. There was no systematic effort to search out and eradicate these local pests. They suffered attrition only when they were caught by a reconnaissance-in-force, a night ambush, or while they were attempting an offensive action. No one was keeping the pressure on them.

Armed with this information, we went one step further. We charged subordinate units with responsibility for the specific small elements known or suspected to be in their areas of operation. This was a combined Free World–South Vietnamese Army program resulting in close coordination of all forces down to district level. Periodic reporting on results was required so as to assess progress. The 25th Division refined this process to a high art.

Within several months, we could see positive results from this effort. Marginal Viet Cong units that had survived at minimum strength when they were left alone began to fold up under pressure. Many were simply inactivated because of ineffective remaining strength.

This was all accomplished without flash or fanfare. Attrition was by twos or threes. When the word got out that we were looking for locals by name, the pressure caused them to move out, hide deep, or Chieu Hoi.

The overall result was to hasten the decay of local forces and to further weaken the link between the Communist apparatus and the people. This device institutionalized the Constant Pressure Concept and allowed one to keep tabs on its success.

Sub-Region 1

On a multi-division scale, our effort against Sub-Region 1 was an excellent example of the Constant Pressure Concept. For a period of years, this key sub-region had survived under the noses of two U.S. and two South Vietnamese Army divisions. It did so by being slippery and alert. During these years, it had suffered enormous casualties but relying on North Vietnamese Army replacements, it always managed to survive and to rebuild. The North Vietnamese Army headquarters was usually underground in the deep jungle of the Trapezoid. (Map 4) Its subordinate elements holed up along the Saigon River in secondary growth Rome-plowed areas, in the Boi Loi Woods, and in the Trapezoid. They lived off two separate lines of communication—one across Hau Nghia Province to the Angel's Wing in Cambodia and the other from the Fishook south down the Saigon River corridor. (Map 4)

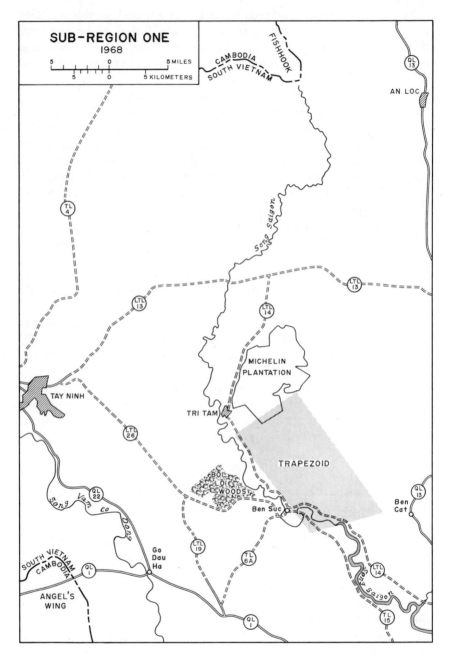

SUB-REGION ONE
1968

5 MILES
5 KILOMETERS

FISHHOOK

CAMBODIA
SOUTH VIETNAM

AN LOC

QL
13

Song Saigon

LTL
13

TL
4

LTL
13

LTL
14

MICHELIN
PLANTATION

TAY NINH

TRI TAM

LTL
26

TRAPEZOID

BO
LOI
WOODS

QL
13

Ben
Cat

Ben Suc

Song Vam co Dong

QL
22

LTL
19

Go
Dau
Ha

TL
6A

SOUTH VIETNAM
CAMBODIA

QL
1

Song Saigon

LTL
14

ANGEL'S
WING

QL
1

TL
15

MAP 4

Aiding Sub-Region 1's survival was the fact that it was near the boundary between our divisions and as pressure mounted on one side it could slide away. Our units tended to concentrate on what was in their area of operation. Cross-boundary co-ordination was not a strong point.

Starting in July 1969, we hit the problem head on with a full-court press by all U.S. and South Vietnamese Army forces in the area. First, we moved the divisional boundary to the Saigon River—the 1st U.S. Division and 5th South Vietnamese Army Division to the northeast of the river and the 25th U.S. Division and 25th South Vietnamese Army Division to the southwest. U.S. Navy and Vietnamese Navy boats worked the river. A floating boundary was established on either side of the river to enable rapid exchanges of territory and responsibility.

To kick off the effort, a co-ordination conference was held by all participants to exchange intelligence and co-ordinate operational details. The Commanding General, 1st Infantry Division, was designated co-ordinator for the operation. He maintained the books on current operations, insured an exchange of information with all participants, hosted weekly staff co-ordination meetings, and monthly commanders' conferences. Within the first week, Sub-Region 1, was on its way down. Co-ordinated effort by ground forces and Navy elements along the river started exacting a nightly toll on resupply efforts across the river. At the same time, a South Vietnamese Army airborne battalion and a U.S. battalion moved in on top of the 268th Viet Cong Regiment in Boi Loi Woods and the 1st Division and 5th South Vietnamese Army started a major tactical effort supported by Rome plows in the Trapezoid. Although not a formal element of the Sub-Regional 1 effort, the 1st Air Cavalry to the north choked down on the enemy and impaired his resupply via the Saigon River corridor.

Progress was not spectacular. There were no big fights but every day there was a steady toll of the enemy. Prisoners told tales of not wanting to go on rice resupply details because it was sure death. In addition, major headquarters type elements of both Sub-Region 1 and the 268th Regiment were overrun and captured. The pressure was so great that the 101st North Vietnamese Army Regiment moved completely out of the area.

We were, of course, very pleased with the erosion that Sub-Region 1 suffered in this operation as it was the strategic link pin of the entire Communist effort towards Saigon. There was an important bonus. This was our first real test of the Dong Tien (Progress Together) program. The improved performance of the 8th

South Vietnamese Army Regiment working with the 1st Infantry Division showed us clearly that we had chosen the right path in that the South Vietnamese Army was ready to assume a major combat load.

While we were keeping full pressure on Sub-Region 1, pacification in nearby populated areas was proceeding in a very satisfactory fashion. Sub-Region 1 units were fully occupied in self-survival and could not interfere. Under the umbrella of our pressure, Regional Forces, Popular Forces, and Popular Self Defense Forces gained strength and capability.

By early 1970, when the first sizable U.S. troop withdrawal took place, Sub-Region 1 was so debilitated and the South Vietnamese Army and regional forces so improved there was no noticeable change in security ratings.

Dong Tien Program

In June 1969 we started a major effort to upgrade South Vietnamese forces in III Corps as part of the Vietnamization program. The program, announced jointly by the Commanders of III Corps Tactical Zone and II Field Force Vietnam, was called the Dong Tien (Progress Together) Program. It paired U.S. units with South Vietnamese Army and Regional and Popular Force units for operations—the objective being to allow each force to learn something from the other. Because of the key importance of airmobile skills in the Vietnamization program, we put particular stress on combined airmobile operations. Each U.S. commander shared his air assets with Vietnamese units. At first Vietnamese elements merely went along on U.S.-planned and managed operations but progressively the Vietnamese took over and ran their own operations.

There were two very obvious benefits that accrued from this effort in short order. First, Vietnamese commanders and units developed real skill in using airmobile assets (without depending on U.S. advisors as in the past). Secondly, Vietnamese units using air assets followed the U.S. example and started operating in areas they had avoided for many years.

The program was then extended to operations as a whole. The payoff here was substantial. The Vietnamese began to operate continuously—both day and night—and in some cases performed as well or better than their U.S. partners. As a battalion or regiment showed that it was really effective, it was "graduated" from the system and took over an independent mission.

This program was nothing new. It was directly copied from I Corps where we concluded that an important element in the suc-

DONG TIEN

cess of the 1st South Vietnamese Army Division was an informal
arrangement of the same sort. The only "new" element was to
formalize the system as a command directed program. This was
done because the South Vietnamese Army in the III Corps area had
historically resisted combined operations. It also gave the program
more status and visibility.

The upshot and final test of the system came as U.S. units began
to withdraw from III Corps. The success of the Dong Tien program
was attested to by the manner in which Vietnamese units were able
to pick up the load and effectively keep the pressure on the enemy.
Throughout mid-1969, U.S. and other Free World Forces were
carrying about 80 percent of the combat load in III Corps as
measured by the numbers of enemy killed in action. Beginning in
November 1969 South Vietnamese units began to increase their
share, until by April 1970 the situation had changed dramatically
with the South Vietnamese Army carrying almost one half of the
combat load. This was partially due to the redeployment of some
U.S. units. Chart 25 indicates one way in which we pragmatically
measured the actual progress of the Vietnamization Program. The

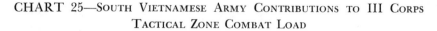

CHART 25—South Vietnamese Army Contributions to III Corps Tactical Zone Combat Load

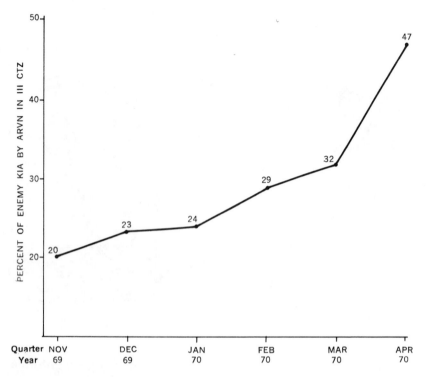

South Vietnamese Army units that operated so effectively in Cambodia with no U.S. advisors were the products of this Dong Tien program.

Helicopter Allocations

Following the defeat of Communist main force efforts in the *Tet* period of 1969, we took a hard look at our method of allocating assault helicopter company and air cavalry support. The purpose was to see if we were getting all that was possible from these relatively scarce and valuable units.

At the time, our Standing Operating Procedure was to make a daily allocation of assault helicopter companies to U.S. and South Vietnamese units. Units that wanted air assets for a particular day put in their bids. We sorted out the requests and assigned use of the assets based on our evaluation of the Corps-wide situation and the unit's part in it. Since there were never enough helicopters to fill all valid requests, some requests always went unfilled. Because of the dynamics of the situation, a unit could not plan very far in advance.

Until all requests were considered, a unit did not know if it would get the air assets which it had requested. This was, of course, the standard system of allocating from a central pool when requirements exceed resources.

To get a handle on the problem, we turned to our basic set of statistics on combat results. We found that certain of our units consistently achieved more enemy eliminations on airmobile operations than did others. However, these units did not necessarily receive priority in the allocation of air assets, since allocation was based on what a unit said it was going to do without consideration of its past achievements. At the same time, the uncertainty of getting assets impaired the units' efficiency in keeping full pressure on the enemy.

In an effort to improve results, we stopped daily allocation of assets and went to a monthly allocation, which was weighted in favor of the units that were producing results or had a high priority mission overall. For instance, the 3d Brigade, 9th Infantry Division, our most proficient user of air assets, which worked Long An Province—the first priority pacification target nationwide—received 45 Assault Helicopter Company days per month, while a like-sized unit and area with a poor track record and a less important mission, received only 25 Assault Helicopter Company days per month.

For planning purposes the allocation was spread over the month, and a tentative schedule issued. Thus, a unit knew in advance what it would have for air assets on a given day and could plan the rhythm of its operations accordingly. This schedule was not set in concrete, however. When the situation dictated, we pulled the assets and put them where they were needed at the moment.

In announcing the new system, we made it clear that allocations were "results" oriented and that those units which used assets most efficiently would continue to receive a proportionately greater share of available assets. However this was more of a gambit to stimulate good performance than a factual description of the actual allocation process.

Our experience proved that this change was both timely and beneficial. Coming at a time when the enemy was changing his tactics (breaking down to small units), it allowed units to plan effectively for future operations and gave them incentive to try more imaginative ways to employ their assets. It also allowed us to assign the same air units to the supported ground unit, thus facilitating the development of closer coordination and teamwork. In other words, the units could work their way up the learning curve.

TRANSPORTING ARTILLERY FIRING PLATFORMS

This is cited as an example of departure from the "standard" or "reasonable" system to achieve better results.

Full Response to Antiaircraft Fire

In the summer of 1969 the three Communist main force divisions in the III Corps Tactical Zone north of Saigon were in the process of being driven up against the Cambodian sanctuary areas. In flying over War Zone C, it became apparent that we were receiving rather heavy .50 caliber antiaircraft fire. We soon found out from captured documents that the Communists had initiated an intensive campaign to shoot down American choppers. As a result, our aircraft losses went up, although modestly. After observing the enemy tactics, it was theorized that they were selecting an area along the upper Saigon River logistical and infiltration corridor which they wished to protect, positioning an antiaircraft battalion in it and then letting fly.

The normal U.S. response in the past had been to attack any guns which were a problem and detour around the rest. However, in this case, it was decided, for largely psychological reasons, to try to defeat the tactic head on.

It was decided to:

(1) **Report and record all firings.** (Maximizing our information.)

(2) Attack all located guns with maximum firepower (gunships, artillery and Tactical air) .

(3) Work the area over on the ground when feasible and desirable.

After a period of weeks, our aircraft losses went back to normal or below. It was found that it took only a matter of days to either destroy or neutralize an entire battalion (say 9 to 15 guns) . Whether this was due to destroying the guns, killing off the crews, or exhausting their ammunition supply was not known. However, it was quite apparent that they were cycling in fresh battalions to replace the old. After some months the enemy gave up, but the full response technique on a less generous scale was retained against any fire (light machinegun or rifle) . Eventually the enemy antiaircraft fire subsided to normal proportions or less. Unfortunately, the statistics on this interesting operation could not be located.

The Night Hawk Kit

In retrospect, it is observed that most of the improvements or innovations described in this monograph were ideas which usually involved people—whether concepts, management, tactics, techniques or training. This was a surprise—that doing something a little different or a little better with people could result in substantial improvements. However, the Night Hawk Kit was an example of a *hardware* solution developed by analysis.

Earlier we described the success of the Night Search technique, Although very profitable, a Night Search operation involved a major investment of two Cobras and one Huey plus additional back-up helicopters and required a high degree of skill on the part of the sniper spotters.

The 25th Infantry Division studied this technique and, over a period of time, developed a kit consisting of a coaxially mounted mini-gun, Night Observation Device, and a small pink and white searchlight. This was ideal as the Night Observation Device gave maximum efficiency for normal night observation, the pink searchlight could be used for very dark night conditions, and the mini-gun had ample firepower for the job and replaced both Cobras. Being a "plug-in" kit for a Huey, it could be removed in the day and installed in any operational plane at night. The coaxial feature allowed one man to operate it, thus removing the need for "handing off" targets. The final refinement was the use of both a right and left hand kit which eliminated the effect of stoppages.

This clever development with on-hand components allowed one plane to do the job of three or more and gave better results with less highly trained operators. This program was so successful that U.S. Army, Vietnam eventually fabricated the kits and issued them to all units, thus providing an improvised night gunship which could perform fairly sophisticated tasks under night light conditions.

Arc Light Program

In Vietnam, ARC LIGHT (B–52) strikes were one of the most valuable and effective weapons available to higher commanders. However, as with many good things, they were limited in number and hard to come by. Demand always exceeded availability. During the period covered by this report, available sorties per day varied from 60 down to 47 for the entire theater. Allocation of sorties rested at Headquarters Military Assistance Command, Vietnam. There was no suballocation of strikes. Rather, subordinate units nominated targets to Commander, U.S. Military Assistance Command, Vietnam who approved strikes based on the overall situation in Southeast Asia and the quality of the target. By quality, one means the importance of the target, plus the reliability of the intelligence concerning it and its location.

At Headquarters II Field Force, Vietnam, we utilized a very thorough system of analysis to insure that we represented accurately the importance of our nominations and at the same time did not misuse this asset. To perform this task we created an ad hoc ARC LIGHT element in our G–2 and G–3 AIR shop. They systematically collected every fragment of information available on high priority Communist units and areas in which they were known or suspected to operate. This included:

—Red haze[1] and side looking airborne radar returns
—Ground firings at aircraft
—Visual reconnaissance results
—Aerial photo readout
—Reports from agents, prisoners of war, and Hoi Chanhs
—Results from ground reconnaissance and ground contacts
—Sensor activations
—Other special sources of intelligence

---

[1] Airborne reconnaissance flights to detect heat emissions from the ground.

—Historic patterns of enemy activity—what had he done before and where?

These data were collected and plotted on receipt, resulting in a tactical temperature chart on key areas of the battlefield.

Information from this data bank was available on request to supplement that collected by subordinate units but was used principally at Field Force level to evaluate subordinate unit nominations. On occasion, where a lucrative target escaped the attention of subordinate levels or a target of opportunity emerged, this data bank was used to develop Field Force level targets.

What this system did in particular was to play down the element of emotion and subjectivity in the target selection process. This was particularly important in evaluating targets nominated by South Vietnamese Army units, since they often did not have as much good current technical intelligence available as did we. Their nominations may have been quite valid, but did not always stand up under an analytical screening. Although certainly not foolproof, our system could address the probability of our finding enemy in a target box.

Because of the perishability of intelligence, this data bank could never guarantee the existence of a target in a specific box—particularly since at this point in the war the enemy was fully alert to the B–52 threat and practiced effective passive defense measures.

The great value of the system was that it was rationally organized, so that it could rapidly provide facts to the commander to assist him in target appraisal.

Successful tactics and targeting still depended in great measure on the skill, instinct, and intuition of a commander who knew his enemy. This data bank was designed to assist the commander in fine-tuning the location of targets. In addition the nature of the data bank was such that the addition of one new fragment of information often gave us the opportunity for a highly lucrative last minute diversion of an allocated strike.

The test of any system is the results obtained by it. By this measure ours fully justified the great amount of work that went into it.

We did not nominate targets unless we believed them to be worthwhile. In the great majority of cases, we got what we requested. This was because we had organized facts to back up our nominations and because our active program of ground bomb damage assessment confirmed our prediction of target nature in a high percentage of strikes.

As a matter of historical interest, the use of ARC LIGHTS in the 9th Division area in the delta was almost nil. The populated areas were almost automatically excluded and suitable targets elsewhere were quite infrequent. In the II Field Force Vietnam area in 1969–1970, practically all strikes were way out in deep jungle. However, one can assume the strikes were bothering the North Vietnamese, as their propaganda campaign had as a primary theme the concocted idea that tremendous damage was being done to the South Vietnamese people by indiscriminate use of ARC LIGHTS.

Indicators

With the passage of time in Vietnam, we developed a feel for our operations and the enemy, which enabled us to pick up strong or weak points by focusing on certain elements. These elements varied from individual areas to broad spectrums of activity. Some illustrations follow:

Gross eliminations were important but highly variable as to significance. A good unit in an area with lots of enemy consistently did a lot of damage. A unit in such an area that didn't cut up the enemy needed expert help to determine what it was doing wrong. Obviously, some units were in a dry hole (not much enemy around) and showed low elimination rates. It took considerable skill to determine the unit's knowledge of the enemy situation and its basic skill level in order to ascertain if their lack of results was due to lack of knowledge and skill or lack of enemy. As the enemy strength in an area declined this factor became more and more unreliable.

The exchange ratio (kill ratio) was of considerable value in assessing the professional skill of a unit. The matrix below gives a general idea:

Exchange Ratio	Skill Level of Unit
1 to 50 and above	Highly skilled U.S. unit
1 to 25	Very good in heavy jungle
	Fairly good U.S. unit in open terrain
	Very good for ARVN in open terrain
1 to 15	Low but acceptable for U.S. unit
	Good for South Vietnamese Army unit
1 to 10	Historical U.S. average
1 to 6	Historical South Vietnamese Army average

These exchange ratios applied to combined arms teams, including of course, airmobile and air cavalry support. The figures were highly variable due to local conditions. Also as the enemy strength declined, they became more erratic and of less utility.

In connection with the above, we made several efforts to reflect the greater importance of prisoners, Hoi Chanh and Viet Cong Infrastructure eliminations but were never satisfied with our approach. Our final solution was to include them in gross eliminations but with no weighted value. We did not include them in exchange ratios but carried them separately and tried to maximize our intake directly. The figures were inherently unstable over a short period of time but cumulatively fairly stable and showed trends. A low prisoner figure probably indicated lack of strong command emphasis. The Hoi Chanh figure was a valuable measure of overall military pressure although it varied widely according to the stage of progress of military and pacification operations in which one found one's self. As a result, it took much knowledge to interpret correctly. The Viet Cong infrastructure figure was highly erratic and was used only to focus command attention on the area. Although Viet Cong Infrastructive operations were primarily a Government of Vietnam operation, military support by U.S. and South Vietnamese Army forces was often an important assist in getting the Viet Cong infrastructure (or Phoenix) machinery moving.

Contact success ratio.

In dispersed, small unit warfare, the success of a unit was largely dependent on the skill with which small units handled each individual contact. If one visualized a contact as a sighting and a success as one or more enemy casualties, the following matrix gives the general idea:

Contact Success Ratio	Skill Level of Unit
75 percent	Highest skill observed
65 percent	Very professional
50 percent	Unit is beginning to jell
40 percent	Unit has problems but correctible
Below 40 percent	Unit has serious deficiencies in small unit techniques. Probably does many things wrong.

Night contacts and eliminations.

A unit cannot control the battlefield without effective night operations. It was easy to tell how a unit was doing at night from looking at their statistics. However, if their night results were poor it was most difficult to determine why. One approach was to bring in a skillful tactician to observe their operations and determine what the trouble was. For example, one of our units cooled off in heavy jungle at night. After much thrashing around, it was determined by sensors and other means that the enemy had been forced to stop moving at night. This, of course, was good and allowed the unit to ease off at night and thereby generate more daylight effort. Most night problems, however, were failures in basic tactics or technique or poor intelligence appreciation.

Psychological Warfare

Psychological warfare was an area where we wanted very much to improve our performance. We gave it the full treatment hoping to find a handle that would allow us to improve our performance through analysis.

Theoretically, one should be able to develop a matrix between input and output in the form of people who did what the leaflet or broadcast urged them to do. In actual practice, however, this proved impossible to do. There were just too many variables bearing on the system.

Instead of a direct cause-effect relationship between input and output, there was a great spongy glob between them. Sometimes a quick-reaction physchological warfare effort brought immediate results. More often, it achieved no apparent result at all. One just could not predict or detect the relationship.

What may have blunted the effort was the morale and state of discipline in the targeted units. The Communists, themselves masters of the art of psychological warfare, mounted a rigorous defense campaign against our use of it. Before battle, they told their men that they would be tortured and killed if they surrendered. They forbade their troops to read propaganda leaflets. At all times, they practiced internal surveillance where one was always watching someone and being watched in turn.

Thus, when things were going well and the chain of command was intact, a Communist unit was generally impervious to psychological warfare efforts. Individuals might receive the psychological warfare message but do nothing about it because of fear of punishment of themselves or their families in North Vietnam. However, when a Communist unit was beat up and scattered so the chain of command could not function, individuals, who may have been considering the step for months, would slip away and

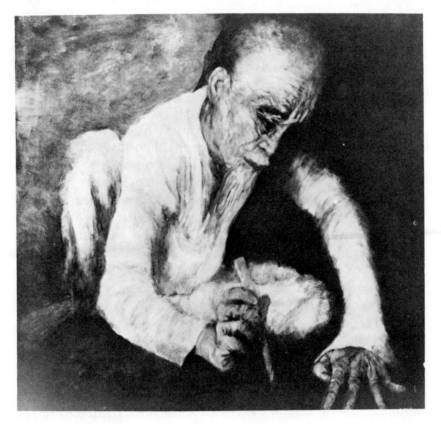

THE INSCRUTABLE EAST

rally. The input-output relation which resulted from these influences was too complex for analysis at field level.

Faced with this impasse, instead of analysis, we relied on a vigorous program broken out in general themes, responsible friendly units, enemy target units and areas. We raised our activity level and insured coverage by this management device. We hoped that the operators would vary the theme and specific content according to the situation in order to get better results. Whenever our intelligence told us a unit was down or beat up, we zeroed in on him and turned up the volume. We stayed with the unit as long as we could fix its location.

One significant observation emerged from our efforts—the more co-ordinated the tactical and psychological warfare effort was on our part, and the more active, the better the overall program. The actual results were difficult to assess, much less measure.

Pacification

The pacification program in III Corps was developed to a very high level of overall effectiveness by early 1970. A full discussion of this development is beyond the scope of this paper as it was mainly achieved through conventional management techniques. However, a key element was a thorough analysis of each of the main sub-programs to isolate the pacing sub-elements, particularly those which could be measured. By means of standard formats and frequent Government of Vietnam–U.S. combined reviews, these key factors were scrutinized carefully and kept moving ahead. Progress in these key factors appeared to pull the whole pacification program along with them. Of equal importance was frequent cross-coordination with military operations which enabled us to focus the military effort to break key log jams in pacification. Of transcendent importance was the general philosophy that heavy military pressure to bring security was the best way to develop an atmosphere in which pacification really took hold and forged ahead.

The tremendous progress made in Vietnam overall in 1968, 1969, and 1970 was due to defeating the North Vietnamese Army and the Viet Cong remnants militarily, continuing the military pressure to improve security, the development of a governmental structure with vitality, strength and growth potential, all of which made pacification possible. Pacification, in turn, reinforced success in the other areas. The point at which pacification develops its own dynamics could never be determined. However, it seems logical that the development of local forces, particularly police, strengthening of local government and economic and social gains over a long period of time, would forge a structure strong enough to smother or convert local dissidence. Of course, the North Vietnamese strategy was to prevent this by applying military power to arrest or upset progress.

As an aside, the Hamlet Evaluation System has been consistently criticized as a cosmetic device. While one can concede that the absolute meaning of the figures was hard to establish, it is an absolute fact that the Hamlet Evaluation System was an invaluable management tool and a meaningful measure of relative progress. Needless to say, its usefulness varied directly with the knowledge and insight of the user. Most press comment was highly critical. However, such comment tended to be quite biased and uninformed as well.

Secondary Road Program

Major engineer effort in Vietnam was put on upgrading the major lines of communication. The end result was a good network of paved roads tying together the major population centers and making possible broad economic progress. This work was done mostly by construction engineers and contract civilian effort. Division and some corps engineers normally worked on military roads and other projects which supported combat operations and sometimes extended this major Line of Communication network.

On the other hand, starting years before but increasingly so from 1964 to 1965 and on, the Communists began to "liberate" large areas in Vietnam. The classical method was to blow up all the bridges and cut the local roads, thus making it difficult for the government forces to move and holding the peasants on the land where their rice, labor and sons could be appropriated by the Communists.

In the spring and summer of 1968, we were forced by various considerations to repair an east-west lateral road in Long An Province between National Routes 4 and 5. The enemy at first resisted, was gradually driven away from the road, and eventually decided to live with it. However, in observing the area, it was apparent that the people who had fled the land were returning, normal life was resumed, and pacification moved ahead.

Based on this experience we began a deliberate secondary road program which marshalled all available bits and pieces of engineer effort left over from other key projects. The road construction priorities were worked out to consider all reasonable factors, with the province chief being the final decision-maker.

Although the figures available were rather sketchy, it was estimated that in 1968, 1969 and 1970 we repaired as many roads and bridges in Long An Province as the Communists had destroyed in 1964–68. Expert opinion has it that this road program was an important element in the rapid decline of Communist strength in the province. Aside from the reasons given above, it also seemed to operate by drying up the small local base areas.

An important element of the program was to design our own criteria and rebuild the most austere road possible which would meet the need. For example, a road which would take bicycles, oxcarts, motorbikes and very small trucks was entirely adequate in many areas as a starter. This "bare bones" approach allowed us to squeeze maximum mileage out of a very modest engineer effort left over from priority projects.

This same approach was tried in Hau Nghia Province with less

ROAD BUILDING

spectacular results. The reasons are not known—possibly because the farm land was less fertile, possibly because the overall integration of military operations, pacification and infrastructure was less intimate.

Our final conclusion was that the secondary road program was more important to pacification than previously realized. Complete concentration on line of communication upgrading was not necessarily the best solution.

Analysis of Rome Plow Operations

Historically, Rome Plow[2] units were one of our most valuable assets. They performed a very important function in the early days in clearing the flanks of highways to remove concealment from possible ambush sites. This allowed us to utilize ground lines of communication and got civilian traffic back on the roads. This

---

[2]The Rome Plow is a big bulldozer with a specialized cutting blade designed to clear heavy brush and jungle vegetation.

ROME PLOW OPERATION

worked directly against the Communist efforts to isolate the population.

Their second important function was the clearing away of traditional Communist base areas. This denied the enemy the jungle concealment that he had long enjoyed in proximity to vital areas. In III Corps Tactical Zone prior to 1967 the Rome Plow effort had been limited to certain key highways such as QL 13 and QL 1 and massive area cuts in places such as the Iron Triangle, the Ho Bo Woods, the Filhol Plantation, the Bien Hoa–Long Binh complex, and the heart of Binh Duong Province. These were all very useful in the situation that pertained at that time.

We opened 1969 with a highly successful effort to reopen the road from Phuoc Vinh to Song Be. This section of road had been closed for four years because of constant Communist presence in the area. Because of this threat, there was interest in making as wide a cut as possible. In an effort to make our effort more efficient, we conducted a simple analysis of enemy ambushes and determined instead that a 200-meter cut on each side of the road would give good visibility, keep effective rifle fire off the road, and inhibit infantry assaults or ambushes. The project was completed at this width and proved to be completely adequate.

As 1969 progressed, aggressive tactical operations wore down the enemy and pushed him back towards his Cambodian base areas. To exploit our success, we pushed teams of Armored Cavalry and Rome Plows out to open the roads in War Zone C which had been abandoned to the enemy for years.

Because of the deteriorating enemy capability and the purely tactical nature of our operations, we elected to further reduce the width of our cuts to 50 meters on each side of the road. This automatically gave us four times the road mileage per day of effort. We found that the resulting 100 meter swath allowed adequate aerial surveillance of the road and did not unacceptably expose vehicles to ambush. Although it allowed the ambusher to get closer to the road, it also narrowed down the observation and exposure zone of the ambush.

Base areas were a more difficult problem. Traditionally, they had been cleared completely. In the case of a large area, this took months of effort. In studying this problem, it was determined that the enemy response to a massive clean cut was to move farther out to the next suitable area and set up for business there. It was, therefore, decided to use a lane clearing technique which would open up the base area for friendly operations but would not automatically drive the enemy out. Initially, a 1,000-meter lane was used with the uncleared interval being left to judgment. If, for example, one diced up the area into 2-kilometer squares of jungle, a 36 percent saving in cutting was achieved. By using a quick and selective cutting technique which bypassed the largest trees and went around difficult areas more rapid cutting was possible and the saving time-wise was greater. As we became familiar with this technique, the lanes were reduced to 500 to 600 meters, thereby increasing the savings.

The most successful use of this technique was in the Trapezoid area south of the Michelin Rubber Plantation and east of the Saigon River. As lane cutting progressed, Sub-Region I Headquarters, the 101st North Vietnamese Army Regiment and a coterie of odds and ends evidently decided they would stay in place. As a result, three to four U.S. and South Vietnamese Army battalions were able to decimate them over a period of months by day patrolling and night ambushes. When they finally had to move further away from the populated areas they were so decimated that they could no longer resist or even affect the Government of Vietnam pacification program.

The One War Concept

The key to operations in the III Corps was General Abrams' One War concept, which in simplest terms meant that all military, pacification and governmental resources and activities worked in coordination towards the same goals. Like most powerful ideas it was very simple. Also, like most ideas in Vietnam it was rather difficult in execution.

However, as has been brought out previously, there were various programs and concepts—constant pressure, working on the enemy system, accelerated pacification, Dong Tien—which in themselves facilitated qualitative and quantitative improvement. When these were all stitched together by divisional, provincial and Corps-wide reviews, the overall result was a rather ponderous but fairly effective coordinated effort. Fortunately, the Communists were not very effective themselves and a fairly effective government effort made steady progress.

Corps-Level Wrap-Up

As one would expect, the conduct of operations at the Corps level was much looser and more diffuse than at the division level.

Although we resorted to considerable fine-tuning (as in the Sub-Region-1 operation), the main energy of the commanders was devoted to crisis management. Whether it would have been possible to have devised a system whereby one kept track of hundreds of enemy units and thousands of friendly units in a systematic and analytical manner is hard to say. The Working Against the Enemy System concept combined with coordinated Regional attacks and the inventory of enemy units—Constant Pressure concept—were efforts in this direction. It should be noted that these three concepts plus an integrated approach to pacification made the Abrams' One War strategy a reality in III Corps. One senses that a red hot review and analysis section with scientist participation and access to a good computer could have systematized many matters which we dealt with in a more informal manner.

One concrete way of stimulating the necessary co-ordination and support was to require all the responsible commanders and officials to keep track of the entire situation—enemy and friendly, military and civilian—with stress on pacification. These rather voluminous statistics, once one became used to using them, gave a clear picture of shortfalls, weak and strong areas, and so forth. It also helped the Vietnamese to get tight control over a complex operation. We are convinced that this approach materially assisted both military

operations and pacification in the 9th Division and later in the III
Corps. Rather than dealing with subjective impressions, the commanders were dealing with cold (fairly reliable) facts.

The Vietnamese Oriental way of looking at things tended to
avoid facts. Once the facts were brought out, the Vietnamese approach to a problem tended to be quite logical and decisive. The
pitfall here was that the Oriental mind often overlooked the factual,
pragmatic approach for various cultural reasons. If one could get
them to use hard facts, their effectiveness gained almost automatically.

This integration gimmick illustrates how one could get hold of
complex problems by reviewing elaborate statistical formats. This
process of statistical review had little overall logic in an analytical
sense—it only pointed everyone in the same direction and uncovered log jams. Once the log jams were cleared, forward progress
ensued. It was the best way we could make the One War concept
really work at all levels.

Whereas one senses we were able to make a sizable dent in
analyzing division-level operations, the feeling persists that we only
scratched the surface at the corps level. In any case, they both constitute interesting problems for future commanders and staffs.

In spite of the fact that the corps level is more difficult to manage
than the division, the combination of the analytic approach, normal
command supervision methods, and selected analysis did produce
results. As had been mentioned earlier, the exchange ratio of the
U.S. units was increased from two to three times (8 : 1 average to
19 : 1 average with a high of 30.1 : 1). At the same time, the attrition of the enemy by U.S. units (not counting prisoners of war and
Hoi Chanhs) was increased appreciably and friendly losses (Killed
by Hostile Action and Died of Wounds) decreased markedly. In
other words, the U.S. units inflicted 70 percent more damage on the
enemy at a casualty cost 56 percent less for an efficiency improvement of 3.8 times. (See Chart 26.) As the South Vietnamese Army
units were brought up to strength, re-equipped, and adopted more
flexible tactics, their performance improved, but more slowly than
the U.S. Chart 26 also illustrates the South Vietnamese Army's
steady and encouraging increase in efficiency. The improvements in
the performance of all units in III Corps (South Vietnamese Army,
Free World Military Allied Forces and U.S.) can be noted in Table
31, All of these units can well be proud of this record as the enemy
at the same time was doing his best to evade tactically and was
progressively shifting units into sanctuary in Cambodia. As could be
expected, pacification proceeded at a rapid rate protected by this

CHART 26—EXCHANGE RATIOS, III CORPS TACTICAL ZONE, JULY 1968– APRIL 1970

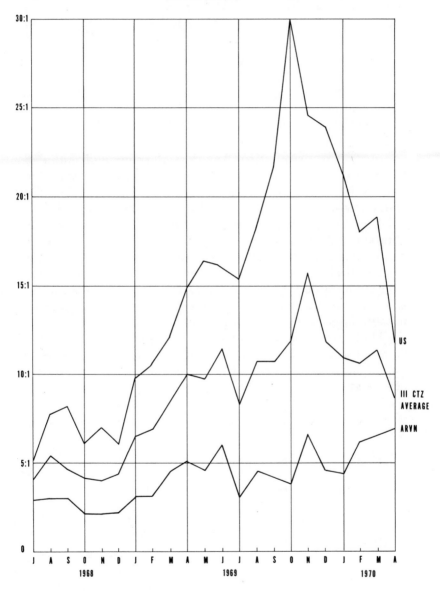

TABLE 31—III CORPS TACTICAL ZONE SELECTED COMBAT STATISTICS
JUL–DEC 68 AND JUL–DEC 69

Date	Enemy KIA	Friendly KIA	Date	Enemy KIA	Friendly KIA
Jul 68	1357	320	Jul 69	3504	424
Aug	4053	766	Aug	4965	462
Sep	3442	727	Sep	4525	422
Oct	2099	514	Oct	3545	299
Nov	2988	743	Nov	4821	307
Dec	2602	594	Dec	4255	358
Average ..	2757	611	Average ..	4269	379

Exchange Ratio: 4.5 : 1   Exchange Ratio: 11.3 : 1

pressure. The 1st Cavalry Division working with three South Vietnamese Army brigades (regiments) and the 11th Armored Cavalry Regiment did a superb job in deep jungle. The 25th Infantry Division essentially worked itself out of a job by driving the 9th Viet Cong Division (actually North Vietnamese Army) into Cambodia. The 1st Infantry Division, in a very quiet sector, by painstaking efforts, was able to achieve a very fine exchange ratio of 55 to 1. (The best division performance seen in a quiet sector.) The 25th South Vietnamese Army Division, under an able commander, was able to work up to a 25 to 1 exchange ratio—a 300 percent improvement.

There are many problem areas remaining which space does not permit listing. But, by late 1969 or early 1970, the nature of the war began to change and the Cambodian operations ushered in a new phase.

CHAPTER XI

On Controlling the War

The problem facing American units in the Spring of 1968 and subsequently, the period of this Monograph, was one of bringing evading enemy units to battle during the quiet periods in between his "high points" of attack and of limiting the damage during these high points so that the pacification program was not interfered with. The situation clearly called for a change in tactics by friendly troops in order to bring the enemy to battle on *our terms* as has been mentioned earlier, rather than on *his terms*. The solution arrived at, as a result of analyses of combat operations and experimentation, was to find, encircle and break up the enemy main force and provincial battalions and as the enemy broke down into smaller sized elements to lower the scale of friendly operations to attack the small enemy units on a continuous day and night basis. The unexpected by-product of this dispersed style and constant pressure was that enemy units at all levels were weakened, reducing their ability to generate replacements from local guerrilla units, and resulting in large numbers of ralliers and the progressive loss of control of the people. The net effect of these interacting defeats on all elements of the enemy system was that the enemy lost capability geometrically rather than arithmetically. The general philosophy that unrelenting military pressure to bring security was the most important way to develop an atmosphere in which pacification could flourish was transcendental. It was the best pragmatic way to control the war.

The Attrition Strategy

Some observers of the Vietnamese war have criticized its "attrition" strategy, particularly in its earlier phases. It could have been more properly termed a strategic defense initially and gradually became more and more active as the South Vietnamese government and forces became more organized. It ended up as an offensive defense.

It is interesting to note that most wars, since the "nation in arms" concept of the French Revolution, have relied heavily on attrition—World War I and II and our own Civil War being prime

PURSUIT

examples. Wars which have been won primarily by maneuver have
been the exception rather than the rule. Usually maneuver, attrition, interdiction, and direct attacks on the enemy's base have been
combined, according to the nature of the war itself, to gain a victory
or a draw. The Vietnamese war has been no exception—direct pressure, that is attrition, was applied to neutralize the enemy units and
to strain his personnel and logistic support organization. Interdiction of seaborne supplies was made effective and efforts were made
to cut off landborne supply lines by in-country operations and by
bombing the Ho Chi Minh Trail. Bombing of the enemy's home
base was conducted within certain limitations. Pacification completed the circle by progressively cutting the enemy off from in-
country resources. It could be theorized that attrition was more important than in Western European wars because enemy units, if
out-maneuvered, would not surrender and in many cases could
avoid encirclement or envelopment by slipping away in the dense

jungle. As a result, they had to be rendered ineffective over a period of time through the cumulative loss of manpower, equipment and supplies. In summary, the Vietnamese strategy by 1969 and 1970 was reasonably classical considering the problems posed by political limitations (sanctuary, bombing halt, and so forth), but attrition did assume an important central role. Our conclusion, considering the circumstances, is that it was not an attrition strategy, although attrition was important, but a fairly complete strategy. This complete strategy was not fully effective until late in the war as it took considerable time to organize some aspects of it. However, it should be recognized that the many constraints on operations in Vietnam made the allied operations most difficult to carry out effectively. The bombing pause, the partial Laotian sanctuary, the complete Cambodian sanctuary, the inherent difficulties of a semi-guerrilla situation, the instability of Vietnamese society and government, the tremendous will and ruthlessness of the Communist North Vietnamese, the difficult conditions of terrain and jungle, made the Vietnamese War an uphill struggle all the way.

Body Count

The 9th Infantry Division and II Field Force, Vietnam have been criticized on the grounds that "their obsession with body count" was either basically wrong or else led to undesirable practices. While the basic inference that they were "obsessed with body count" is not true, one could advance the thought that keeping tabs on enemy killed and kill ratios might lead to a more cold blooded approach than would otherwise be the case. It seems desirable to take this criticism head-on lest some readers assume that the general approach inevitably leads to undesirable practices.

In the first place, the Constant Pressure concept and Working on the Enemy system were based on the reasoning that the best way to defeat the enemy and to protect the South Vietnamese people was to utilize maximum force against the entire Communist system. This theory has been proven correct many times and in many places in Vietnam. The soft approach has been tried many times with a noticeable lack of success. The deceptive aspect of the soft approach was that it worked well on the surface for a period of months until the enemy organized a response and then retrogression set in.

The Malaysian experience tended to support the soft approach as it was quite successful in that case. What the casual observer missed was that the Malaya insurrection was a relatively weak and soft Communist effort, whereas the Vietnamese effort was a real war made possible by massive external support and intervention. As a result the rules in Vietnam were almost the opposite from Malaya. This was graphically illustrated by the experience of the Australian Task Force. This fine outfit, one of the best in the theater, had every advantage. It had Malaysian experience in the jungle, stabilized units, extensive training and so on. Yet its successes were based on innovation and its least productive efforts were based on Malaysian type operations.

Once one decided to apply maximum force, the problem became a technical one of doing it efficiently with the resources available. In many areas this required real skill and iron determination as the enemy was usually able to stay alive and at least stay even for years under moderate pressure. However, the Constant Pressure concept, well applied, did not lead to a brutalizing of the conflict. In fact, the reverse was true. It was a provable fact that it led to more prisoners of war and Hoi Chanhs than a soft approach. It also led to less civilian casualties and damage. It resulted in fewer friendly casualties in both killed and wounded. More importantly, pacification progressed more rapidly. Thus we see a system which entailed maximum force and higher enemy casualties initially, but, in the long run, wound the war down and facilitated all the developments necessary to defeat the enemy and protect the people. The avoidance of civilian casualties and body count padding was more a matter of training and standards regardless of the approach involved.

Thus, it can be said that the 9th Division and II Field Force Vietnam approach which emphasized maximum damage to the enemy ended up by "unbrutalizing" the war, so far as the South Vietnamese people and our own forces were concerned. The Communists took a different view, as could be expected.

The Search and Destroy Operation

It will be noted that there is little mention of the Search and Destroy Operation in this Monograph. This omission was not deliberate but incidental. In the first place, the Search and Destroy Operation was rapidly falling into disuse during this period, and we personally had very little experience with it. In the second place, we did not wish to discuss operations with which we were not personally familiar.

As we understand it, the original idea of the Search and Destroy Operation was a multi-battalion reconnaissance in force which sought out large enemy units and then attempted to encircle and destroy them. It not only gave good ground coverage in jungle terrain, but during the period when enemy units were strong and combat effective, it enabled friendly battalions to be kept in hand in order to render support to a hard pressed unit if necessary. As the enemy units were ground down, the friendly units spread out and conducted independent battalion reconnaissance in force operations (sometimes called sweeps) and then gradually worked down the scale to small unit reconnaissance operations. Unfortunately, the term hung on longer than the operation and tended to become a blanket term for any offensive operation. To the best of our recollection, the term was cast into limbo by Military Assistance Command, Vietnam during this period, but it died hard due to the tendency of returnees to use terms that were current during their previous tours.

In 1968, in the 9th Division, the Search and Destroy Operation had been overtaken by events although the battalion reconnaissance in force was used to deal with really tough base areas. We gradually worked into the company reconnaissance in force coordinated at battalion level, followed by the platoon reconnaissance coordinated at company level.

In II Field Force, Vietnam, with large enemy units and heavy jungle, the phaseout of the operation was not as rapid. The last large scale Search and Destroy Operation that can be identified was a sweep through the Michelin Rubber Plantation in the winter of 1969. As the enemy began to deteriorate, the friendly units spread out, even in the jungle, and by the winter of 1970, company level reconnaissance was the rule even up against the Cambodian border.

The Search and Destroy Operation described in the press as a sort of scorched earth tactic was beyond our experience. We have read that Search and Clear Operations, particularly those involving the destruction and resettlement of a tough Communist fortified village, were resorted to earlier in the war. We can recall no instances of such operations in our area of responsibility, either actual or played up in the press. We do recall a few very small resettlement operations which were undertaken, most reluctantly, at Government of Vietnam initiative in areas where the Government of Vietnam could not generate adequate security forces. These required high level approval, both U.S. and Government of Vietnam.

In connection with the above discussion, the Vietnamese Army was slower to abandon mass sweeps. It was difficult for a Vietnamese commander to send a company into a place where a regiment had been decimated four or five years earlier. (The American commanders had the advantage of not being aware of the earlier catastrophe.) However, the Vietnamese finally worked their way down the scale also.

Controlling the War

In examining the Vietnamese war, particularly in its early stages, one could see many situations in which the Communists, although not necessarily successful, were able to give the Allies a hard time. The set-piece ambush, the set-piece attack on an isolated post, the seizure and defense of a populated area, and the development of a fortified village or hamlet were all examples of operations which the Communists executed many times and were difficult to handle without incurring excessive friendly military casualties and, in some cases, undue civilian casualties or damage. The Communist style of making war was inherently destructive to the people and physical resources of a country. The Communists "liberated" the countryside by destroying roads and bridges. They controlled the country by breaking up its social and governmental structure and applying force and terror against the people. By fortifying villages or by seizing inhabited areas, they forced the government into heavy combat which harmed the people and destroyed civilian resources. Their organization of the masses to support the Communists absorbed the total manpower and financial resources of the country, leaving nothing for economic progress. Many other examples can be cited of the inherent destructiveness of a Communist inspired war. It was that way by philosophy, doctrine, and choice.

On the other hand, an aggressive and skillful Allied effort could seize the initiative and damage the enemy severely with low casualties and little, if any, harm to the civilian population. The casual observer of the Vietnamese War would resist this conclusion. He has been so conditioned by reading dramatized newspaper accounts of the war that he visualizes Vietnam disappearing under the smoke and flame of bombs, artillery shells, and unnamed nefarious devices even at this late stage. However, if one looked at the facts, it was quite apparent that the more the Allied side gained control of the war, the less destructive the war became. If one studied the III Corps Tactical Zone (around Saigon) in 1968–1970, the picture was quite clear. The enemy units became weaker and weaker, friendly military losses declined, civilian casualties declined, damage to houses and crops was relatively rare, B–52 and Tactical air sorties declined markedly, and were delivered in uninhabited jungle areas, artillery usage declined, rice and other crop production increased, roads and bridges were rebuilt, economic and social conditions improved, the government operated more effectively, and so on. Inherently, the Allied effort tried to protect the people and rebuild the country.

NEGATIVE CONTROL

An interesting theory can be developed from these observations. If the Communists were able to seize the initiative and conduct the war according to their own rules, Communist successes would have been more frequent, friendly losses higher and the general damage to and disruption of the civilian community more widespread. On the other hand, if the Allies had grasped the initiative and imposed their own rules, the reverse would be true.

POSITIVE CONTROL

This theory was difficult for the Government side to apply. In the Vietnamese context, at least, there seemed to be some basic superiority of force ratio that had to be reached. While it was not the classical 10 to 1 ratio, it did seem to be somewhere in the 4 to 6 to 1 area. Then, of course, the friendly government had to get itself organized well enough to function while being subjected to Communist attacks and interference. There were also innumerable localized problems—geography, terrain, the nature of the people, and so forth. The proper tactics were not easy to define— heavy firepower, light firepower, large or small unit operations—there were many possible approaches.

However, with all these explanations if one observed the Malaysian experience and the Vietnamese experience, it appears possible over a long period of time to defeat a Communist insurgency if the resources and will can be assembled. However, and of equal importance, if the government side and its allies can seize the initiative and control the war, it can "win" with fewer losses and less damage to its civilian structure than otherwise.

CHAPTER XII

Limitations and Problems
in the Use of Analysis

The use of operations analysis was inherently a difficult task in Vietnam. As mentioned previously, to analyze a problem one should be able to describe the process in some detail, obtain reliable data inputs, and establish an adequate feedback system. These tasks varied widely in difficulty and seemed impossible in some areas.

Combined arms operations at all levels (that is Corps, division, brigade and even battalion) were too large and complex to study in toto by analytical methods. Pacification was similarly complex. The technique employed was to isolate pieces of the problem which could be analyzed. The remainder had to be attacked by means of judgement, professional skill, experience and sometimes intuition. The overall intergration always had to be done on this basis. Even in areas such as small unit techniques which responded well, on the surface, to analysis, the actual cause and effect relationships could not be traced out with confidence. These comments should not discourage attempts to improve operations by analysis and otherwise; they should merely underline the obvious point that the human mind can somehow grasp large problems by means which are difficult or impossible to duplicate on paper.

It should also be understood that many "new" doctrinal concepts (such as the constant pressure idea) were actually not "new" but well-established doctrine which proved to be more pertinent in a particular phase of the war. Some concepts were implemented because the necessary organizational measures had finally been taken (for example, pacification), others because a real technical breakthrough had been made (for example, the Jitterbug). In sum, Vietnam was full of people with good ideas; but people who could select useful ones and implement them were not as easily found.

A confusing element in the equation was and is that outstanding leadership (military or civilian) transcends or overrides the standard rules. One must always ask whether something works because it is executed by an artist, whether it is basically a good idea, whether it is too difficult for general use, and so on. To the artist with a deep knowledge of the war, a decision may appear simple and logical. To a less gifted person, the decision may seem illogical or based on intuition. One man's knowledge is another man's intuition.

The process of analysis and improving efficiency while desirable tended to confine one's thinking in a set framework. This could be prejudicial to change and innovation. The Communists were fairly clever at eventually devising defensive measures against a new tactic and as a result it could be expected to be less and less profitable as time went on. This placed a premium on changes to keep ahead of the Communists and to retain the initiative. The Communists' reaction to continuous changes and innovation was relatively slow and uncertain so the cumulative effects of many innovations was quite productive. In sum, while using analysis, one should foster change and innovation.

One should avoid working on the flat part of the learning curve and "gold plating" projects. This could lead to large effort for small return. If one stayed on the steep part of the efficiency curve, a little extra effort could bring back modest but worthwhile returns. This idea of doing a fairly good job with reasonable effort was hard to get across to Americans as their nature was to try to do the best job possible.

Statistics were effective and necessary. However, the quantity of reports and the amount of detail had to be watched, so the chain of command would not become a reporting machine.

Computers were quite useful. Unfortunately, the division level computers available were glorified business machines with the usual handicaps of slow speed, low capacity, and overscheduling. More advanced computers would have been helpful. A more general problem was the rigidity of computer data bases and programs. As the situation changed, they tended to become outdated.

Some specific examples of these internal problems may serve to illustrate them more clearly.

The standard mines and booby trap approach was to progressively elaborate and sophisticate the overall program. The analytical approach was to isolate the few most important elements and to focus a simpler program on the individual soldier. The innovative approach was to partially finesse the problem by emphasizing night ambushes.

The use of analyses and its factual approach was useful in deflating the idea that the Communists were "six feet tall." There was a tendency to assign to them many capabilities, as a matter of course, which were quite rare or almost non-existent. The U.S. tendency, at least, was to assume that the Communists were tricky and skillful adversaries. Actually, they were pretty dull and pedestrian, and if one faked them out of their standard approach, they were almost helpless.

Problems involving social, sociological, cultural and language patterns were very difficult to handle. Our Prisoner of War program produced satisfying results, both absolutely and relatively, but we could never break the language and indoctrination barrier. The South Vietnamese Army was more successful than we, probably due to a minimal language and racial obstacle. Psychological Warfare was a most difficult area in which to pin anything down.

As previously mentioned, pacification and combined arms operations were primarily managed by normal civilian and military management techniques and analyzed on the fringes.

The Vietnamese War was replete with other examples where the reasons for success or failure were not completely understood.

This lack of knowledge or understanding was the greatest problem in Vietnam for both sides. One could speculate that five honest men could study any aspect of the war and prove to their satisfaction that five different things were true. A biased person could always find enough information to prove his point to his own satisfaction. A good rule in Vietnam was to assume that a study which clearly proved something was either superficial or loaded. This difficulty worked both ways—the Communists were so captive to their own doctrine that their operations were sometimes quite unproductive. The Central Office for South Vietnam, the North Vietnamese headquarters which essentially ran the war in southern South Vietnam, both politically and militarily—was very dogmatic and hidebound. In III Corps at least, our greatest ally was the Central Office for South Vietnam—their reaction or action was quite predictable. They were completely locked on to a big unit war approach which played into our hands completely. Even the South Vietnamese who really understood the war required tremendous mental flexibility. Westerners had a similar problem in sloughing off their western ideas. The end result was that a relatively small percentage of people had the insight and grasp to deal with the war constructively and creatively.

We are not suggesting that operations analysis was impossible in Vietnam. We are only suggesting that the "fog of war" and the rapid changes placed a high premium on the element of military experience and judgment in guiding the application of the analytic process. Some areas clearly fell outside the scope of the analytical art at that time.

One could question whether the approach described here would be readily transferable to a more classical "western type" conflict.

In Vietnam, with all its ambiguities, one was dealing with a highly repetitive operation. It was somewhat comparable to an assembly line—whereas one could visualize a "western war" as an episodic or climactic affair with periods of intense decisive activity followed by longer periods of low activity. It would appear that this type of conflict might require a different approach from an analytical point of view.

CHAPTER XIII

Overall Conclusions

This Monograph covers primarily the systematic blending of military judgment, data collection, and the simple problem-solving techniques as performed by the 9th Division and II Field Force, Vietnam in the period 1968 to 1970. We did not elaborate on the normal military decision-making methods which are well understood and which were utilized extensively in Vietnam. However, we have stressed the extension of these more normal decision-making devices by analytical methods. We have felt obliged to adhere to the standard military modus operandi, and, consequently, have drawn the following overall conclusions:

1. Normal military command and management techniques, aggressively pursued, were adequate in Vietnam to keep military and pacification operations working reasonably well. The "analytic approach" was a useful complementary technique.

2. The judicious use of operations analysis and analytical techniques when melded with military judgment was quite effective in improving performance in many areas of activity.

3. The 9th Infantry Division's analytical results-oriented efforts to optimize resources and increase combat effectiveness (which had as a base the goal to provide the maximum number of fit, motivated, well equipped and properly supported infantry soldiers to the field on a daily basis, night and day) worked.

4. The combination of the Constant Pressure concept, pacification, working against the enemy system, and Vietnamization made the One-War concept a reality and proved to be very effective tactically and strategically in the III Corps Tactical Zone around Saigon in 1969 and early 1970.

5. Analysis worked best at division level; it was more difficult to apply with precision at Field Force or Corps level.

6. The individual commander's ability, skill and knowledge transcended the more tangible factors.

7. Innovation and changes in tactics had to be aggressively pursued while continuing the optimization of ongoing operations which were well understood.

8. Many aspects of the situation resisted analysis.

THE AUTHORS LISTEN TO COLONEL GERACI

There is no doubt that the overall system described in this monograph worked. The $64 question is, why? Was it due to the way the war was developing in Vietnam at that particular time, or was it due to the use of combat analysis or to some other reason?

Most objective observers would agree that the Allied policies, strategy and grand tactics improved as the war went on. The improvements in the organization and effectiveness of the Government of Vietnam, the national mobilization of 1968 and thereafter, the increasing military pressure on the enemy system, and the accelerated pacification campaigns all contributed. Not all was done that should have been done, but for any imperfect world, the cumulative effect was one of impressive gains.

There was also a concurrent improvement and tightening up in the tactics and techniques utilized in Vietnam. As a body of doctrine solidified and was refined by battlefield experience, our operations became more effective.

Linked with the above was a definite deterioration in the strength and quality of the enemy units. The Viet Cong losses during *Tet* were substantial—in many areas the Viet Cong began to disappear. As their combat requirements expanded and combat losses of the North Vietnamese began to accumulate, their experienced cadre became fewer and fewer. In the overall balance, their gross capability and their skill levels both declined.

A not inconsiderable factor in our favor was the high quality of the people involved. Down through the major level at least, practically every position was filled with top-notch people. These high quality leaders, from battalion level up, enabled us to come rapidly to grips with an unfamiliar type of war and to succeed.

The use of a system for coordinating all military and civil aspects of the struggle was widespread. However, in the III Corps Tactical Zone around Saigon, this system was elaborated and strengthened to a point that the One War concept became a reality in many areas. This focusing effect was very important.

A tremendous intensity of operations or concentration of effort was a factor. If one realizes that infantrymen were in the field about 100 hours a week and that units from battalion up were in operation 24 hours a day, seven days a week, the physical, mental and nervous demands on the commanders can be visualized. If one superimposed on this a tremendous will to damage the enemy and move the war in a favorable direction, substantial progress ensued. This intensity of effort had to be achieved and maintained at a very high level. Whether this intensity is feasible across the board is debatable.

The analytic approach helped to put all this together. Its concentration on results rather than activity was important. Its assistance in understanding the key aspects of complicated operations was valuable. Combat analysis helped to guide and control the myriad small engagements which added together meant progress.

A measured and rational development of combat analysis as a tool of command deserves emphasis in the future.

APPENDIX

Milestones

1963

November	President Diem assassinated.

1964

August	Gulf of Tonkin incident

1965

March	First commitment of U.S. combat units
May	173d Airborne Brigade arrives
September	1st Cavalry Division arrives
October	1st Infantry Division arrives

1966

April	25th Infantry Division arrives
August	4th Infantry Division arrives
December	9th Infantry Division arrives

1967

February	Elements of the 9th Infantry Division begin Delta operations from Dong Tam
December	101st Airborne Division arrives

1968

January	*Tet*-1968 enemy offensive
May	Mini-*Tet* enemy offensive against Saigon
June	9th Infantry Division Headquarters moves from Bearcat to Dong Tam
July	Operation Safe Step commences

1969

January	IV Corps Dry Weather Campaign commences
January	9th Infantry Division Night Cavalry Tactics commence
February	9th Infantry Division Night Raids commence
April	Peak of 9th Infantry Division sniper program success
June	Construction of Dong Tam completed
June	Dong Tien Program commences
August	Majority of 9th Infantry Division returns to the U.S.

Index